BOOKS BY KENNETH KOCH

POETRY

Ko, or A Season on Earth
Thank You and Other Poems
When the Sun Tries to Go On
The Pleasures of Peace
The Art of Love
The Duplications
The Burning Mystery of Anna in 1951
Days and Nights
Selected Poems 1950–1982
On the Edge
Seasons on Earth
On the Great Atlantic Rainway, Selected Poems, 1950–1988
One Train
Straits

FICTION

The Red Robins
Hotel Lambosa

THEATER

Bertha and Other Plays
A Change of Hearts
The Red Robins
One Thousand Avant-Garde Plays
The Gold Standard: A Book of Plays

NON-FICTION

Wishes, Lies and Dreams: Teaching Children to Write Poetry
Rose, Where Did You Get That Red?: Teaching Great Poetry to Children
I Never Told Anybody: Teaching Poetry Writing in a Nursing Home
Sleeping on the Wing: An Anthology of Modern Poetry with Essays on Reading and Writing (with Kate Farrell)
The Art of Poetry: Poems, Parodies, Fiction, Interviews and Essays

MAKING YOUR OWN DAYS

The Pleasures
of Reading and Writing Poetry

K ENNETH K OCH

A Touchstone Book
Published by Simon & Schuster

TOUCHSTONE
Rockefeller Center
1230 Avenue of the Americas
New York, NY 10020

First Touchstone Edition 1999

TOUCHSTONE and colophon are registered trademarks of Simon & Schuster Inc.

DESIGNED BY ERICH HOBBING

Set in Minion

Manufactured in the United States of America

3   5   7   9   10   8   6   4   2

Library of Congress Cataloging-in-Publication Data is available.

ISBN 0-684-83992-X
0-684-82438-8 (Pbk)

Permissions appear on page 313.

To Karen

Acknowledgments

This book owes a lot to friends and other readers, for their encouragement, their criticism, and their ideas. Andrew Epstein was important to my writing the book to begin with. Once the writing began, Jordan Davis was my indispensable assistant, listening to and reading every version of every chapter as I wrote it and telling me what he thought. His part in the book went quite a way beyond textual criticism; he thought through the whole subject with me and was thus able to be a keen critic of the tone of the book and of what needed to be in it and what didn't. Karen Koch, my wife and thus around even more often than Jordan, heard at least as many versions as he did and was able to give it her best and most continuing thought. This was a great help. Barbara Fischer and Roosevelt Montas did most of the typing, retyping, and editing of the manuscript. Barbara also did research for me in the Columbia University library; her technical expertise was more than matched by her literary intelligence, which made for research as creative as it was supportive. Once a first version was finished, I sent the book to my friend, the poet Mark Halliday. He fearlessly told me all he thought was right and wrong in it; I agreed with him about almost everything and the book is a different one in substance as well as in detail because of his comments. For reading early versions I am also grateful to Frank Kermode and Ron Padgett. The book owes a good deal to Kate Farrell and to what I learned about writing and poetry from working on several books with her. To her I also owe the idea of the "Poetry Base," which is a variant on her idea of a "happiness base." My editor, Trish Todd, has been like the sunshine and rain that made the book happen at all. I thank all these persons and can only hope the book reflects some of the clarity and intelligence they gave to helping me write it.

Contents

And now that you
are making your own days
—FRANK O'HARA,
"A True Account of Talking to the Sun at Fire Island"

A Brief Preface

In sober mornings do not thou rehearse
The holy incantation of a verse
—HERRICK,
"When He Would Have
His Verses Read"

Poetry's part of your self
like the passion of a nation
at war it moves quickly . . .
—O'HARA,
"To Gottfried Benn"

The aim of this book is to say some clear and interesting things about poetry. Poetry, because it stirs such strong feelings and because great examples of it are so rare, has often been written about in ways that make it seem more difficult, mysterious, more specialized, and more remote than it actually is—it is written about as a mystery, as a sort of intellectual/aesthetic code that has to be broken, as an example of some aspect of history or philosophy. Non-specialist readers are likely to find such writing more difficult to understand than poetry, and in fact not always on the subject of poetry, so it ends up being not much help. Other writing about poetry is, if anything, too simple, enthusiastic maybe, but vague and imprecise. "A lyric triumph!"; "These are the voices of America," etc. What's not clear here is a sense of what, artistically, is going on. There has also been some brilliant writing about poetry—by Valéry, Saintsbury, and Pound, for example— from which I've borrowed in my attempt to make this a clear and readable guide, a sort of introduction to a large subject.

The second half of the book is an anthology of poems that illustrate what is said in the preceding chapters and which, in turn, I hope, the chapters will make it more of a pleasure to read. With poetry—as with baseball, or architecture, for example—one has to understand a little in order to enjoy it, and also one has to enjoy it a little in order to want to understand it. The poems and the prose should work toward the same ends—pleasure and understanding—the text by clarifying, the poems by giving the experiences the text is talking about.

I have written not only about reading poetry, which is probably the main relation to the subject most people have, but also about writing it—specifically, about inspiration, and about what happens while a poet writes. My remarks on these subjects can only be tentative and suggestive, since a good deal of the information I'd need to be thorough there is no way to get: I would have to *be* Keats, Homer, Shakespeare, Dickinson, and so on. However, I say some things I am pretty sure are true—I am one poet and have known and read a lot of others—and saying them seemed useful for readers of poetry, as well as for those who write or wish to write it. Knowing how poems are made is a help in knowing how to read them: the ideal experience of reading a poem is, in many respects, close to the experience of writing it: one goes through uncertainty, flashes of perception, small satisfactions, puzzlement, understanding, surprise. A reader who knows how poetry is made has a better chance of responding to what is there.

Included in the "Reading" chapter are brief discussions of long poems, dramatic poetry, and poetry in other languages. These are all often neglected in presentations of poetry; they seem to me, however, an important part of the subject.

The main innovation in the book is probably the discussion of poetry as a separate language. I liked that idea because it was dramatic and also because it seemed to help clarify a great many things. That poetry is a (somewhat) separate language helps to explain what poetry is able to communicate; how it is inspired—both at the beginning and while the poem is being written; in what way what it says is true; and the excitement poets feel when they sit down to write it or even think about writing it; as well as the most intelligent and pleasurable way to read it. The discussion of the "poetry language" is divided into a number of parts: its relation to ordinary language; music—rhythm, meter, rhyme, stanzas, forms; its other features, or inclinations—comparisons, personification, lies, etc.; and a part called "The Poetry Base," about how this language can be learned.

Poems were chosen for the anthology to exemplify and illuminate what is said in the chapters. The selection isn't meant to be inclusive or, even, representative. This will, I hope, serve as an apology—to poets, especially living ones, who aren't in the book, and to readers who like to find the poets they are fondest of in all collections. And, from the past, there is no Mallarmé, no Neruda, no Smart, no Virgil, no Ariosto—these are marvelous poets, and any regular anthology would have to include them. There are also, I know, some odd choices—Dante's "Guido, vorrei," for example—from the great poets who are included in the anthology, which, not in any sense definitive, is rather, in Wallace Stevens's phrase, "Pages of Illustrations."

PART I

The Language of Poetry

CHAPTER ONE

The Two Languages

Poetry is often regarded as a mystery, and in some respects it is one. No one is quite sure where poetry comes from, no one is quite sure exactly what it is, and no one knows, really, how anyone is able to write it.

The Greeks thought, or at least said, that it came from the Muse, but in our time no one has been able to find her. The Unconscious has been offered as a substitute, but that, too, is hard to locate. How anyone is able to write it is explained in this way: the poet is a Genius who receives inspiration.

One way to get a little more clarity on the subject was suggested to me by something Paul Valéry said when he was thinking about the things that could be said in poetry and not otherwise: he said that poetry was a separate language or, more specifically, a "language within a language." There would be, in that case, the ordinary language—for Valéry French, for us English—and, somehow existing inside its boundaries, another: "the language of poetry." Valéry let it go at that; he went on to talk about other things. I thought it worth taking literally and seeing where it might lead; I thought it might explain something important about how poems are written and how they can be read.

According to this idea, a poet could be described as someone who writes in the language of poetry. Talent is required for doing it well, but there are things that can help this talent to appear and to have an effect—for example, you have to learn this particular language, which you do by reading it and writing it. The language itself helps to explain inspiration, which is always, at a certain point in its development, the appearance of some phrase or sentence in the poetic language. You may be moved by the West Wind, but until the words come to you "O wild West Wind," the inspiration is still in an early, pre-verbal phase. Once "wild West Wind" is there, it leads to more of this oddly useful language; once the tone, the channel, the language level is found, the poem can take off in a more purely verbal way.

Before I came on this idea of poetry as a separate language, I had been thinking of the analogy of a verbal synthesizer, computer, or pipe organ.

You sat down at this instrument and *played;* you didn't tap out a clear message in teletypical prose. Whatever you said would be accompanied by music, and there were keys to press, to make comparisons, to exaggerate and lie, to personify, and so on. This idea of a synthesizer seemed to help explain the joy, even the intoxication, poets may feel when about to write, and when writing, and the similar joy and intoxication others may feel in reading their works. This joy seemed to me an element that was left out of most explications of poetry, or of the "poetic process." The synthesizer idea finally seemed to me a little askew, though, because it was too far away from language.

I also thought of likening writing poetry to going to a party. It puts you in a good mood. You know there will be music, even dancing; there's no work to be done there, just drinking, talking, and flirting. This analogy was fine for the initial pleasure part but not descriptive of what happens later, since in writing poetry you really do have to work, to make some kind of sense, and to bring things to a conclusion, which you don't usually have to do at a party.

A poet learns the language of poetry, works in it, is always being inspired by it. Just to use this language is a pleasure. I don't remember clearly that time in my childhood when to speak was an adventure, but I've seen it in other children; and I do remember the first year I spent in France, when to speak the French language gave me the same kind of nervous sense of possibility, ambition, and excitement that writing poetry has always done.

Poetry is an odd sort of language in that everyone who uses it well changes it slightly, and this fact helps to explain poetic influence and how poetry does change from one time and one poet to another.

Poetic purposes of a sort—a magical, religious sort—may be at the very origins of language or may have appeared very early on. To name things or beings was a first step to speaking to them and to trying to control them. Since its unknowable beginnings, however, language has become mainly a vast, reasonable, practical enterprise, with vocabulary and syntax and grammar to enable you to say almost anything you wish. The part the "almost" applies to is what can be said only by poetry.

If we take the idea of a poetic language seriously, it can be defined first as a language in which the sound of the words is raised to an importance equal to that of their meaning, and also equal to the importance of grammar and syntax. In ordinary language, the sound of a word is useful almost exclusively in order to identify it and to distinguish it from other words. In poetry its importance is much greater. Poets think of how they want something to sound as much as they think of what they want to say, and in fact it's often impossible to distinguish one from the other. This is an odd position from which to speak, and it's not surprising that strange things are said in such a language. The nature of the language can be illustrated by the way a nonsensical statement may, simply because of its music, seem to present some kind of truth, or at least to *be* something, even, in a certain way, to be memorable. For example:

> Two and two
> Are rather blue

"No, no," one may say, "two and two are four," but that is in another language. In this (poetry) language, it's true that "two and two are rather green" has little or no meaning (or existence), but "two and two are rather blue" does have some. The meanings are of different kinds. "I don't know whether or not to commit suicide" has a different kind of meaning from that of "To be or not to be, that is the question." Repetition and variation of sounds, among other things, make the second version meditative, sad, and memorable, whereas the first has no such music to keep it afloat. The nature of prose, Valéry said, is to perish. Poetry lasts because it gives the ambiguous and ever-changing pleasure of being both a statement and a song.

The music of language needs to be explained, since most often in reading prose or in hearing people talk we aren't much aware of anything resembling music. There are no horns, no piano, no strings, no drums. However, words can be put together in a way that puts an emphasis on what sound they make. Sound is part of the physical quality of words. "To sleep" means to rest and to be unconscious, and usually that is all it means, but it also has a physical nature—the sounds *sl* and *eep,* for example—that can be brought to the reader's attention, like the sounds hidden inside a drum that emerge when you hit it with a stick. Once you are listening to the sound as well as to the meaning—as you won't, say, if you read "Go to sleep" but will, almost certainly, if it is "To sleep, perchance to dream" (Shakespeare)—then you are hearing another language, in which that sound makes music which in turn is part of the meaning of what is said. The poetry language is used by persons who have things (known to them or not known) that they need to say, and who are moved by this need and by a delight in making music out of words.

The poet is led in uncustomary directions by the musically weighted language, and readers are led there in their turn. Poetry would just as soon come to a musical, as to a logical or otherwise useful conclusion; and in fact its logical or useful one would have to be also musical for the work to be poetry at all. In the ordinary language of ordinary experience, the thought or the remark "The sun is shining this afternoon" is likely to lead to other words related to these in a practical way: "Why don't we go out?"—or in a familiar and sociable way—"Yes, isn't it lovely?" If a person is "thinking in poetry" and speaking its language, the sounds—and the arrangement of these sounds, which is the rhythm—are more likely to determine what follows: after "The sun is shining this afternoon" may come "The moon will shine tonight/And I shall see my darling soon/By sun or candle light"; or "It is shimmering shafts of incalculable densities"; or "Yes, shining! Shine, sun, and warm us with your beams!" None of these is of much practical consequence but has an aesthetic consequence in that it gives pleasure and insight or does not. One is thinking of that kind of consequence when one writes or reads poetry.*

Music contributes to "sense" in various ways—in this Herrick poem, for example the rhyming of *laid* and *maid*:

> In this little urn is laid
> Prudence Baldwin (once my maid)
> From whose happy spark here let
> Spring the purple violet.
>
> (HERRICK,
> "On Prue His Maid")

Ordinarily one wouldn't say that ashes were "laid" in an urn—a body might be laid in a grave but hardly in an urn. And ashes aren't laid but put. The illogic of what is said is made "all right" by the rhyme, which gives enough pleasure to allow the reader to enjoy what is being said and to understand it. The happy lightness of Prudence's spirit is what the poem is about. Were you to say, instead, "In this little urn is laid Prudence Baldwin, once my housekeeper," that elusive meaning (along with the emotions it brings) wouldn't be there.

Along with communicating a meaning, music may make whatever is said convincing, by the beauty of the way it is said:

---

* The lexicon of this language, if one existed, would give a different emphasis to the information it gave about a word: the music would be given as much space at least as the meaning. Of *Sunday* it would certainly say, as ordinary dictionaries do, that it was a proper noun and a day of the week; and a description of its music would begin with its being composed of two separate sounds (which are also words) or "notes": *sun* and *day*, with the first sounded more strongly than the second, so that one says SUNday not SunDAY. But the phonetic description of the word wouldn't stop there. Examples might follow to illustrate its musical possibilities: its rhyming, say, with "Monday," "gun day," "fun day"; its partial rhyming in such phrases as "Sunday lunch," "summer Sunday," "Sunday and in love"; its metrical "rhyming" with "backwards," "speaking," "Irish," "motions"; its alliterative pairing with "secret," "south," "scouting," "sleep," "sandy." If it were a large dictionary, passages from poems would be cited to show how the sound of the word *Sunday* was part of their music and their meaning.

> Let me not to the marriage of true minds
> Admit impediments. Love is not love
> Which alters when it alteration finds
> Or bends with the remover to remove.
> Oh, no, it is an ever-fixed mark . . .
>
> (SHAKESPEARE, Sonnet 116)

It's possible that only a very few people have ever experienced the kind of noble unchanging love that Shakespeare refers to in these lines, but there are probably even fewer who don't believe it exists when they read them. Thanks to the music, emotion becomes stronger than reason—who wouldn't *wish* that such a feeling existed, or that one had felt it oneself?

Music can not only make an emotional statement convincing; it can also give an emotional content (and a clarity) to a statement that without it is nonsense and has neither.

> The sun is ten feet high.

Adding a line that rhymes with it can give feeling and meaning to this nonsensical statement:

> The sun is ten feet high
> Suzanne walks by.

Evidently, the speaker is in love. Suzanne's presence dazzles him like the sun, it makes the sun feel that close to him. The lines have meaning—the reader has an experience—a sort of miracle has taken place, all because of the sound equivalence of *high* and *by;* without it, not much would happen:

> The sun is ten feet high
> Suzanne walks past.

This is just a senseless statement followed by an irrelevant one. An equivalent in ordinary language to such a musical failing in poetry language might be a subject and verb that aren't in agreement; so that one can't "make sense" of what is said, as one can't here with *high* and *past* but can with *high* and *by.*

The language of poetry doesn't stay the same for poet after poet. Every time music creates (or contributes to) meaning, the way it does so becomes part of what other poets can do. And poets not only use what other poets have discovered but change it. It's a language that doesn't (can't) hold still. Each poet shows other poets how to write and how not to, as if saying, "Use me but don't sound like me; use me to make something else." Every speaker of this language, by speaking it differently, changes the language that later poets will be able to speak. Other poets' poetry, for poets, then, is a dictionary, a grammar, and a vocabulary, a place to begin. A passage of Marlowe's dramatic verse, like this one in which Tamburlaine is praising Zenocrate may please everyone, but for poets it may also be immediately seen to be *useful*—it shows a way to write sensuous, stately, yet natural-sounding lines of blank verse.*

> Zenocrate lovelier than the love of Jove,
> Brighter than is the silver Rhodope,
> Fairer than whitest snow on Scythian hills
> Thy person is more worth to Tamburlaine
> Than the possession of the Persian crown . . .
> (*Tamburlaine the Great,* part I)

Or this passage of Milton, or this much later one of William Carlos Williams, each of which shows other ways to write:

> Not that fair field
> Of *Enna,* where *Proserpi*n gath'ring flow'rs
> Herself a fairer flow'r by gloomie *Dis*
> Was gather'd . . .

> I have eaten
> the plums
> that were in
> the icebox

Along with its emphasis on music, poetry language is also notable for its predilection for certain rhetorical forms such as comparison, personification, apostrophe (talking to something or someone who isn't there), and for its inclinations toward the imaginary, the wished-for, the objectively untrue. Music either simply comes with these predilections or is a main factor in inspiring them. The sensuousness of music arouses feelings, memories, sensations, and its order and formality promise a way to possibly make sense of them.

The ordinary language is of course where the poetry language comes from. It has the words, the usages, the sounds that the poetry language takes up and makes its own. It constitutes, along with thoughts and feel-

---

* For more about blank verse, see p. 33.

ings, what may be called the raw materials of poetry. If you think of each word as a note, this ordinary language is like an enormous keyboard and wherever it is, the poet has a medium, just as the painter has, wherever there are paints, the sculptor wherever there is wood or stone. On the poetic keyboard, each note (each word) refers to or stands for something that is not physically present and that is not itself. This is easiest to see in regard to nouns. Here, on this page, is the word *horse* and over there, beside that tree, is a horse. The word *horse* can make a reader see, smell, touch, even feel as if riding on a horse. Since it isn't really a horse, it can't really be ridden or engaged to pull a cart; but it has advantages for the writer that its real-life counterpart lacks. It's lighter and infinitely more transportable; it can be taken anywhere and put with anything—the horse is in the harbor; the silence was breathing like a horse.

Words can be handled this way and the material world they represent can't be. As space yields to nouns, time may yield to verbs and their agile tenses: "The Russian army marched through Poland" is said in an instant; as is "I have loved you for ten thousand years." Wishes, spoken or on a page, are as physically real as facts: Would that it were evening! The future is easy to manage: "Once out of nature I shall never take/My bodily form from any natural thing" (Yeats, "Sailing to Byzantium"). With pronouns, identity can be altered: I am you. Adjectives are there to make possible every sort of modification hardly existent outside: an eighteenth-century sleep, mild sandals. Language also has grammatical and syntactical rules and structures that organize and clarify the world and experience: "If Napoleon hadn't lived, we wouldn't be here tonight." Another great gift of language is the enormous quantity of its words, and their variety—colloquial words, scientific words, slang, archaic words, etc. It's a huge medium, so much larger than any possible palette or keyboard that comparison seems foolish.

Given such a medium, it is hard to imagine not wanting to play with it, to experiment to see what might be said with it, to take its powers, as it were, into one's own hands. Bringing out its music is the first step in doing this. The language, musically inert but filled with promise, is there waiting. The poet comes at it somewhat like a translator, as Valéry said, a "peculiar kind of translator, who translates ordinary language, modified by emotion, into the language of the gods." I would call it the language of poetry, which may or may not help us to speak to the gods but does enable us to say great things to one another.

Poetry can do this because of one extraordinary characteristic of language, which is that it is without any impediment to saying things that are not true. Language has no truth- or reality-check. You can say anything. The only things it's strict about are grammar and spelling, and, in speech, pronunciation. You can say "Russia is on my lap" but not "Russia me lap am on." The conventional use of language does have restrictions: what we say must be clear (understandable) and true (verifiable) or, at least, familiar. A wild statement if it is sufficiently familiar will be allowed; "Life is a dream," but not "Life is two dreams." Poetry can say either one. Language is like a car able to go two hundred miles an hour but which is restricted by the traffic laws of prose to a reasonable speed. Poets are fond of accelerating: "In the dark backward and abysm of time" (Shakespeare); "They hurl with savage force their stick and stone/And no one cares and still the strife goes on" (John Clare); "I effuse my flesh in eddies and drift it in lacy jags" (Whitman).

Poets looking at language are enticed by it and want to use it, at least on those lucky days when the connection seems to be there between their feeling for the language and their power to do something with it. That connection is emotional and musical.

CHAPTER TWO

Music

Music can make us do what it wants.

(PYTHAGORAS)

Poetry searches for music amidst the tumult of the dictionary.

(BORIS PASTERNAK)

It's hard to say if the music of poetry creates the emotion in a poem, or if it is the poet's emotion that creates the music. Probably both are true. The intention to write with music, and the fact of doing so, are likely to put the writer in a state in which any emotions present have a good chance of coming out. It's a well-known quality of music that it can get to feelings very fast; and when a person writes, it can deepen and color whatever is there to be said. There have been poets who wrote poems while listening to music— but usually they are just finding their own, in the words they write. This music is the most essential part of the "translation" a poet makes from ordinary to poetic language.

The musical elements, the sounds that words have, are usually hidden, or mostly hidden. They can be brought out and made hearable by repetition. In ordinary prose and in conversation they are subjugated for the benefit of practical aims: the sentence has a point unrelated to music and which in fact it would disturb if it became too audible—"No dogs are allowed on the beach" is, as far as music goes, pretty much of a blank; the purpose of the sentence is to keep dogs off the beach. If you read, instead, "No dogs, and no logs/Are allowed on the beach," or "No poodle however so trim/And no dachshund unable to swim," etc., you might smile, grow dreamy, or begin a little dance, but in any case might lose the practical message. Individual words in non-literary prose and in conversation are like persons holding on to a rope and hauling a boat out of the water; the practical end, the beaching of the boat, matters infinitely more than the beauty or the graceful movement of the haulers. Poetry, by means of repetition, makes us aware of the words that are hauling in the meaning so that we have to respond to them, both as music and as sense.

REPETITION AND RHYTHM

Repeating sounds and rhythms makes them physically apparent and demanding of attention. In the sentence "I was wondering if you'd like to go for a walk today" there is no word that stops us and makes us experience the words, nothing that makes a noticeable musical sound; the person responding to it is likely to say simply yes or no. This situation is changed by a translation into the language of poetry: "I wondered if you/Would like to go out/To walk in the park,"—here all three lines have the same pattern of strongly and weakly stressed syllables: de*DUM* da da *DUM;* or, "The sky is so blue!/I wonder if you/Would like to go out/and wander about," in which sound is repeated (rhyme). There is no beautiful music here, but one does hear the sound of the words and phrases, which is the beginning of its being possible. An appropriate answer to the poetry-language question would be in the same language: "I very much would/So I will get dressed/And go walking with you."

Rhythm is easier to understand once you realize that every word in the language already has one. Each word has a little music of its own, which poetry arranges so it can be heard. The rhythm in words is a matter of stresses: one syllable is emphasized—or, one might say, "pronounced"— either more or less than the syllable next to it: the word *father* is a *DUM* da—one pronounces it *FATH*er; the word *before* is a da *DUM;* *CAT*alogue a *DUM* da da; after*NOON* is a da da *DUM;* one-syllable words can't have a rhythm any more than one drumbeat can, but in a rhythmic series they can be either das or *DUM*s, unstressed or stressed: *TRY* this; try *THIS.*

It's hard not to hear repeated rhythms, as in "Father! Father! Laughter! Laughter!" which is four *DUM* das in a row; or as in "Alone beneath the shining autumn moon," which is five successive da *DUM*s.

It is easier to write in rhythm than might be supposed. By saying any simple phrase and listening to where the strong stresses are, then saying three other phrases that "sound right with it," that have stresses more or less in the same place, you have caught on to rhythm and have written four lines that have it—by continuing, for example, "Is there any butter on the table?" with:

Is there any sugar in the coffee?
Are there any comics in the paper?
Are there any dolphins in the sea?

Here there is pleasure in the music of *sugar, coffee, comics,* etc., because of the "unnaturally" regular order in which these words occur.

Something similar can be seen in bodily movement. Raising your right leg once to walk forward probably means you are going somewhere, perhaps to the door, and the gesture (raising the leg) passes unnoticed. But if you raise your leg in precisely the same way a few times more, it becomes noticeable—and you are probably not walking but dancing.

LINE DIVISION

Line division is a part of rhythm. It establishes the place where the rhythm temporarily stops. It helps to determine in fact what the rhythm is, by means of the stop—or what in music is called a "rest"—that it creates. "O my luve's like a red,/Red rose" has a different rhythm from that of "O my luve's like a red, red rose."*

Lines can divide statements up in a balancing and rhetorical way—

A little learning is a dangerous thing;
Drink deep, or taste not the Pierian spring;
(POPE, "Essay on Criticism")

or in an unsettling way—

moving a perhaps
fraction of flower here placing
(CUMMINGS,
"Spring is like a perhaps hand")

or they can give an apparent (rhythmical) order to jagged and unconnected statements—

---

*When poetry is written out the way prose is, the breaks between lines are indicated by slashes. So "O my luve's like a red,/Red rose" is meant to be read as two lines:

O my luve's like a red,
Red rose

To employ her
Construction ball
Morning fed on the
(ASHBERY, *Europe*)

As far as prose sense is concerned, line divisions are an interruption for no reason—ordinary English, unlike music, doesn't include "rests" except for those necessary for understanding the prose sense of what is said; these are indicated by punctuation marks. Line breaks cause stops the way periods and commas do, but, instead of being necessary for sense, draw attention to tone and sound. In doing so, they make poetic sense, but that is a different kind. The fact that they are interruptions is what they are all about. Reading, and having to stop for them, one becomes more conscious of the words as units in themselves. For example, if I put the line breaks in part of what I've just said, I get:

One becomes
More conscious
Of the words

And here, because of the lines, I feel, as I didn't before, the pleasantly similar sounds of *becomes* and *conscious* and also the repetition and variations of the rhythm:

da da *DUM*/da *DUM* da/da da *DUM*
One be*COMES*/more *CON*scious/of the *WORDS*

It's a music that it's tempting to go on with: "One becomes/More conscious/Of the words/When one looks/At a person/One has loved/For a long, long time/And one knows/That one is saying/What one should/Have said a long/Time before. . . ." In my original sentence, I was aware neither of the music of the words I was writing nor of any poetic promise in them of any sort—certainly no love story. But the hesitations caused by the line breaks resulted in my speaking in a way I speak when I am unhappy, and this seemed to lead inevitably to my speaking of something sad.

METER

Rhythm can be metrical or non-metrical. Metrical means that the rhythm is to a great degree regular and fixed: a pattern is already set and waiting for the poet to use, a pattern of alternating stressed and unstressed syllables like the da *DUM* da *DUM* da *DUM* da *DUM* in which Marlowe wrote "The Passionate Shepherd to His Love":

> A *BELT* of *STRAW* and *Ivy BUDS*
> With *CORal CLASPS* and *AMber STUDS*

or the unrhymed iambic pentameter line (which goes da *DUM* da *DUM* da *DUM* da *DUM* da *DUM*, having one more da *DUM*—foot—than Marlowe's lines) Shakespeare used in his plays:

> But *SOFT*! What *LIGHT* through *YONder WINdow BREAKS*?
> (*Romeo and Juliet*)

Writing in meter, the poet chooses a pattern and stays in it. The beauty of metrical music comes from the slight variations that are made on the pattern.

Meters are identified by two characteristics: the kind of stress pattern they have and the number of times this pattern is repeated in each line. Or you could say, by the kind of metrical unit and the number of these units in a line. Almost always, each unit contains one stressed syllable and usually one, and less often two, unstressed syllables. These units are called "feet." The number of words is irrelevant: "feet" are about syllables. The word *good-bye* is a foot and is pronounced da *DUM*. There are different kinds of feet, depending on where the stressed syllable comes and how many other syllables there are. The most common foot in English poetry is called an iamb or iambic foot. *Good-bye* is an iamb, as is the phrase "as if," an unstressed syllable followed by a stressed one. A line composed of da *DUM*s is an iambic line. *Baby*, a *DUM* da, a stressed syllable followed by an unstressed one, is a trochee. Less frequently used feet include the anapest—under*NEATH*, after*NOON*, da da *DUM*—and the dactyl—*HOL*iday, *SEM*inar, *DUM* da da. Words like *afternoon* and *seminar* may be made part of iambic or trochaic lines by placing them so that there is an expected stress on their more lightly stressed syllables, *AFT* and *NAR*:

> This afternoon we'll hold a seminar
> This *AFTerNOON* we'll *HOLD* a *SEMiNAR*

That is to say, depending on the metrical pattern set up, *AFTERNOON* can be pronounced after*NOON*, as in "In the long afternoon underneath the arcades" or *AFTerNOON*, as in "This afternoon we'll hold a seminar." It can't ever be pronounced af*TER*noon; that pronunciation makes the word unrecognizable.

Familiar phrases also have a meter to begin with: "in *LOVE*," for example, is iambic, as is "worn *OUT* "; and "*KISS* me" is usually trochaic. What you mean to say of course can change the pattern:

> For I am *IN* love and not *OUT* of love.

An iambic line doesn't have to be composed of iambic words or phrases, but rather of iambic feet, which may include parts of non-iambic words. In Romeo's "But soft! What light through yonder window breaks?" both *yonder* and *window* are trochaic, but fit into the iambic pattern of the phrasing—the "feet" they're part of are "through *YON* " and "der *WIN*."

Most lines of English metrical poetry are of from three to five feet. A three-foot line is called trimeter, and a line with three iambic feet is called iambic trimeter:

> My heart keeps open house,
> My doors are widely swung
> (ROETHKE, "Open House")

A line with four iambic feet is iambic tetrameter:

> Had we but world enough, and time
> This coyness, lady, were no crime
> (MARVELL, "To His Coy Mistress")

with five, iambic pentameter:

> That's my last Duchess painted on the wall
> Looking as if she were alive. I call
> That piece a wonder, now . . .
> (BROWNING, "My Last Duchess")

with six feet, an alexandrine:

> Fool, said my Muse to me, look in thy heart and write
> (SIDNEY, "Astrophel and Stella")

Seven-foot lines, called fourteeners because of their fourteen syllables, haven't been used much since the Renaissance:

> Well (quoth Apollo) since my Feere and Spouse thou can not bee,
> Assuredly from this time forth yet shalt thou be my tree
> (OVID, *The Metamorphoses,* tr. Golding)

The secret of writing well in meter—and of reading it well—is being aware of the two kinds of rhythm in any metrical line: the imposed metrical rhythm, and the natural speech rhythm, which isn't eliminated, but simply modified, by the meter. One doesn't want the natural rhythm to be lost, or the line will sound "stilted" and stiff and deprived of the emotion there is in natural speech; one also wishes to keep the elevation and force and elegance that the metrical music may bring with it. So one writes—and reads—hearing them both, in a way, at the same time.

When the natural rhythm seems to *be* the main rhythm and the metrical rhythm is mostly unheard (seeming to give no more than slight highlights to the natural rhythm), one may have something especially effective and beautiful, as, for example, in Prospero's lines to Ferdinand:

> Our revels now are ended. These our actors,
> As I foretold you, were all spirits, and
> Are melted into air, into thin air . . .
>
> *(The Tempest)*

When this kind of meter (unrhymed iambic pentameter, also called blank verse) first came into English poetry, it had no such beautiful variety, subtlety, and nuance, but often sounded mechanical and robotic: natural speech rhythm seemed blocked by stresses too mechanically regular:

> Your wonted true regard of faithful hearts
> Makes me, O king, the bolder to resume,
> To speak what I conceive within my breast
> Although the same do not agree at all
> With that which other here my lords have said
> Nor which yourself have seemèd best to like
>
> (SACKVILLE & NORTON, *Gorboduc*)

This is meter defeating speech in the sense of keeping it from expressing feeling. It needs variations—and maybe something like Shakespeare's genius—to lift it up.

Blank verse (unrhymed iambic pentameter), Shakespeare's and Milton's meter, has been the standard English meter for plays and for narrative poems. (For examples of blank verse in the anthology, see pp. 167, 168, 171, 180, 189, 228, 232.) In the ways it has changed, it's a good example of how the poetry language itself changes, how at different epochs it puts different kinds of music in poets' heads. At first, blank verse was often clumsy and mechanical, as in the (above) *Gorboduc* example. It wasn't much of a pleasure to say aloud. Christopher Marlowe created a blank verse line that was at the same time speechlike, elevated, and melodious:

> And ride in triumph through Persepolis
> (*Tamburlaine*)

Marlowe also invented, or at least perfected, a way of harmoniously joining together a series of blank verse lines (a "verse paragraph") so that a whole passage had a unifying music, the way a lyric poem does. Shakespeare, who was happily influenced in his blank verse by Marlowe, added to what Marlowe had done his perfection of the technique of "enjambment"—that is, of runover lines, lines in which there is no natural syntactical stop at the end of the line, just a metrical one. Contrast these two passages, one early, one late Shakespeare:

> But soft! What light through yonder window breaks?
> It is the East, and Juliet is the sun
> (*Romeo and Juliet*)

These lines are "end-stopped," not enjambed. There is a strong reason to pause at the end of each line. The following lines are enjambed:

> My desolation does begin to make
> A better life
> (*Antony and Cleopatra*)

One pauses only slightly after "make," there being no syntactical reason to stop, and with the natural music of the phrasing such that it hurries one on. This enjambment addition to poetry language permitted greater subtlety and flexibility and naturalness in blank verse lines. A later change was the introduction of extra unaccented syllables in the line. This practice is noticeable in Wordsworth and other Romantic poets. Before this time, blank verse lines had to be strictly ten syllables, except for the allowable extra unaccented syllable at the end of the line—"To be or not to be, that is the question." (In this line there's also what's called a "reversed foot"—"*THAT* is" instead of "that *IS*," which is allowable and apparently sounded all right to Shakespeare.) If there was what seemed to be an extra syllable elsewhere in the line, it was meant to be elided (skipped over, melded with the next syllable)—"Of man's first disobedience, and the fruit": the reader was meant to read this as ten syllables, not eleven, by hearing "dis-o-be-dyence" rather than "dis-o-be-di-ence." However, eighteenth-century poetry critics misunderstood Milton's practice and thought he was putting in extra unaccented syllables, writing eleven- or even twelve-syllable lines. Since Milton was the most highly esteemed of poets, this was thought to be acceptable. Somewhat mysteriously, then, eleven-, twelve-, and even thirteen-syllable iambic pentameter lines began to sound all right.

> Inscrutable workmanship that reconciles
> Discordant elements. . . .
>> (WORDSWORTH, *Prelude*)

Here the second "foot"—*ableWORK*—has three syllables, two unstressed, one stressed. This change brought blank verse closer to ordinary speech while at the same time depriving it of a certain elegance. Some modern writers have found any kind of blank verse too regular, too "old-fashioned" and too "poetic" and have written instead non-metrical lines with about five stresses in each; other poets, Frost, for example, used blank verse but with even more freedom than Wordsworth's:

> Right past both father and mother, and neither stopped it
>> (FROST, "The Witch of Coös")

Meter is attractive because it gives an instant feeling of form, of things being well-organized, well-considered, neat, and clear. It organizes what is said into a recognizable musical pattern and allows us to enjoy variations on that pattern. It can lift what is said so it sounds as if it were being pronounced in a great place, part of a celebration; with it, even the simplest statements may sound momentous:

> Keep up your bright swords, for the dew will rust them
>> (SHAKESPEARE, *Othello*)

It can help, in conjunction with rhyme, to make a formally elegant work, like a Ben Jonson song (see anthology, p. 174) or a very funny one, like Byron's *Don Juan* (pp. 190–96).

The kinds of meters (like the kinds of rhyme schemes and stanzas) are part of the language of poetry, as verb forms, subject-verb agreement, and idiomatic ways to say things are part of the ordinary language. They may be hard to use, or hard to read, at first, but usually not for long. For a poet, writing (or speaking) in iambic pentameter may become as natural and as automatic as speaking in grammatically correct sentences. The formal aspect of meter gives to both poet and reader, when it is well used, a sense of technical grace and expertise, even of perfection. It proposes clear artistic standards for the poet to meet, and also may be, by its incessant demandingness, inspiring.

By our own time most poets have been willing to give up the good qualities of meter for qualities they found, and preferred, in non-metrical poetry. Almost all non-metrical poetry also does without rhyme (rhyme will be our next subject). Metrical poetry began to sound "poetic," as if it were mainly living off other poetry and had lost too much connection with the life outside it—with the way people think, talk, and feel.

Non-metrical music can be created in various ways. One is by taking phrases that already have a strong natural speech rhythm and putting a few together in every line; if they are parallel with each other, i.e., have the same or approximately the same rhythm, the result may be something like:

> I am the poet of the body and I am the poet of the soul
> > (WHITMAN, "Song of Myself")

Even a less pronounced parallel syntactical construction can create non-metrical music—as in these not-by-Whitman lines each divided by a preposition:

> The anemones are blossoming beside the poet of the body
> The roses bloom above the dwelling of the five-hundred mechanical engineers
> The rocks are falling and the birds are making their circles of tu-whit tu-wu beyond the old gulch.

Strong accents can be forced by means of punctuation and repetition:

> I am the poet! the poet of the body!
> And where, tell me where, is the poet, the poet of the soul?

In all these cases when there are very strongly accented syllables, the mind tends to make music out of their patterns.

Similar effects can be obtained, or intensified, by the way the poem is divided into lines. Line division obliges the reader to put accents where they might not ordinarily be. For example, if Whitman had written:

> I am the poet/Of the body/And I am the poet/Of the soul

there would be a distinctly different music from that in the line he actually wrote:

I am the poet of the body and I am the poet of the soul

There are more extreme ways of ending lines that bring accents to syllables that ordinarily would have none:

> I have eaten
> the plums
> that were in
> the icebox
> (WILLIAMS, "This Is Just to Say")

One of the great pleasures of non-metrical rhythm is the chance it gives to find music in ordinary ways of talking and writing rather than (the metrical pleasure) in infusing it into or imposing it on them. Another pleasure is in being "plain." Sometimes it seems there is nothing more beautiful that one could read (or write) than lines with that "plain" music:

> That's not a cross look, it's a sign of life
> but I'm glad you care how I look at you
> (O'HARA, "Poem")

> oh god it's wonderful
> to get out of bed
> and drink too much coffee
> and smoke too many cigarettes
> and love you so much
> (O'HARA, "Steps")

Line endings can be obviously connected to feelings, as in the lines by O'Hara, or not, as in Williams's lines.

Once the rhyme and meter barriers were broken, poets tried out all kinds of ways to write poetry without them; among the more radical experiments are Williams's one-word-per-line poem "The Locust Tree in Flower," Apollinaire's calligrammes, "concrete" poems, Ashbery's numerous experiments, including *Europe,* of which the main formal element is the interruption and altering of everything with each new line, Cummings's jumping-around-the-page poems, and the Italian Futurist* poet Marinetti's

---

* Futurism was an artistic and literary movement in Europe just before and during World War I which opposed traditional art with an art that incorporated the violence and rapid movement of modern machines.

poems made up entirely of imitations of the sounds of war. These are all in the Experimental Division of non-metrical poetry, which is a different place from the more usual one, in which the new technique is directed more toward expression than toward experimentation. The two can hardly be separated, though: Apollinaire's calligrammes are often lyrical and tender (see anthology, p. 234), and whatever is discovered by the experimenter is then available for use (and further changed) by the lyricist; and these two are sometimes the same poet.

The first consistently non-metrical poet in English was Walt Whitman. He brought into poetry the heightened prose of nineteenth-century political orators and preachers and that of the King James translation of the Bible:

> It avails not, time nor place—distance avails not,
> I am with you, you men and women of a generation, or ever so many
>   generations hence,
> Just as you feel when you look on the river and sky, so I felt,
> Just as any of you is one of a living crowd, I was one of a crowd
>
> (WHITMAN, "Crossing Brooklyn Ferry")

The rhythm is the natural rhythm of the speaking voice; not one syllable is changed even slightly—as it would be, for example, if the lines were metrical:

> Not distance, no, nor time, nor place avails
> O men and women of a future time
> To separate us, for we are the same
> When looking at the river or the sky
> Or being members of a living crowd

This metrical version isn't the way anyone speaks—there is a musical heightening of such syllables as VAILS, OF, FOR, AT, OR, and again OF that has no relation to natural colloquial emphasis. The meter is like a rhythmic piano accompaniment that changes the way the words are said. The reader "sings along" with it. Whitman's non-metrical lines are more like natural speech, but not quite: someone talking is more likely to say "Neither time, place, nor distance can keep us from being together" or, even more likely, "Time isn't going to keep us apart, and neither is distance; and I don't think where we happen to be is going to either." One skips over these versions as if there were no music in them at all. Though colloquial, Whitman's lines are full of stops and repetitions and variations that make us aware we are at a concert and not out on the street:

It a*vails* not, time nor *place*—*dist*ance a*vails* not . . .

While it loses the particular heightening of metrical poetry, this non-metrical poetry gives the impression of being natural and artistic at the same time. As with most artistic changes, something is gained and something is lost.

To readers, what is gained is of more interest, since what is lost can still be found in other poems.

Once it was discovered that non-metrical verse could give such pleasures, it became an important part of the language of poetry; many poets wrote it, and most of these wrote it in ways different from Whitman's. One Whitman-like quality most poems held on to, though, was closeness to natural speech:

> Sweep the house clean,
> hang fresh curtains
> in the window,
> put on a new dress
> and come with me!
> (WILLIAMS, "Love Song")

The new rule was that everything could be a poem as long as it "sounded right." The poem still had to sound right, but there were many more ways in which it could do so.

The appeal of non-traditional poetry (to sum up a little) was its seeming more "natural" (no artificial regimenting of syllables), more "modern," practical, plain, down to earth, with less decoration and less fuss—more permissive, freer, offering a much greater variety of possible kinds of poems; thus, potentially, more surprising and unpredictable (writing or reading a poem you never know what you're going to get); and connected to this uncertainty, the "metaphysical" interest of not knowing whether or not it is "really poetry," i.e., the pleasure of living, as it were, on the edge of art.

All this, along with the main appeal of the new poetry: its offering, by being colloquial, a more immediate connection of language and feeling:

> don't be shy of unkindness, either
> it's cleansing and allows you to be direct
> like an arrow that feels something
> (O'HARA, "Poem")

Non-metrical rhythm made a big change in the language of poetry. Poets didn't entirely stop using meter (and, often along with it, rhyme), but poems are now written with the possibility of either using meter or not.

This change hasn't diminished the resources of the language of poetry but has increased them.

RHYME

Rhyme is a poetic use of the sound of words, as meter is a poetic use of the order (and thus the rhythm) of syllables. Rhyme is part repetition and part variation: the beginning consonant sound has to be different and all that comes after it has to be the same: *hat/cat, horse/force, tomorrow/sorrow, attitude/latitude.* As can be seen from these examples, the rhyming has to begin on the stressed syllable of the word: *so*rrow, to*mo*rrow.

The most familiar kind of rhyme is complete rhyme: *sleep* and *keep.* These complete rhymes are the kind that traditionally come at the ends of lines, and along with adding music to the poem help to give it an organization. But there are other kinds of rhyme, too, sound similarities that echo through poems and give them music of a subtler, less noticeable kind. These are called partial rhymes and may be repetitions of the vowel sounds of accented syllables—*sleep* and *reef*—or of their beginning and ending consonants—*sleep* and *slap.* There is also the minimal sound similarity called alliteration, in which the only thing that is the same in two syllables is the beginning consonant sound: *bus* and *bed; sleep* and *slender.* When end rhymes determine the tune of a poem, these partial rhymes contribute to its nuances. In poetry without end rhymes, these partial rhymes may to a greater degree carry the main burden of the music.

Rhyme is more obvious than meter. It's louder. It draws attention to itself and can be heard right away.

> Farewell, too little and too lately known,
> Whom I began to think and call my own;
> For sure our Souls were near ally'd; and thine
> Cast in the same Poetick mould with mine
> (DRYDEN,
> "To the Memory of Mr. Oldham")

When rhymes come at the ends of two lines in a row, as they do here, the lines are called couplets. (Three rhymed lines constitute a triplet, which is much rarer.) These loud, quickly occurring rhymes tend to create an effect of neatness, compactness, and convincingness.

Rhymes at the ends of alternating lines give more the pleasure of surprise and of satisfaction after a little suspense:

Who says that fictions only and false hair
Become a verse? Is there in truth no beauty?
Is all good structure in a winding stair?
May no lines pass, except they do their duty
    Not to a true, but painted chair?
        (GEORGE HERBERT, "Jordan(I)")

In the old English ballads, only the second and fourth lines of the four-line stanza have rhymes.

O long, long may their ladies sit
    With their fans into their hand
Or ere they see Sir Patrick Spens
    Come sailing to the land
        (ANONYMOUS BALLAD,
        "Sir Patrick Spens")

Rhyme schemes are sometimes more intricate, as for example in some poems by Jonson and Donne (see anthology, pp. 174–175). Rhymes may be also used very irregularly, as in Milton's "Lycidas" or in Eliot's "The Love Song of J. Alfred Prufrock."

In most poems written before our time, rhyme is loud and clear and is meant to be noticed. It creates pleasing sounds and a rich musical texture. In some poems written as songs, rhyme and other noises seem to be the main things there:

Whenas the rye reach to the chin
And chopcherry, chopcherry ripe within
    (GEORGE PEELE,
    "Whenas the Rye Reach to the Chin")

When roasted crabs hiss in the bowl,
Then nightly sings the staring owl,
                            Tu-who;
Tu-whit, tu-who: a merry note
While greasy Joan doth keel the pot.
    (SHAKESPEARE,
    "When icicles hang by the wall")

The rhymes and the repetitions add to the festivity: the words "sing" more than they "say." This richness of rhymes—here, of all kinds, including alliteration—has also been used for more difficult and less familiar celebrations:

Enough! The Resurrection
A heart's clarion! Away grief's gasping, joyless days, dejection.
Across my foundering deck shone
A beacon, an eternal beam. Flesh fade, and mortal trash
Fall to the residuary worm; world's wildfire, leave but ash:
In a flash, at a trumpet crash,
I am at once what Christ is, since he is what I am, and
This Jack, joke, poor potsherd, patch, matchwood, immortal diamond,
Is immortal diamond.

(HOPKINS, "That Nature is a Heraclitean Fire. . . .")

Hopkins's rhyming words strike quickly, with an effect like lightning; a reader is rushed from one to the other. Rhymes can also slow down reading:

Anon his heart revives: her vespers done,
Of all its wreathèd pearls her hair she frees;
Unclasps her warmèd jewels one by one;
Loosens her fragrant bodice; by degrees
Her rich attire creeps rustling to her knees:
Half-hidden, like a mermaid in sea-weed,
Pensive awhile she dreams awake, and sees,
In fancy, fair St. Agnes in her bed,
But dares not look behind, or all the charm is fled.

(KEATS, "The Eve of St. Agnes")

It's natural to pause at each musical effect to enjoy the sensations it gives, sensations that may be both of music and of other kinds of experience. In the Keats stanza, for example, the sweet musical harmony of *knees,* after *frees* and *degrees,* encourages the reader to pause there, and, in so doing, to get more of an experience of Madeline's knees as well as of the music. Of course, both in the Keats and Hopkins lines, there is a lot of other musicality to go along with the complete rhymes: alliteration ("Flesh fade . . . fall"; "half-hidden"; "in fancy, fair"), half-rhymes of all sorts ("resurrection/clarion"; "beam/worm"; "sea-weed/dreams"), and sequences of strongly stressed syllables that make the meter slower and richer ("world's wildfire, leave but ash," "attire creeps rustling," "mermaid," "sea-weed"). The complete rhymes, though, are the stars, or at any rate the bandleaders that keep all these others in tune.

Organizing is the other main thing rhyme does—along with making a pleasing music. Rhymes at the ends of lines do the most obvious organizing—they are like the bows dancers might make at the end of a series of steps. The poem stops for a moment, then starts up again. The new line may continue or may take the poem in a new direction. But the rhymes create a kind of unity of the music that carries over to the thought. They tie the lines together—in couplets, in quatrains, or in some other way.

For poets, rhymes provide a way to make things fit; and they give them something to go toward. Poets may have a meaning in mind, something they want to say, but as their poem heads for that sense, it is also headed for a "sound sense," the rhyme that will keep it musically on course. It can be difficult to find rhymes, and frustrating, but it can always be done (in an emergency, one can change the first rhyme word, after all) and the effort, momentary or lasting, may be inspiring. There must be an uncountable number of wonderful things in poetry that have come from the need to find rhymes. Often, I'd guess, poets aren't even particularly aware of searching for rhymes. Conversant as they are with the language of poetry, it may be more that the sound similarities are there in advance, to influence and to organize what they end up saying. A rhyme may in fact be the first sign of a poem the imagination gets.

The reader shares the poet's pleasure in the simultaneous appropriateness and surprisingness of the rhymes—appropriate to the meaning, and surprising that they are so. Good sense and communication don't ordinarily go with such foolishness as *done/one, frees/degrees/knees;* and it's agreeably surprising when they do.

This surprising appropriateness can also have a comic effect; Byron is a great master of that. Of sixteen-year-old Don Juan's taking meditative walks in the woods, Byron says,

> You may think 'twas philosophy that this did;
> I can't help thinking puberty assisted;

and of Juan's prudish mother,

> In virtues nothing earthly could surpass her
> Save thine "incomparable oil," Macassar!
> (BYRON, *Don Juan*)

It's a happy surprise to see a poet being so frivolous, masterful, and free with what is supposed to be so serious a responsibility and one of the things his performance will be judged by—proper rhymes.

NON-RHYMING
AND IRREGULARLY RHYMING POETRY

Rhyme of course was a big issue in the evolution of modern poetry. To a lot of poets, rhyme, like meter, seemed part of the old dispensation and an outmoded technique for poetry to use in dealing with the new life of the twentieth century. The very virtues of rhyme, the things it accomplishes best, were what was wrong with it: its "beautifulness" and its "efficiency," its capacity for organizing poems and for making what they said convincing and precise (the world didn't seem so beautiful, so well ordered, or so understandable). Also rhyme seemed to limit "freedom": the lure of being absolutely free in what one wrote was that one just might, in that way, come on something true. Or perhaps just new—that was also an attraction and a reason for giving up the old ways. Rhyme seemed to go with a past world.

Different poets, as might be expected, reacted in different ways. Yeats held on to rhyme but let it be rougher, less exact, rhyming *blood* with *aloud, summon* with *superhuman, work* with *dark, lap* with *escape.** Stevens held on to rhyme, as to other features of the poetic language, but put it in unexpected places—like the rhymes with *gown* in these lines:

> no thread
> Of cloudy silver sprinkles in your gown
> Its venom of renown, and on your head
> No crown is simpler than the simple hair. . . .
> (STEVENS,
> "To the One of Fictive Music")

Or rhyme could be used for a few line endings and then dropped:

> When the rain stops
> and the cat drops
> out of the tree
> to walk
> (ROBERT CREELEY,
> "Midnight")

Or a poet might be attracted to a kind of rhyming so quiet and subtle as to pass almost unnoticed:

---

* One can even see a little of this in Keats—*sea-weed* and *bed*—though in Keats the effect is to make the sound more sensuous, not rougher, as in Yeats.

There is a great amount of poetry in unconscious
	fastidiousness. Certain Ming
		products, imperial floor-coverings of coach-
wheel yellow, are well enough in their way but I have seen something
	that I like better—a
		mere childish attempt to make an imperfectly bal-
			lasted animal stand up,
	similar determination to make a pup
		eat his meat from a plate.

(MARIANNE MOORE, "Critics and Connoisseurs")

The rhyme of *Ming* and *something* is hard to catch; and so, in the predominantly colloquial prose rhythm of the lines, is the rhyme of *up* and *pup*. The pleasure a reader may get is hearing a not-quite-identifiable or findable music.

Williams, on the other hand, gave up rhyme (and meter) completely. He said he wanted to get to the music of the American spoken language because that's where the poetry was—there, and as he says in one of his poems (see anthology, p. 241), in the sound of such wholly urban, contemporary things as a concrete mixer. Giving up rhymes, he came on other sound similarities that intruded less on the sound of talk: "I have eaten/the plums/that were in/the icebox/and which/you were probably/saving/for breakfast." *Icebox* and *breakfast* seem unrelated plain words, but when put together like this they make music with their *s, b,* and *k* sounds and their trochaic (*DUM* da) rhyme.

The end of conventional rhyme—complete rhymes at the ends of lines—makes other sound similarities—the various kinds of partial rhymes—suddenly more audible and more important to the music. The poet, having given up rhyme, doesn't stop hearing the music of the poem: that the poem "sounds right" is essential to its being a poem, and sound similarities have everything to do with that—the sound, of course, being not only related to the emotional and intellectual content but infused with it and an integral part of it. So the poet must start hearing a music that is just as beautiful as before but now not sustained by regularly recurring notes. The intervals between one thought, between one musical impulse or one musical idea or sequence and another can be smaller or greater, according to the secret ways in which the mind is led by its desire for it, without the necessity of anchoring it down at given and expected points. Along with making for a subtler kind of music, the displacement of sound similarity from its role as an organizing force in the poem to being entirely something the poet is more or less unconsciously drawn to may result in a correspondingly irregular and less rationally controlled train of thought.

The end rhymes are gone which completed thoughts and which organized them into a whole; the poet's mind is left floating among possible musics, at the ends of lines or more likely in their middles. This new music is appealing because it is surprising and fresh and to some poets is irresistible, too, for where it leads them, for giving them power to find a new order in the apparent disorder of sounds and thoughts. The new irregularly heard music can lead to a big, fragmentary collection of clearly depicted anecdotes and scenes, held together by invisible connections of sound and emotion, like Williams's "Della Primavera Trasportata al Morale: April," or to quite another kind of poem, like John Ashbery's "Clepsydra," in which meaning and music seem to have melted into one another so as to be indistinguishable:

> and you
> Must wear them like clothing, moving in the shadow of
> Your single and twin existence, waking in intact
> Appreciation of it, while morning is still there and before the body
> Is changed by the faces of evening.

There are certainly "meanings" here, but of a kind that were not possible to poetry before the displacement of ordinary rhyme. The kinds of "partial rhyme" here include pure vowel rhymes like *waking, appreciation, changed,* and *faces,* all with their stressed *a* sounds; and the quieter rhythmical repetitions of *clothing, moving, waking, morning,* and *evening.* There is also the intriguingly paradoxical rhyming of *single* and *twin existence* (of which one accepts the logic before thinking, because it sounds right); and, clearly illustrative of how sound can influence meaning, especially when the intellectual content is so kept in abeyance, is the effect *changed* has on *faces* (in the last line quoted). One has no idea what the faces are, but the stress that the *a* in *changed* obliges one to put on the first syllable make these faces, whatever they are, momentous, moving, and perhaps even a little frightening, in a way they wouldn't otherwise be—if, for example, the lines read "before the body/Is altered by the faces of evening."

The Ashbery passage is very difficult—i.e., unfamiliar, and takes a while to get used to—and so is probably not an ideal example for this early stage of the book. However, the latest, most hair-raising developments in the language of poetry are out there, too, along with Shakespeare and Shelley, and may as well be looked at, at least, as soon as possible.

Another aspect of poetic music is the stanza, which can be thought of as a very formal sort of version (in poetry language) of the paragraph; and there are, beyond that, the predetermined forms of entire poems—sonnets, sestinas, villanelles, and others. Stanzas and forms are pure poetry language, being, essentially, nothing more than ways of organizing other forms of poetic music—rhythm and rhyme. Stanzas, with their "rests" that are even more definitive than those at the ends of lines, orchestrate the repetitions and variations of meter and rhyme, and divide what is said into units—as do the different "movements" of symphonies, or of string quartets. This division adds possibilities to what the writer can do. Stanzas may continue directly from one to the next, or take off in new directions, for example. The most commonly used stanzas in English are couplets, two rhyming lines together, and quatrains, a four-line stanza usually rhyming lines 1 and 3 and lines 2 and 4, or just lines 2 and 4. Other stanzas include the three-line terza rima (see "Ode to the West Wind"), the eight-line ottava rima (see *Don Juan*) and the nine-line "Spenserian" stanza (see *The Faerie Queene*). Stanza forms have an obvious influence on what is written and on how that is read. You would probably find that the same story, if told in couplets, in quatrains, and in ottava rima, for example, would be in noticeable and interesting ways a different story. The stanza is part of the music, that "can make us do what it wants."

To both readers and writers, stanzas give extra pleasures of form within the larger form of the whole poem. A stanza can be admirable in itself; a harmony of good stanzas can be even better. *Stanza* is the Italian word for room; it's derived from the Latin word for "stopping place" or "place to take a stand." Each stanza may be paused in or quickly moved on from. In modern poems without rhyme or meter, a stanza may still be there that frames the music, as in Stevens's "Thirteen Ways of Looking at a Blackbird" (see anthology, p. 229), or Williams's "Young Woman at a Window":

> She sits with
> tears on
>
> her cheek
> her cheek on
>
> her hand
> the child
>
> in her lap
> his nose

pressed
to the glass

Poetic forms for whole poems tell the poet in advance how long the poem will be and what demands must be met on the way. The requirements inspire and provide a challenge to do something new in an old situation. Sometimes a form has become very successful, a great international star, as the sonnet did. The sonnet, as Petrarch wrote it in the fourteenth century (see anthology, p. 158), was a fourteen-line poem made up of two main parts, one eight lines long and rhyming ABBA ABBA, and the other six lines long, rhyming DEF DEF or some variation of that. Better known to readers of English is the kind of sonnet Shakespeare wrote, which may be divided into four parts: three quatrains rhyming ABAB CDCD EFEF and one final couplet rhyming GG (see anthology, p. 173). The Shakespearean version is, in English at any rate, easier to write than the Petrarchan one, which demands many similar rhymes. The sonnet form allowed for repetition and variation of a witty kind; it was long enough to get something said and short enough to "think in" and write in one sitting. It appealed to poets and to readers for several hundred years, and was obviously a form that caused poems to exist, caused poets to write them, as the form of the blues has caused songs to exist (see anthology, p. 269).

Modern poets, as would be expected, given their feelings about rhyme and meter, have had doubts about conventional stanzas and forms. Some, like Yeats and Auden, went on using them; others didn't. Some poets invented new ones. Ashbery's sixty-six-page poem "Litany" is written in two columns on each page which are meant to be read "as simultaneous but independent monologues"; O'Hara's "Day and Night in 1952" begins as a page and a half of prose poetry and concludes with thirty-three lines of verse, each ending with the word *of*. Stevens invented a blank verse stanza for lyric poems ("Sunday Morning," "Le Monocle de Mon Oncle") as well as the numbered variations-on-a-theme format of "Thirteen Ways of Looking at a Blackbird."

There is a reason, beyond the simple wish for newness, for new forms. After a certain time, a poetic form, somewhat like a style of dancing or painting or a way of dressing, begins to have a "period atmosphere," which adds a certain kind of meaning to the poem. Immediately, whether intended or not, it says, "I am a traditional form, and in being so I invite you to consider the past time that used me, as well as the different view of life that my form represents." A sonnet can no longer be just what it says any more than a Renaissance costume can be just a smart outfit. This doesn't mean good sonnets can't be written in our time, but that when they are written they are likely to have an additional sound and sense due to their history.

This discussion of music is brief but should give an idea. For more, George Saintsbury's *History of English Prosody* is a wonderful big book on the subject.*

---

* The music of poetry can be perceived without being understood intellectually: a poet can read Milton and begin writing Milton-like lines without counting syllables and a reader can enjoy Milton's steady beat in the same way. Music in poetry is "catching" as well as catchy. A poet can be a great poet, a reader an acute and happy reader, without being conscious of all the technical details of the art of poetry. There are, however, reasons for knowing the most important of these details. Technical knowledge helps one to recognize differences, and these differences in turn inspire ways of saying things. For a poet, a variation in poetic music almost automatically means a variation in what can be said. Knowing the technical aspects of poetic music can also be a help in revising, even in continuing a poem that may have gone off track, be musically changed, and the poet can't quite see why. Being able to analyze the difference between the rhythm in line one and in line ten may help get the poem back in tune. And of course if you want to sound like Shakespeare for a few lines, it's good to know what his iambic pentameter is like. For the reader, there is the pleasure of recognizing the music and being better able to enjoy its variations—to be stirred by a bravura performance, say, in decasyllabic lines or in the repetitions of a sestina (see anthology, p. 156). Recognizing the musical pattern of lines also improves the chance of reading them right and thus getting not only the music but the sense.

CHAPTER THREE

The Inclinations
of the Poetry Language

Poetry is recognizable most obviously by its music, but there are other features, too, that are often found in it. Among these are comparisons, personifications, apostrophe, and various forms of saying what is not exactly
true. These, less fundamental than music is, might be called rhetorical
and emotional tendencies or inclinations of the language of poetry. That
is, to be poetry, it has to be musical; and if it is poetry, it may well have
these other features, too. They aren't necessary, but poetry has had so
much success with them that they tend to be in poets' heads as lively possibilities when they write. Speakers of the poetry language must make
music or they aren't speaking it at all; and they have a tendency, these
speakers, to exaggerate, to compare, to talk to things, and so on, in a way
that escapes ordinary sense, to some degree, in order to make sense of
another kind.

> And I will luve thee still, my dear,
> Till a' the seas gang dry.
> (Burns, "A Red, Red Rose")

It's impossible to love that long because of the limitation of the human life
span, but a lover can feel that it is possible, and in that feeling the falsity of
the statement becomes a truth. And when Burns, earlier in this poem,
compares his luve to a red, red rose what is a reader to make of it? The young
woman presumably is much taller than a rose, has greater life expectancy,
has the power to move and to speak, and, even, has markedly different
looks. Actually, of course, there's no problem if one has the slightest familiarity with the poetic language. For an idea of how he feels the freshness,
fragile sweetness, and beauty of the girl, there is nothing so true as Burns's
statement. To another observer Burns's luve may seem to be a "young

female Scotsperson," or a nineteen-year-old daughter of X and Y; but these views of her don't seem truer or more important than Burns's. Her "rose-likeness" is one thing that causes things to happen around her, that makes being on the earth with her worthwhile. To speak to the wind, as Shelley does, is childish, impractical, and seems based on a false assumption that the wind can hear and respond; but it's also based on the true assumption that it's possible to talk to the wind—why be restricted by being told that you can't? The conviction that this talking is real and useful may be as strong as a similar conviction people have when they pray.

Poets anticipate what may be called the sense-breaking liberties these conventions, or inclinations, provide them, as singers may anticipate certain liberties of voice, and painters the expressive freedom of the splash of their brushes, and may be inclined from the very start of their writing a poem, to have ideas that derive from them. To walk into a room in a mood for making comparisons is not like being there to make an inventory of its contents.

COMPARISONS

Shall I compare thee to a summer's day?
(SHAKESPEARE, Sonnet 18)

And the fact that you move so beautifully more or less takes care of
      Futurism.

(O'HARA,
"Having a Coke with You")

Comparisons can be used to clarify something, which is usually what happens in prose; or to make things vivid, exciting, and emotionally appealing, which is what usually happens in poetry.

A cardinal
Passes like a flying tulip, lights and nails the green day
Down

(SCHUYLER, "Hymn to Life")

She burns like a shot glass of vodka
She burns like a field of poppies
at the edge of a rain forest
(YUSEF KOMANYAKAA,
"You and I Are Disappearing")

Comparisons are sometimes the only way some necessary thing can be said; this may be true even if part of the comparison is something not completely understood. "It was cold and dreary being without you" is general and vague, and doesn't include the springtime sense of being with the person, nor any thought of the fierce winds, snow, ice, and duration that are all suggested in Shakespeare's line "How like a winter hath my absence been."

Comparisons have to be fresh in order to have the best effect: if you write "red as a rose," few readers will see a rose, fewer still will smell one, or remember a particular rose on a particular day—thus, few will be emotionally affected. If you write "white as a rose," on the other hand, or "white and orange as a rose," you have a better chance of causing the little shock that makes reading a poem a live experience. "Red as a rose" is so familiar that a reader is most likely to take in the whole phrase at once, to accept it automatically, and to not see or feel anything.

A comparison not only compares but brings in more of the world. Explanatory sentences tend to restrict and even to reduce the amount of reality in what is being said; poetry, with its comparisons, expands it. In Shakespeare's expression of his feeling of missing his friend, there are winter days. If Rilke, in one stanza of a sonnet (from the *Sonnets to Orpheus*) about mirrors, compares the mirror to a gateway, the gateway is there in the poem, along with the wide forests the dawn has been compared to and the sixteen-point stag that he has compared to a chandelier:

> You, spendthrift, still giving yourself away to the empty ballroom—
> When the dark dawn comes, as wide as the forests,
> And the chandelier goes, like a sixteen-point stag
> Through your impossible gateway

This is a lot of life to have in so short a space, a big cast one might say, brought together by means of comparison.

Comparisons can be illuminating and reassuring—as if our senses had found an instant and convincing order in things that our reason couldn't see. They give a sense of control, of being in a position of power from which things can be seen and judged, where experience is expanded, and where knowledge is instantaneous and needs no study. It gives strength and pleasure to find likenesses—to write them, and to read them.

The sense poetry makes, with the aid of comparisons, doesn't replace ordinary intellectual sense but joins it to make more sense. No one will mistake Homer's "rosy-fingered dawn" for either a woman's hands or flowers, nor Shakespeare's "darling buds of May" for newborn babies, and no one is likely to confuse the two elements in

> Kisses on the breast, like water from a pitcher!
> (PASTERNAK, "Sparrow Hills")

but will have, instead, a sharper sense of all of them.

Comparisons are usually divided, in school, into two kinds, simile and metaphor. Similes are open, visible comparisons that make their intentions clear: I am saying that this resembles that. They use *like* or *as* to do so. Metaphors are quicker and more secretive: they skip the *like* or *as* and simply assume the likeness of A and B by having A behave as if it were B. "Love is like the sun" is a simile. "Love lights up the picnic" is a metaphor.

Metaphors are often more powerful than similes because they hit before the reader knows what's happening: we have accepted what was said, then find it doesn't make sense (intellectually), and yet it does.

> Steam wheezes between the couplings
> (RUTH STONE, "Winter")

In a simile, also, two things are experienced at once but more slowly:

> Steam came up through the couplings like an old person wheezing

Similes and metaphors can appear together, as they do in Schuyler's lines quoted above.

> A cardinal
> Passes like a flying tulip, lights and nails the green day
> Down

The *cardinal/tulip* comparison is a simile, out in the open; the *cardinal/carpenter* comparison (he nails down the day), however, isn't. The bird in this comparison isn't *like* a person nailing, he *is* one. Of course, there is also here the pleasure of the other meaning of "to nail down" (to settle the matter).

As elsewhere in poetry, things don't stay the same in what Wallace Stevens called the "realm of resemblances." Taste in comparisons has changed and gone on changing. Many Elizabethan comparisons were "set," artificial, and seemed to be "thought" or "figured out" likenesses rather than naturally sensed ones: the loved woman's eyes were compared to the sun, her mouth to a "gate of pearls" (Spenser), tears to thunderstorms, and so on. Sonnets would be built around one or two elaborately worked-out comparisons, like Sidney's comparing his beloved to a book, or Spenser's comparing courtship of his lady to a deer hunt. Spenser and Sidney have some more natural, fresh, and sensuous comparisons, as well; and finally, in Shakespeare, these fresh images become the most frequent kind:

> and then my state
> Like to the lark at break of day arising
> From sullen earth sings hymns at heaven's gate
> (SHAKESPEARE, Sonnet 29)

Donne's comparisons brought new parts of the world into love poems: his and his mistress's souls are compared to compasses; their eyes are hemispheres; his enduring though increased love is compared to national taxation policy.

Among the Romantic poets, Keats used comparisons to elaborate on and linger over physical sensations:

> Her rich attire creeps rustling to her knees:
> Half-hidden, like a mermaid in sea-weed,
> Pensive a while she dreams awake
> ("Eve of St. Agnes")

Shelley's comparisons do some of that, too, and also give unseizable abstractions a degree of sensuous life:

> The everlasting universe of things
> Flows through the mind, and
> rolls its rapid waves,
> Now dark—now glittering—now
> reflecting gloom....
> ("Mont Blanc")

Modern poets have used comparisons with the same kind of freedom, and even violence, with which they have used meter and rhyme. Traditional comparisons, to some, seemed so out of date as to be irrelevant, purely "poetical." (The wish for a somehow "non-poetical" or in any case less poetical poetry has been strong in many modern writers.) One somewhat violent use of comparison has been expanding the range of what may be compared, so as to include contemporary kinds of ugliness, harshness, and danger. Walking in the Realm of Resemblances, then, with this part of life in it, the poet has a chance of getting to a deeper and stronger truth, of perceiving undeniable new connections. "I love you as the bee loves the flower," or "as the evening loves the sea" seems lost in the world of old poetry and with nothing like the force of

I will cherish you
As a returning veteran
Cherishes
His only remaining leg
(VLADIMIR MAYAKOVSKY)

The poet's violence may be not toward the subject matter of comparisons, or toward their traditional appropriateness, but toward their reasonableness and even their comprehensibility. It is possible to think that if poetry remains faithful to what is rational and clear, then it will also remain a prisoner of what is already known: it will say, no matter what the poet intends, essentially the same old things. To Breton and other Surrealist poets, the existence of the form of comparison suggested one main thing: to stretch the comparison as far as it would go, preferably farther. Doing this, a poet might be able to free likenesses that before had been locked, with the key of rational intellect, in the unconscious. The Surrealists were excited by the idea of a great, fresh source of knowledge in the unconscious, which poetry could get to—and comparisons seemed one of the best ways. The further apart the terms of a comparison are, wrote Breton, the better it would be: "As beautiful as the chance encounter of a sewing machine and an umbrella on an operating table" (Lautréamont, *Les Chants de Maldoror*). This was the model for Surrealist comparisons. Breton wrote a whole poem of "surreal" comparisons about his wife:

My wife with wrists of matches

My wife with fingers of chance and of the ace of hearts.
(BRETON, "Free Union")

If poets like Breton, Mayakovsky, and Lorca ("coins in mad swarms/Devour the abandoned children") bombarded and stretched poetic comparisons, others subdued them so much as to make them almost invisible, as Williams did in "Queen-Ann's-Lace" (see anthology, p. 238), a poem that talks simultaneously about a woman's body and a field of white flowers but never compares the two. In doing so of course, Williams's poem is truer to actual experience than a comparison would be: one doesn't experience a likeness, not at first; first one is "fooled," one thinks X *is* Y; then a split second later one sees it isn't but is like it. For the reader the opposite happens: the poem seems disconnected and about two unrelated things—then, surprisingly, they're seen to be the same.

In the work of some poets there seems to be an abandonment of comparisons and replacement of them by a sort of layered language, one could say a language of rapid and rich juxtapositions, by means of which the collage and superimposition and bringing-together work of comparisons is accomplished with none of the "comparison machinery" showing.

> O white-chested martin, God damn it,
>   as no one else will carry a message
>   say to La Cara: amo.
>
> (POUND, Canto LXXVI)

Pound doesn't say "My feelings and my situation are like those of a Renaissance Italian lover," nor "A vow of love is like a military or civil message to be conveyed by a messenger," nor "a martin (bird) is like a human messenger who can speak Italian," yet all these things are implied, and since they go by so fast are more believable. The comparisons are assumed; they happen before you know they are there. In the following lines by Ashbery, it would be hard to know even what the unspoken comparisons might be; what one has is a sense of a lot of disparate things put together in a way that seems to enrich their poetic sense:

> To employ her
> construction ball
> Morning fed on the
> light blue wood
> of the mouth
> *(Europe)*

These seem comparisons at the outermost limits, more collecting than connecting, but making a connection anyway by the mysterious accident of their coming together.

Like rhyme and meter, comparisons are so fascinating and productive a part of the language of poetry and have in it such a grand and varied history of success, that poets, though they rebel against them, don't quite want to give up the good they bring, and promise to bring, when they write in that language. So rather than complete renunciation there are experiments, expansions, and substitutions. The Realm of Resemblances is still there, like a forest outside the intellectual window, and it's hard to see what poetry would do without it.

PERSONIFICATION AND APOSTROPHE

With how sad steps, O Moon, thou climb'st the skies
(SIDNEY, "ASTROPHEL AND STELLA, 31")

and the farm, like a wanderer white
With the dew, come back, the cock on his shoulder . . .
(DYLAN THOMAS, "FERN HILL")

Personifying ideas, concepts, objects, and other non-living or non-human things makes them easier to talk about; poets may be led to personification, too, by the sheer drama of it, the Night walking by in beauty (Byron), Love shooting all its arrows into the poet's heart (Sidney), Death stopping by to pick one up in his carriage (Dickinson). Like comparison, personification brings more of the world into the poem and also connects what isn't known directly with what is—Death has a chariot, Love has a bow with arrows. Poets tend to personify such things as it seems essential to deal with, to be familiar with, to try to control; left in their alien, non-human state, they may be of a species too far outside our own for us to have any contact with them. Love, Death, Autumn, Sorrow, April, the Past, the Future, Tigers, Sunflowers, Chance, once humanized, are brought into the realm we inhabit. In Sidney's sonnet beginning "With how sad steps, O Moon, thou climb'st the skies" the moon is personified (it is taking steps) and at the same time talked to. This kind of talking to is called apostrophe and it brings powerful, essential, and unmanageable things into the poem even more forcibly than either comparison or personifying does: there is a little intellectual distancing about both of those, whereas talking to something means assuming it is there and can both hear and respond. Being able to converse with Death, with Time, with "Visions of the hills!/And Souls of lonely places!" (Wordsworth) gives a feeling of power and control, at least of being beyond one's ordinary range.

In a general sense, both personification and apostrophe help us to resolve our disconnectedness, not only from the natural world (and in the case of apostrophe, too, from the dead and the as yet unborn), but also from the very abstractions we have invented in order to help us to understand it and ourselves. Personifications reinvent abstractions, bringing back their force:

And Joy, whose hand is ever at his lips
Bidding adieu . . .
(KEATS, "Ode on Melancholy")

Poor soul, the center of my sinful earth
(SHAKESPEARE, Sonnet 146)

Personification is a main feature of many religions—Greek religion personified and deified almost everything: the sun, the wind, death, wisdom, war, beauty. In ceremonies of other religions, men and women who are dressed as gods of Rain, the West, Terror, and Death, come close to people, touch them, dance with them, and are prayed to. The animistic belief that natural phenomena are alive and have souls, which is rarely found in its religious form in our civilization, persists in poetry, where, like other beliefs cast aside by rationality and science, it serves a purpose of dramatizing and of connecting things.

For Shakespeare and other Elizabethan and Jacobean poets, the main forces that seemed to define existence were Death, Time, and Love—these were the important ones to personify and to talk to:

> Nor shall Death brag thou wandrest in his shade
> (SHAKESPEARE)

> Death be not proud, though some have called thee
> Mighty and dreadful
> (DONNE)

> Love's not Time's fool
> (SHAKESPEARE)

The other great force was God, and those poets who believed in God might address Him in their poems. Talking to God is a special case of apostrophe, since it is based on a public tradition and on a private conviction that God actually exists, can hear, and can respond. Poets may believe they are talking to Time or to Death in the heat of writing a poem, but don't usually have a continuing feeling that such a conversation is possible. It is a contact by speech invented for the occasion, whereas talking to God (and His replying) may be felt to be possible at any time. This kind of apostrophe, then, may have, more than others, the tone of an ongoing conversation:

> Batter my heart, three-personed God; for You
> As yet but knock, breathe, shine, and seek to mend
> (DONNE, Holy Sonnet 14)

> Lord, how can man preach thy eternal word?
> He is a brittle crazy glass:
> Yet in thy temple thou dost him afford
> This glorious and transcendent place,
> To be a window, through thy grace....
> (HERBERT, "The Windows")

Talking to God is almost always praise or prayer. Or, as in Milton's sonnet, an urgent request:

Avenge O Lord thy slaughtered saints whose bones
Lie scattered on the Alpine mountains cold ...
（MILTON,
"On the Late Massacre in Piedmont")

For the Romantic poets, apostrophe and personification had another kind of value, enabling them to be close to Nature in a particularly intense way: so Shelley, speaking to the wind, the skylark, the moon; Keats, to a nightingale, to autumn, to a bright star; Byron, in *Childe Harold* to heroic landscapes—cliffs, oceans, mountains; Wordsworth, to the familiar as well as the most spiritual aspects of nature, addressed sometimes as specific individuals and sometimes as presences:

O sylvan Wye! thou wanderer through the woods ...
（WORDSWORTH,
"Lines, Composed a Few Miles
Above Tintern Abbey..."）

Ye Presences of Nature in the sky
And on the earth! Ye Visions of the hills!
And Souls of lonely places!
("The Prelude")

Poets and poetry itself, and other works of art that caught and preserved beauty, were also addressed, especially by Keats, who addresses sonnets to Homer ("Standing aloof in giant ignorance/Of thee I hear and of the Cyclades"), to "Romance" ("O golden tongued Romance, with serene lute!") and, most famously, an ode, to a Grecian urn ("Thou still unravished bride of Quietness").

Talking-to brings closeness and, also, it may be a feeling of power: "Roll on, thou deep and dark blue ocean, roll!" Byron says to the ocean, and for a moment he and his reader are the equals of the mighty sea and may feel strong rather than relatively helpless before it—so enormous, so powerful, and so wet. Under ordinary circumstances how could one imagine it would do as one wishes? And when Donne took on an even more fearsome force, in "Death Be Not Proud," even if Death could not hear or reply, Donne's own fear of death could hear him, and the conversation could be stirring for that.

Walt Whitman may have been the champion apostrophizer of all time; he talked to everything:

Outlines! I plead for my brothers and sisters!

Naturally enough—everything for him partook of the same selfhood and the same soul:

> Be firm, rail over the river, to support those who lean idly yet haste with
>   the hasting current;
> Fly on, sea birds! fly sideways, or wheel in large circles high in the air!
> Receive the summer sky, you water, and faithfully hold it till all
>   downcast eyes have time to take it from you!
> Diverge, fine spokes of light, from the shape of my head, or any one's
>   head, in the sunlit water!
>
> (WHITMAN,
> "Crossing Brooklyn Ferry")

Whitman uses apostrophe dramatically, to join in with everything, by telling it to do what it must, inevitably, do. This passage, from "Crossing Brooklyn Ferry," is in its entirety thirty-two lines long and all apostrophe. It begins with "Flow on, river!" and ends with "You furnish your parts toward eternity,/Great or small, you furnish your parts toward the soul." A line like Byron's to the ocean could have been, one may imagine, for Whitman just the beginning of a whole series of commands.

Whitman was a great transformer of the poetic language. No one ever repeated what he did with apostrophe, but what he did can be heard, usually in more modest and at least partly ironic ways, in the work of twentieth-century poets: in Williams, talking to his nose:

> Oh strong-ridged and deeply hollowed
> nose of mine! what will you not be smelling?
>
> ("Smell!")

in Pound's talking to his "songs" (his poems) and to Whitman himself; in Stevens's "To the Roaring Wind": "What syllable are you seeking,/Vocalissimus,/In the distances of sleep?/Speak it." For Frank O'Hara, talking to things is a part of the general excitement:

> Oh! kangaroos, sequins, chocolate sodas!
> You really are beautiful!
>
> ("Today")

> you, Motion Picture Industry,
> it's you I love!
>
> ("To the Film Industry in Crisis")

He uses it in a deliberately "showy" way.

Auden, as part of his general program to clarify and to explain, to bring the new world within the bounds of old wisdom (or the old world within those of the new wisdom), often personifies abstract concepts:

> Time will say nothing but I told you so
> > ("If I Could Tell You")

> Defenseless under the night
> Our world in stupor lies
> > ("September 1, 1939")

However, personification and apostrophe are not used much by modern poets. Concepts such as space and time and death and melancholy haven't often been personified and conversed with. Our linguistic sophistication has made it hard for us even to believe in abstract words, much less to start talking to them as if they were human.

Personification and apostrophe seem unable to bring us close to nature as they did Wordsworth nor make us one with it as they did Whitman. But, as is the case with rhyme, meter, and comparisons, the good these features give to poetry—the fullness, the feeling of power, connection, and control—has not entirely gone away, even in the work of poets who rarely use them, but has reappeared in subtler forms:

> Oh! Blessed rage for order, pale Ramon,
> The maker's rage to order words of the sea,
> Words of the fragrant portals, dimly starred,
> And of ourselves and of our origins,
> In ghostlier demarcations, keener sounds.
> > (STEVENS,
> > "The Idea of Order at Key West")

Here exclamation takes the role of apostrophe. It isn't the "rage for order" that is being addressed, which would be the case if this were an apostrophe, but "pale Ramon." However it is really the "rage for order" which is evoked so strongly and which we're enabled to feel close to, as if it were with us in the room. Similar in their effect to such exclamations are questions addressed to no one, to the void, to some Unknown Answerer:

> How much longer will I be able to inhabit the
> > divine sepulcher
> Of life, my great love? Do dolphins plunge
> > bottomward

To find the light? Or is it rock
That is searched? . . .

(ASHBERY,
"How Much Longer Will I Be Able to Inhabit
the Divine Sepulcher?")

Is the bird mentioned
In the waves' minutes, or did the land advance?

(ASHBERY,
"Le Livre est sur la table")

The presences evoked in these poems of whom the strange questions are
asked, are not such (formerly) clear ones as Death, Time, Nature, or God,
but are no less powerful for being undefined: the sense is of the presence of
the Unknown, which Ashbery talks to here as Keats talks to the star in his
sonnet.

Related to comparison, personification, and apostrophe, in its way of
bringing parts of experience closer together is something called synesthesia, which, in poetry, means talking about details of one sense as if they
were those of another: a green fragrance, a loud yellow. Psychologists
say that in an early stage of infancy people don't distinguish between
what different senses give to them. Even as adults, people can get into that
state, if asked to close their eyes and listen: a bell rings; everyone, if feeling appropriately receptive that day, will be able to say "what color" the
sound was. There is no "right" color; everyone has particular associations,
all of which are right: the point is that the associations exist. When teaching elementary school students to write poetry, I proposed a poem in
which some Spanish words would be used. To help prepare my students
for writing, I asked them to close their eyes and tell me which word was
darker, *night* or *la noche*. Everyone in the class thought *la noche* was
darker and one little boy couldn't wait to tell me that *la noche* "also has a
little purple in it." The language of poetry is receptive to that kind of association—"a green thought in a green shade" (Marvell); "Catches tigers/In
red weather" (Stevens).

LIES

I am beginning to alter
The location of this harbor

(BERNADETTE MAYER,
"Poem")

I went to Egypt to escape
The Indian, but the Indian struck
Out of his cloud and from the sky.
(STEVENS,
"The Cuban Doctor")

In Xanadu did Kubla Khan
A stately pleasure dome decree
(COLERIDGE,
"Kubla Khan")

But thy eternal summer shall not fade
(SHAKESPEARE,
Sonnet 18)

That apparent lying is so much a part of the language of poetry may at first seem strange in light of the fact that one thing a good poet is always trying to do is to tell the truth. However, this truth may be a new truth, felt only by the poet in the heat of inspiration, and for which there is no familiar form of expression; and it will be a truth in the language of poetry, in which "two and two are rather blue" and "The sun is ten feet high/Suzanne walks by" have some claim to veracity. A poet may be able under these conditions to say something that is true only by saying something that on the face of it seems false. "The truest poetry," Touchstone says, in Shakespeare's *As You Like It,* "is the most feigning."

One quality of poetic truth is that it isn't a general truth that can be separated from its expression in a particular poem. What truth could there be in the poetically very convincing "nobody, not even the rain, has such small hands" (cummings) if you separate it from cummings's poem. Even Donne's "Death, thou shalt die" is John Donne in an exalted state saying it. You can't deduce from it, "Yes, Donne is correct. Death will die."

You could say, then, that recognizing the truth of what you are saying, if you're the poet, is a matter of recognizing the genuineness of your feeling. But that is hard, too, for the excitement of writing poetry may incite you to say things you might never feel except when you are writing it.

So one goes along and does the best one can, in this matter of poetic truth. Having written something, one looks at it and then looks at it again, and again. What may not have been, or seemed, true, before you wrote it, may have become true by your having written it. "I love this tree," for example. Before writing, you may never have paid the tree much attention.

Outside of art, the aim of lying is usually to deceive: "I didn't steal the oranges." This is transformed into a lie with a different object if you say, "It was the sunlight that stole the oranges," or "Yesterday the sunlight remembered oranges." Here, presumably, you aren't trying to deceive but to register an elusive feeling or impression.

Perhaps the commonest kind of poetic lying is stating a feeling as if it were a fact: "She's all states, and all princes, I" (Donne, "The Sun Rising"); "And I will luve thee still, my dear/Till a' the seas gang dry" (Burns, "A Red, Red Rose"). Such statements are in one sense lies, in another sense true: they are the truth of feelings.

Lies may also be stories, like the story of Kubla Khan or Stevens's Cuban doctor, that end up revealing some kind of truth. Metaphor and analogy may also take the form of lies:

> With my red veins full of money,
> In the final direction of the elementary town
> I advance for as long as forever is.
>
> (DYLAN THOMAS, "Twenty-four Years")

If you read this as ordinary language it says nothing, because nothing it says can possibly be true. To someone led by its music to read it as poetry, it says a lot: blood is power to the living, as money is—one spends it till one dies—one has a lot at the beginning; "final" and "elementary" are vague but clearly suggest death and the grave—the grave is a very elementary town, nothing in it but space for one body. "Forever" is the forever of one person's consciousness—forever, for me, is the space of time I live; after that, time won't exist. All this is communicated by the shortcut of evidently untrue statements.

Surprising, apparently "impossible" images can be seen as a kind of lying. In poetry their purpose may be to give a sharp quick impression of something on the borders of consciousness but that doesn't fit in with ordinary thinking:

> La terre est bleue comme une orange
> (The earth is blue as an orange)
>
> (PAUL ÉLUARD, "Premièrement")

It seems to be a lie—an orange is undeniably orange. There is a thrill of understanding, all the same. This understanding is experiential and sensuous, like suddenly seeing the ocean; we see the earth, an orange, and the color blue. Having had the experience, we may find a logic in it, a visual truth that is in certain paintings, perhaps even in real oranges seen in shadow. Éluard may have been thinking of this or not. It's possible that in writing the line he simply wished for the orange to be blue because he was tired of orange ones.

Something close to lying is pretending to know more than one does know, or possibly could know, and/or pretending to have more power than one has or could possibly have. The impulse to so pretend may be highly emotional. Happy and in love, one may feel as strong as the wind, and one's love may feel as great and as eternal as the sea. Writing, one may in fact have the feeling of knowing things that may be unknowable, that come to one in a flash and for which one has no proof; and with such knowledge one may make grand pronouncements:

> Love is not love
> Which alters when it alteration finds
> (SHAKESPEARE, Sonnet 116)

> Life, like a dome of many-coloured glass,
> Stains the white radiance of Eternity
> (SHELLEY, "Adonais")

These exhilarating statements have an uncertain relation to reality. But, occurring as one writes, they may have the flash of true revelation—"It just came to me!" the poet says, as if to verify the truth of a perception—and a convincing moment of truth is, well, convincing. If one can catch such a moment, it will be there, on the page, perhaps to cause revelations (and exhilarations) in others. The reader, raised to the height of inspiration at which the poem was written, may see, and be convinced, as well.

Some poetic "lies" are visions of the future: the poet sees beyond the present and ordinary truths:

> But thy eternal summer shall not fade
> Nor lose possession of that fair thou owest
> (SHAKESPEARE, Sonnet 18)

> Death, thou shalt die
> (DONNE,
> Holy Sonnet 10)

> The world should listen then—as I am listening now
> (SHELLEY, "To a Skylark")

> Once out of nature I shall never take
> My bodily form from any natural thing,
> But such a form as Grecian goldsmiths make
> Of hammered gold and gold enameling
> (YEATS, "Sailing to Byzantium")

Boasting, which may be sheer lying or just exaggeration, often isn't offensive in poetry: "I am large, I contain multitudes" (Whitman). Readers may be buoyed up along with the writer and share the exhilaration of being so grand, of being more than they usually are—in Donne's sonnet, for example, stronger than Death and able to taunt it.

Giving advice doesn't necessarily include lying, but does sometimes seem based on a kind of omniscience that the giver of it may not actually have:

> Man, being reasonable, must get drunk;
> The best of life is but intoxication
> (BYRON, *Don Juan*)

> Gather ye rosebuds while ye may,
> Old time is still a-flying
> (HERRICK,
> "To the Virgins,
> to Make Much of Time")

It is reassuring to be told things in a confident tone, and poets like to write that way, to happily state their opinions or feelings as truths—which, with the articulation made possible by the language of poetry, they may turn out to be.

A FEW OTHER INCLINATIONS

> This hour I tell things in confidence,
> I might not tell everybody, but I will tell you.
> (WHITMAN, "Song of Myself")

> ... Il faut être absolument moderne.
> (It's necessary to be absolutely modern.)
> (RIMBAUD, in a letter to a friend)

Telling secrets is part of being completely open and free, of being able to say anything one wants. If one tells secrets in a poem, they are part of a poem, not of a confession or an autobiography; like wrecked car parts used to make a sculpture, or the sounds of birdcalls or traffic in a musical piece, their function is changed; so for poets it may be a relief to tell them and make them part of something else. A common experience poets have is finding themselves able to say things in poems that either they were aware of but had never said to anyone or else were things that had been, until that moment, secret even to themselves. These moments occur in writing for various reasons; music moves one's mind in unexpected directions; and poets, while writing, are positively inclined to look for "secret" things—that is, heretofore hidden from or banished from their consciousness—to help inspire and support what they write.

When I asked my poetry-writing students in a nursing home to write about secrets, about things they had never told anybody, doing so seemed to be inspiring: finding what they themselves had forgotten, as well as what they hadn't spoken of before:

> I once had a secret love but I never told anybody
> I once ran away but I never told anybody
> Once when I was walking down the street
> I saw a man running with a gun in his hand
> But I never told anybody
> Once I found a pocketbook, I was a little girl, and I never told anybody
> I planted a rosebush at the corner of my house
> Every month it had a different-colored rose—a white one, a pink one, a
>   red one—
> And I never told anybody.

> (MARY L. JACKSON)

The "person" the poet is telling secrets to may be a strange combination of everybody and nobody. One expects to be forgiven for what one tells if it's a good poem.

Another poetic inclination is to say something new, and in a new way. Williams's poem beginning "Among/of/green stiff/old bright/broken/branch . . ." gives the pleasure of looking at a locust tree and also of reading about it in a way that has never before existed. The two pleasures are connected: if the tree is described in an old, familiar way, you don't see it as well:

> I saw the lovely locust tree
> and on its ancient boughs . . . etc. . . . .

Instead, you "see poetry." Poetry has to be constantly renewed. This happens at different speeds. In "experimental" periods like ours newness tends to be more prominent and more accelerated.

Newness may in fact be one main thing a poet sets out to achieve. The deliberate choice of an odd way of dividing lines or of deliberately saying things that make no sense can't in itself make a poem worth reading, but the oddness, the feeling of being in new territory and away from the usual way things are done may lead to something good, like Ceravolo's

> Oak oak! Like like
> it then
>   cold some wild paddle
>   ("Drunken Winter")

or George Herbert's seventeenth-century poems in the shape of an altar and of wings.

This impulse to be new is uncharacteristic of ordinary speech and prose. For the poet, it heightens the feeling of adventure. It's like searching for Shangri-la in a winged vehicle of your own invention. Fortunately, there is a great deal of technology behind you: all the poetry other poets have written.

The need to be new takes one far from regular discourse—asking for directions to the train station, the first time you might say "train station/where is it?" and the next time, "I/must/must/find/find/the/the" etc. But then, too, each request for information would have to be communicating a different message, giving emotional experience of a different kind: "Oh where is that train station, tell/That I so long to find?"

The last inclination of the poetry language I'll mention—though there are more—is specifically addressed to making whatever is said a work of art. Without this one, of course, you may be writing, but you're not writing poetry. You may write "When we woke up lying together, at dawn, her body felt as cool as the pale wet leaves of the lily of the valley," and you will have *something*, a sensitive impression of a moment, but not something memorable, that for its sense and for its music will make a reader enjoy it each time it's read, as is the case for me at any rate, with these lines by Ezra Pound, which constitute his poem "Alba":

> As cool as the pale wet leaves
>   of lily of the valley
> She lay beside me in the dawn.

There isn't the same effect if the order of the lines is changed:

> She lay beside me in the dawn
> As cool as the pale wet leaves
>   of lily of the valley.

Obviously, in the first version you end up with the dramatic presence of the woman; in the second, you end up with wet leaves. Nor is the music as satisfying when the short clause comes first and the long modulated phrase second—not for this poem, in any case. The short declarative line at the end tends to make the reader spend as much time on it as on all that's come before—being said more slowly, it seems more momentous.

Consciously or not, poets are always concerned with such matters—with the length of lines, with the order in which things are said, with the rightness of every word, as well as with there being a shape to the whole utterance that will make it a pleasure to read again and again. A similar concern is fundamental to creating art of any kind. I include it here so it can be seen also as one of the unusual inclinations a poet feels—like the inclination to exaggerate, to personify, and so on—when writing in the language of poetry.

To sum up: the poetry language is distinguishable from ordinary language, out of which it is made and of which it is a variant, by the structural role played in it by music. This musical language shows inclinations to compare, to personify, to apostrophize, to lie, to boast, to tell secrets, to give advice, to constantly change, and to organize what is said in it into works of art; these characteristic kinds of utterance tend to bring together a multiplicity of words and experiences and to connect them in ways that confer, at least momentarily, knowledge and power on those who speak the language. Thanks to this intellectual and verbal power, poets are able to say things—important, enhancing, and empowering things—that can't be said without it. It's a language that gives pleasure and communicates while doing so. It is not the "perfect language" which Cabalists and others have been searching for since the Middle Ages, but it does go toward making any language a more nearly perfect one, able to express things never said before and that never could be expressed except by poetry:

> And the hapless Soldier's sigh
> Runs in blood down Palace walls
> (BLAKE, "London")

> The snow falls by thousands into the sea
> (THOMAS LOVELL BEDDOES,
> "The Ivory Gate")

It is understandable that poets, sitting down to write in such a language, would be stirred as painters are entering their studios, as composers are touching their pianos; and that readers would be stirred in a similar way by reading it. To be so affected, of course, one has to learn the language.

CHAPTER FOUR

The Poetry Base

Learning the language of poetry may be described as getting a "poetry base." Once one has it, good things follow: one can read better, and, if one is a poet, write better. The difficulty of learning it, however, may seem overwhelming. It is a language that, in its modern English version, has existed for at least five hundred years, has been used by persons of great intelligence and sophistication, and has been changed to some extent by every one of them. It is full of references, innovations, complexities that might take more than a lifetime to learn were it not for the fortunate fact that one can pick it up in its most advanced state by reading the work of poets who use it, who use it now and who have used it in the past. A transfer takes place: by reading, a young poet can possess what has taken hundreds of years to develop. Keats wrote *Endymion* when he was twenty-two years old. *Endymion* is all Keats but the Keats who wrote the poem is made up partly of Shakespeare, Spenser, and Milton. Poets can use what they haven't invented in order to invent what they want to invent. "Ode to the West Wind" is pure Shelley but without Dante's terza rima it would be much less so, as it would be without Miltonic phrasing—"Thou, from whose unseen presence the leaves dead." Poets "cut in" on other poets and whirl partners away into their own poems. They are able to pick up new steps and do variations on them in what seems no time at all.

Almost always this process happens more than once in a poet's life, sometimes even dozens of times. Some of these "cut-ins" are much more important than others, such as those of Shakespeare on Marlowe, Wordsworth on Milton, Stevens on Keats, Williams on Pound and on Keats, O'Hara on Mayakovsky.

Poets don't usually develop strong original styles all at once, even if they are quick learners. They read and read, they pick up something here and something there. As they go on, they build up what may be called a "poetry base," a knowledge of the language of poetry which will enable them to respond to inspiration when it comes and will itself be part of their inspiration. To be "fluent" in this language is to have a chance to be good at writing poems. At any point in the learning, one may stop and write; but the learning goes on. Changes in one's experience may require aspects of the poetry language one had no need for before—the poems of Li Bai, or of John Dryden, for example, encountered at fifty may be just the thing to turn one's work around in the right direction.

What the poetry language actually *is* for a poet amounts to what he or she knows of it at any particular moment. At first a poet is likely to be an imitator, an aspiring candidate stammering out the equivalent, in poetry language, of grammar exercises. To give an idea of how this process of learning the language works, I'll give two examples—my own, and that of the children I taught to write poetry. The first part of the language I learned was rhyme. I had been read nursery rhymes. I noticed that, along with rhyming, there was rhythm, a bouncing along in a regularly repeated way. That was meter, though I didn't know its name. I was able, however, to imitate it, to do it on my own. And that, at the age of six or seven, is all I knew about poetry, or was, rather, the part that I was aware that I knew. In the first poem I remember writing, however, when I was seven, there are other poetic characteristics noticeable to me now that I wasn't aware of then:

> I have a little pony
> I ride him up and down
> I ride him in the country
> I ride him in the town

It rhymes, it's metrical; it also uses repetition with variation in a quite sophisticated way. Riding up and down is not parallel with riding in the country and in the town. United by rhymes as by the words "I ride him" the unlikeness becomes a likeness that is a pleasant surprise. This intention was certainly (one hundred percent) not conscious. I had no idea of what parallel or non-parallel meant. My little work shows another predisposition of poetry: it's a lie. I did not have a pony. I am not sure that I really wanted to have a pony, there in the fairly urban suburb of Cincinnati, Ohio, where I lived. But the shadow of such a wish had come to me at least a few times, when I saw some other child riding a pony or when I read a story about such a child. So my work was characteristic in this way, too, that it expressed a wish, and, even more characteristically, a momentary or fleeting one.*

---

* My poem probably has another odd poetic characteristic, that of being influenced by another poem and even of appropriating part of it. In a book of nursery rhymes, I recently came on the following poem. I have no memory of seeing it before, but I wonder—

> I had a little pony
> His name was Dapple-Grey

Much of what I have learned about poetry since writing that poem has come about in the same way, unconsciously, without my knowing it, as a result of my reading and of my feelings. This combination, working in secret, accomplishes a lot for a writer, but at a certain moment, for me it was when I was fifteen, another factor appears as well, which may be called the deliberate will to do some particular thing. This happened for me when I read Shelley. I very quickly wanted to write like Shelley—I think, in fact, I wanted to *be* Shelley, with his open collar, his flowing hair, and most of all his incomprehensible ability to put something like this on a page:

> I met a traveler from an antique land

> I arise from dreams of thee
>   In the first sweet sleep of night

> Life, like a dome of many-coloured glass

> O wild West Wind, thou breath of Autumn's being

Reading Shelley, over and over, without understanding too much, but picking up some of the spirit of it, I added certain things to my "poetic language." I learned "O!," the knack of evoking and talking to no matter what or whom; and personification—if the wind is talkable to, it's a person, and so is autumn, whose breath it is. I was also trying grand, bold, distant comparisons (Life, like a dome). I wrote "serious," aspiring poems, poems about grand things beyond my knowledge and experience, intricately rhymed poems about war, cancer, youth and age:

> And as a growing eaglet feebly tries
> To spread his new-formed wings and soar through space,
> Alas! He cannot leave his nesting place
> So I . . .

Adolescence was a part of this, too. It was my age and Shelley together that led me to write what I did write. Emotionally, I was "ready" for the language of "Ozymandias" and "The Indian Serenade." I used for the first time "lofty"

> I lent him to a lady,
> To ride a mile away.
> She whipped him, she lashed him,
> She rode him through the mire;
> I would not lend my pony now
> For all the lady's hire.

language, lofty syntax: "And as . . . Alas! . . . So I . . ." and lofty words and phrases: "growing eaglet," "new-formed wings," "soar through space," "Alas!" No one I knew spoke this way—it seemed to me something like the language of the gods. Speaking it, I was instantly aloft, in a realm of thought and feeling that connected me to the other speakers of that language, the mighty dead; speaking it, I felt far from school, from friends, from sports, from Avon Fields Place where I and my parents lived. Two years later, when I read William Carlos Williams, I found the new pleasure of being able to include the familiar things in my life in my poems, without losing any of the exaltation:

> Little girls smearing
> the stolen lipstick
> of overheard grown-up talk
> into their conversation,
> unconscious of the beauty
> of their movements
> like milkweed in the wind,
> are beginning to drift
> over by the drinking fountain
> where they will skip rope
>
> ("Schoolyard in April")

Lofty language and distant subjects, for me, came first, however; and with them, at fifteen, "wisdom," the power to define and to pronounce, and omniscience far beyond my years, since I was, as my eaglet poem concluded "Not yet a man, and still no more a child!" Reading Shelley significantly advanced my knowledge of the poetic language. It was as though I had bought a much more complex and up-to-date poetry machine. Still not "state-of-the-art," because discoveries were being made and had already been made in poetry that I knew nothing about (by Williams, just for example) but sophisticated enough for me to keep going. When I did discover "modern," non-rhyming, non-metrical, non-hifalutin poetry, it transformed my poetic language like a happy virus. The eaglet gave way to my dog, Cokey; "nesting place" was "nest," if it was there at all; "space" was "sky"; "Alas!" became "Too bad!"

What I had learned before (in the pony and Shelley phases) wasn't gone, only altered. The metrical regularity—the da DUM da DUM—of "I HAD a LITtle POny/I RIDE him UP and DOWN" and "And AS a GROWing EAGlet FEEBly TRIES" gave way to the non-metrical DUM da DUM DUM da of "LITtle GIRLS SMEARing." Instead of complete rhymes, like down and town or space and place, there were partial rhymes—mitts, drift, skip— and words with the same rhythmical patterns: LIPstick, converSAtions, FOUNtain. Altogether this made a music that was more like the way I talked. As for subject matter, the April poem wasn't less serious than the eaglet one (both poems are about youth and age), was perhaps even more serious, because it was closer to me (I had seen little girls but no eaglets desiring to soar). Comparison was still there, though this time to things I was familiar with—milkweed and lipstick—and still my new poem kept the omniscience, the declamatory confidence, that I already knew how to have in writing a poem:

> They speak in whispers
> about the omnipotent teachers
> while the little boys
> scoff over their ball-mitts.
>
> The teachers themselves
> stare out of windows,
> remembering April.

The "wisdom" in this poem is certainly a wisdom I didn't have as I went about my seventeen-year-old life, but, as I believe is characteristic of much of the wisdom of poetry, is what might be called a "wisdom breeze" that blew on me as I was writing. Clearer perhaps is to say that it was a wisdom created largely by the language of poetry I had learned so far, which was encouraging me to be musical, to make comparisons, to concentrate on sensuous details (*smearing, drift, graceful*) and on feelings (*scoff, stare, remembering*) and to use beautiful and unexpected combinations of words ("remembering April"), and also to balance things and to complete them.

By seventeen I had learned some of the poetic language, enough to write in a way that was recognizably poetry. Everyone learns this language somewhat differently.

In 1967, I worked in a New York public school looking for a way to teach schoolchildren to write poetry. Thinking of what children might be good at doing, I gave them a series of writing assignments (I called these "poetry ideas"), wish poems, comparison poems, dream poems, lie poems, and so on. What I called "poetry ideas" I realized later were something more like the elements of a sort of grammar of poetry. I noticed that after writing their wish poems, children sometimes put wishes into their comparison poems, and, later, comparisons in their dreams and lies poems, and so on. They were in fact learning the poetry language and seemed excited more each time they used it. For music, the most essential aspect, I limited my suggestions to some simple forms of repetition, such as starting every line with "I wish" or putting a different comparison in each line. This provided two ways of "disrupting" the flow of ordinary prose: division into lines, and repetition of words. This disruption made music, gave a little lilt to what was said, and replaced the pleasure of continuity with the pleasures of repetition and variation.

Given the means to make verbal music without the strain of looking for rhymes, and being given flat-out directly as subjects various other features of the language of poetry—write wish poems, write lie poems, write comparison poems—my students wrote well enough to show they were learning the language, not just practicing or doing exercises:

A breeze is like the sky is coming to you . . .
(IRIS, fourth grade)

I was given a piece of paper made of roses,
I have a red, blue and white striped rose . . .
(ELIZA, third grade)

I used to be a design but now I'm a tree
(ILONA, third grade)

These lines are in one way already "accomplished"; the whole poems they're in aren't as good as the individual lines are. Later, when my students knew more, they were sometimes able to put together whole poems.

THE DAWN OF ME

I was born nowhere
And I live in a tree
I never leave my tree
It is very crowded
I am stacked up right against a bird
But I won't leave my tree
Everything is dark
No light!
I hear the bird sing
My eyes, they open
And all around my house
The Sea
Slowly I get down in the water
The cool blue water
Oh and the space
I laugh swim and cry for joy
This is my home.
For Ever.

(JEFF, fifth grade)

The "poetry idea" for this poem was to tell a Lie. Having already written poems about wishes, comparisons, dreams, and contrasts of the present and past, Jeff was ready to be in the ambiance of these things when he started to write. His line endings are reinforced by the repeated words, *tree, sing, water;* and there are also the nice variation/repetition of *house/home* and the striking short last line "For Ever," and the breathlessly incomplete line "Oh and the space." Where did all this come from? From Jeff, obviously; he wrote it. He told me, though, that he didn't know what it was about, that he "just wrote it." It's to take nothing away from the author, I think, to say that his poem came from his intelligence, his feelings, and from the language of poetry he had learned—as he was able to use it, on this lucky, inspired afternoon.

The poetry ideas I used in my classes were ideas extracted from poems. The next year I used poems directly (by Donne, Blake, Lorca, and others). I explained and dramatized them and found poetry ideas in them for the children to follow. Their new poems showed other acquisitions from the language of poetry. In this poem, for example, inspired by Blake's "Tyger," there are things that seem affected by the earlier experience of writing about colors, comparisons, and dreams, but there is also something of the grand tone of Blake's language and of its strangeness and intensity:

> Giraffes, how did they make Carmen? Well, you see,
>> Carmen ate the prettiest rose in the world and
>> then just then the great change of heaven
>> occurred and she became the prettiest girl in the
>> world and because I love her.
> Lions, why does your mane flame like fire of the
>> devil? Because I have the speed of the wind and
>> the strength of the earth at my command.
> Oh Kiwi, why have you no wings? Because I have
>> been born with the despair to walk the earth
>> without the power of flight and am damned to do
>> so.
> Oh bird of flight, why have you been granted the
>> power to fly? Because I was meant to sit upon the
>> branch and to be with the wind.
> Oh crocodile, why were you granted the power to
>> slaughter your fellow animal? I do not answer.
>>>> (Chip, fifth grade)

Carmen was a girl in the class Chip apparently was fond of, which was part of the inspiration that enabled him to use so well what he already knew, and what he had just learned, from reading Blake.

In learning the poetry language, both I, at the age of seventeen, and my students, at the age of eleven, had a long way to go, but we had begun.

Whatever knowledge of the poetic language one has is there ready to combine with feelings, ideas, events, anything one "has to say." It is affected by inspiration, like a mirror catching the light of what comes in. Shelley, when he wrote his "Ode to the West Wind," knew Dante's terza rima and Shakespeare's exhilarating iambic pentameters. They were part of what enabled him to create his world-sweeping wind.

PART II

Writing and Reading Poetry

CHAPTER ONE

Inspiration

Learning the language of poetry, and establishing a poetry base, can be considered the first part of the work a poet has to do. This phase of the work may be more intensive at the beginning but it doesn't stop; the learning goes on. Another part of the poet's work is to be inspired and to know how best to use the inspiration. After this there is the work of writing the poem and the work of revising it, if need be. These phases of the poet's work are in fact all mixed up together.

"Poetic inspiration" has been used to mean various things. All the meanings are attempts to account for the "unexplainable" parts of writing poetry, which include: How is anyone able to write it? Why are only some people able to write it? Why can even these write only at certain times? How can it be that these people who write it aren't extraordinary in other ways if they can write extraordinary poems? How are these persons (poets) able to say things in their poems that they didn't know before they wrote the poems and that they may not completely understand even afterwards?

These are all good questions and rather puzzling ones. Reading poetry, thinking about it, knowing what we've called the "language of poetry," all these are helps, even necessities for writing a good poem, but they are also quite obviously not sufficient in themselves. One may be all dressed up and ready to go, but the invitation to the party doesn't arrive—or one is there but the music doesn't start.

Everyone who has thought about the matter has agreed that there is some kind of intervention, that there is at least something about poetry that comes from "elsewhere," an elsewhere outside or inside the poet. The early Greeks imagined a Muse, with whom poets had a special relationship; the Muse helped them to write and might be called on at the start of a poem, as she is in the *Iliad:* "Sing, goddess, the anger of Peleus's son Achilleus/and its devastation." Plato said that poets when they wrote were in a state close to insanity—possessed; they didn't know what they were saying and what they did say was beyond their ordinary powers. A romantic extension of this idea is being inspired by a person one loves, in which case the loved person becomes the gloriously disturbing cause of the inspired state. Maud Gonne served such a function for Yeats, as Beatrice had for Dante, and Laura for Petrarch, though none of these poets was reported, at least, to be in so frenzied a compositional state as that described by Plato. These human female Muses were lost or otherwise unattainable women. Wordsworth was inspired by "Nature," by its "beauteous forms" that led him to "see into the life of things." Blake reported receiving messages directly from the Divine; a Voice, he wrote to a friend, dictated to him twenty lines a day of one of his poems. In our own time, the Surrealist poets have deliberately sought inspiration in the "Unconscious" and in chance—anything to free them from the intellect and from ordinary intelligence; once freed of that, the mind, their presumption was, would be open to, and might be flooded by, a deeper and truer awareness and sense of things.

No one can say, beyond such particular examples, where inspiration comes from. Poets continue to look for it in the old places—they read, they travel, they write down their dreams, write without thinking, go for walks, give themselves up to passions of love and loss, listen for voices.

Another way to talk about inspiration is to say that it is something that makes poets feel they have to write, that they must "say something" and that poetry is the only way to say it. Things and situations may have this effect most strongly when they are new for the poet, at the first shock of awareness that they exist: they cause emotions that can't find any outlet but in writing—they have the atmosphere of being "too much." As a child, one might have responded by running and running, as far and as fast as one could; as an adult, one may respond by writing poetry. Passionate love, exaltation, grief, indignation, a sense of disaster, such feelings can have this effect.

People are generally in danger (for poets a productive danger) of being hit by this kind of inspiration. It may in fact make us feel a little "crazy." The odd thing is that, for poets, the lines that may be the product of extreme feelings, if they are "good poetry," may be highly esteemed by the ordinary consciousness and an attempt be made, even, to re-enter the state that produced them in order to write more—or to revise those one has written. It's a strange thing to do, rousing oneself to anger again, trying to re-enter a state of grief for lost love, or a hopeless passion. But this may be part of the poet's "work," for inspiration has not only to come but has also to be utilized to the best effect. One gloriously wild perception can't be allowed to sit by itself in the midst of a lot of plain ones; well, it can, if that is what the poet's best sense of the work suggests, but more often it seems best to go back into the tumultuous emotional state to see what else is there.

This "inspiration extension" is greatly facilitated by the language of poetry, which, having contained and fixed the inspired matter, is there in its physical artistic form to inspire and suggest more like it. The alliteration of "O wild West Wind" may suggest that of "breath of autumn's being." What is inspiredly written, once it is there, is the inspiration caught, in one's words, and sets a standard and shows how it can be met. "With jellies soother than the creamy curd" may not let its author go until, intoxicated by it and by the need to stay at its level or surpass it, he has written (as Keats did) "And lucent syrups, tinct with cinnamon."

Poets are inspired by the work of other poets. This is one of the main sources of the inspirational sparks that fly around, maybe the main source. Poetry inspires poetry, in the most obvious ways. I see a sestina and am impatient to write one. Stevens writes "Catches tigers/In red weather" and I can't be contented until I get that much noise in two short lines. Lorca writes "Ode to Walt Whitman" and I am dying to write a similar kind of poem. Williams has a poem with only one word in each line—my Olivetti rapidly consumes a page, two pages, three pages—I am trying to do the same. Why poets want to do this, why they are driven by the successes they run into may have several explanations. One would be, simply, emulation. The mountain is there, so it has to be climbed: Shakespeare's sonnets, or Stevens's variations, are something I have to be able to do myself. Mixed with this is likely to be the feeling that there is something there in some other poet's poem, that will make you free, enable you to find things in yourself, and in your poetry, that you had no idea were there. Poets may become very excited indeed on seeing a new way of dividing up lines, using colloquial language, of making rapid transitions, of being clear or unclear. These can stir up the expression of feelings, passions for people, for nature, concern about death, the very sense of being alive, that couldn't be expressed and thus in some way remained unacknowledged and over-looked. "Reading Whitman changed my life" may have a very particular meaning when said by a poet who found a new means of expression in Whitman's parentheses, repetitions, and long unrhymed unmetrical lines.

So poets may be passionately devoted to and grateful to other poets, who have given them not only new ways to write but new ways to find themselves and be themselves and go beyond themselves. This is a lot to attribute to a few lines of poetry, or even to five or ten poems, but it does happen.

One reason that an "intervention" may be a necessity for writing a poem is the double nature of language, the fact that we are almost all of our wak-ing lives using language in one way and that, when we write poetry, we use it in another way. To change from one usage to another isn't automatic; poets need some help, a little yeast or other kind of starter, from experi-ences or from "poetically used" words. When you are a practiced poet, this transformation may take place with more ease: a usual place to write, sunlight, quiet, a few untroubled hours, and you may fall as quickly into the aesthetic mode as a painter may on entering his bright studio full of turpentine, paint smells, brushes, and empty canvases. The very intention to write may help effect the change—simply beginning: at this table, on this typewriter, with this pen, writing poetry is what you do, just as in bed, at night, you sleep.

Even the experienced poet at the "poetry-writing" desk, though, needs something for the language to connect with. If there is no revealed feeling, no shock, no exhilaration, there may be nothing the words can do but lay out the silver and the linen—no pheasant is brought to the table. "Experienced" poets in fact may write a lot of dull verse in this way and even be praised for it, but layers out of the table will be all they are unless they are aware that they too, even in their poetic prime, are dependent on something that may or may not come.

One might ask the questions, then, How can a poet be sure it will come? And why does it come at all? The answer to the first question is that you can't be sure but that you can reasonably expect it, just as you can expect a friend to be kind or a large proportion of winter days to be cold. If you've been inspired, have experienced hours, days when you had a gift for writing poetry, it's very likely to go on happening—until you no longer want or need it to, for whatever reason. This leads to the answer to the second question, Why does it come at all? which is that poets want it to so much and need it for their happiness. A person isn't likely to need it if incapable of using it. No one without a talent for writing poetry is likely to desire inspiration for very long, just as no one who hasn't the coordination necessary for skiing will nourish for long a wish for inspired days on the slopes.

Wanting inspiration for poems is likely to mean a person is capable of using it and of having it.

The answer to the first question, on page one of this chapter, How is anyone able to write poetry? is that there is a situation that invites doing so and a certain human capacity for carrying it out. There is a great deal in the world and in our thoughts that has never been mentioned or, if mentioned, hasn't been talked about in a satisfactory way. In the same world of which this is true there is language, full of an astounding assortment of words and equipped with all sorts of technical facilities (grammatical, syntactical) for using them. This combination makes poetry "inevitable"—given such a language, how could people not try to say what so much needs to be said?

Rivers invite bridges, tall buildings elevators, and an exciting and unexplained world invites poetry. Inspiration is part of the talent for writing poetry that poets have—is a part, even though it isn't always available. As for how otherwise unextraordinary persons can write poetry, there seems to be much the same situation in other kinds of work. The last question on page one, how poets can say things they don't actually know is, I think, partly answerable in light of the idea of a poetic language.

This language, as has already been said in some form in the previous chapter, leads poets on to put words together in a way that is unfamiliar, is possibly irrational or in any event unexplainable, but that may be beautiful and musically and formally satisfying, and in fact it may be for these reasons that they are so put together. No one would say that Shakespeare didn't know what he was doing when he wrote "Love's not Time's fool," but those four, stressed, strong words in a row must have sounded wonderful and may in fact have come to him at least simultaneously with what he was intending to say, if not a tiny bit before. What Wallace Stevens was "thinking of" when he wrote "In the moonlight/I met Berserk,/In the moonlight/On the bushy plain./Oh, sharp he was/as the sleepless!" ("Anecdote of the Prince of Peacocks") I can't imagine, but he wrote it, and there it is, and there is nothing in his wonderful letters or in his reported conversations that is anything like it. I think that's because in his letters and in his talking he was not using a language (the poetic one) that invited him to make up a name (Berserk), to repeat a phrase ("In the moonlight"), or to go delightedly riding the *sh* and *s* sounds from *bushy* to *sharp* to *sleepless*. The poetry language swings from peak to peak, and, doing it for the excitement and, even, able to do it because of the excitement, a poet may look back afterwards and find that the wild journey was for a good cause: to escape the apes or the storm, to give a worthwhile example of courage and commitment. That may have been a part of the reason the poet did it in the first place, but wouldn't account for the leaps, which, in ordinary circumstances, would never have been made—that is, in ordinary language. The poetry language allows, and even encourages, saying to go beyond knowing. In it to a certain extent a poet is saying things "on spec," without knowing what in the long run they will be worth.

None of these relatively reasonable things I'm saying is meant to completely demystify the idea of inspiration, since part of its being is that it is mysterious, but rather to bring it into a light where, mysterious or not, it can be looked at.

Some poets have spoken or written about certain things that have inspired them, and other instances of inspiration can be inferred (probably with some accuracy) from the poems themselves and what, in general, one knows about the poets. That William Carlos Williams was inspired by early springtime is obvious from the number and intensity of the poems he wrote about it; and, as well, by early morning. In Stevens it is often noon and summer weather; in Eliot, winter twilight. Donne evidently was inspired by his love affairs and, later, by his relationship with God, and just as much inspired by paradoxes, puzzles, and such hard, prosy subjects as geography, alchemy, and mathematics, which, before he wrote, didn't seem to belong to poetry. Milton was inspired by his Christian fervor, his poetic ambition, and by Virgil and his Italian imitators. Keats was inspired by fantasies of sensuous bliss. He wrote in a letter that before he wrote poetry he practiced "deliberate happiness"—happiness was the state, he thought, at one point in his life, in which he had the best chance to write inspired poetry. He was also inspired by passages in Spenser, Shakespeare, and Milton. Williams, in turn, was inspired by reading Keats and Ezra Pound. Byron discovered the Italian ottava rima of Pulci and Boiardo and was able to begin writing his two great books *Beppo* and *Don Juan*. Some literary inspirations are also influences. Influence is like an inspiration that holds on: you don't dart away from the inspiring work to make something unlike it, but, instead, take it in, and keep it; it becomes a part of yourself.

Poets have talked about different ways a poem begins for them. Valéry said his poem *"Cimetière marin"* started for him as "music." It was a music without words; the next stage was his imagining this music in six-line stanzas (still without words); then suddenly words began arriving—that was the time to sit down and write. Mayakovsky said a poem started for him with recognition of a "social need." There was something affecting a large number of people, a whole society, that had to be dealt with. His fellow poet Yesenin's suicide, Mayakovsky felt, brought on such a need—a need that could be resolved by poetry. Yesenin was a poet of the Revolution. It would be bad for society if his suicide seemed heroic; a poem had to be written that at the same time showed respect for his work and deplored what he had done to himself. Wordsworth said poetry was emotion recollected in tranquility. Lying on his couch, he remembered daffodils he had seen some time before, and this prompted him to write—not walking along and seeing the daffodils.

Pasternak said poetry searches for music amid the tumult of the dictionary, which suggests being directly inspired by words, always looking for them to come together in some right way. Poets may go about (dreamily, Stevens said in a letter) looking for chance inspirations, which they have learned to recognize and to respond to.

Chance inspirations can be deliberately courted. Like Leonardo da Vinci, spattering a brushful of black ink on a sheet of paper when he wanted an idea for a landscape, poets may open books or newspapers at random, with the idea of going on from whatever they find there. The feeling, the theme, of a poem may be already present in the poet, but in need of some chance spark to ignite it into the language of poetry.

Leonardo had already seen a vast number of landscapes. He already possessed landscapes as a subject or theme. In throwing the ink he wasn't looking for a theme but for a way to be able to use one he already had.

If one part of the work of inspiration is knowing what it is, being able to recognize it, and even having some ideas about how to find it, the other part is properly valuing it when it's found, staying with it, putting it to good use.

This means not forgetting it, and, second, using it the best way possible to make a poem. Some poets like to get things down as fast as possible. Williams sometimes wrote on prescription slips; Shelley carried a notebook. Those two mostly wrote poetry, not notes for poetry, when they jotted things down. Hopkins, on the other hand, wrote notes, observations of nature, which maybe as much as fifteen years later would be used in his poems.

Mayakovsky tells a funny story about an inspiration that came to him at an inconvenient time and how he managed to preserve it for poetic uses. He casually remarked to a woman friend that he was a sort of "cloud in trousers." Stricken by inspiration and fear at the same time, he then spent the next hour saying things to make his friend forget what he had said and also to test whether she remembered it. Finally he decided she'd paid no attention to it, and that thus it wouldn't make the rounds among his friends and so be mysteriously unusable for his poetry.

Putting the inspiration to the best possible use is something one learns to do. It's like learning to put to the best use a panther or electricity. Suppose the line comes to you,

I'm like a cloud in trousers

The least productive use of it, aside from simply forgetting it, is to throw it away in conversation: Well, sometimes I'm tough, I know, but other times I'm really very gentle, like a cloud in trousers. But supposing you recognize its possibilities for poetry; you write it down. One minimal use of the statement might be to make it part of a clever list:

Or like a night in gloves
A hurricane in a hat

Such a solution however may seem superficial: one may want to be brought to something important—a strong emotion, a strong view of life. How could "a cloud in trousers" connect with anything like that? Mayakovsky finally used it as part of a long poem, of which one main theme is his strongly desiring, strongly suffering, wildly variable character. "I feel/My 'I'/is too small./Someone stubbornly bursts out of me," he says of himself. And,

> If you want—
> I'll rage on a raw meat
> —or, changing tones like the sky—
> if you want—
> I'll be irreproachably gentle,
> not a man, but a cloud in trousers. . . .

He titled the poem "A Cloud in Trousers" as well.

Of course, inspiration is likely to come from surprising places. A London window display with a tiny waterfall in it inspired Yeats to write "The Lake Isle of Innisfree." It was the sound of the dropping water that did it.

A poet may not know where an inspiration will lead. T. S. Eliot's early poems contain lines that inspired other lines, much later, in *The Waste Land:*

> Come under the shadow of this gray rock—
> Come in under the shadow of this gray rock,
> And I will show you something different from either
> Your shadow sprawling over the sand at daybreak or
> Your shadow leaping behind the fire against the red rock
> I will show you his bloody cloth and limbs
> And the gray shadow in his lips . . .
>
> (T. S. ELIOT, "The Death of Saint Narcissus")*

Nor, if one needs a new inspiration for a poem one is already writing, will one necessarily know where it will come from. For months Yeats had been working on a poem about the Second Coming and a subject with which for him it was closely related—the chaotic state of European politics: he could imagine the world doomed to destruction, from which a new religious cycle would arise. At this time, his wife was pregnant. It seems to have been in some sudden strong emotions about this pregnancy, in the few days before the child was born, that Yeats finally found some of the imagery he needed to finish the poem. "The Second Coming" is full of things that suggest childbirth fantasies and fears: "the center cannot hold"; "the blood-dimmed tide is loosed"; "the ceremony of innocence is drowned"; and the fear of a monster birth (of a beast that "slouches towards Bethlehem").

> * (Come in under the shadow of this red rock),
>   And I will show you something different from either
>   Your shadow at morning striding behind you
>   Or your shadow at evening rising to meet you;
>   I will show you fear in a handful of dust.
>
>   (*The Waste Land*)

Inspiration may raise the sail and a different inspiration fill it with wind. In Yeats's case, the religious and political theme raised it and the birth of a child propelled the boat.

A large class of inspirations consists of "just words." They may come accompanied by clear ideas and feelings or may not—these may be discovered only while writing. Words may be recognized as "good for one's poetry," even if just what that good may turn out to be isn't clear. Frank O'Hara told me that after reading the first (translated) word of a St-John Perse poem (the word "Palms!"), he had to "race to the typewriter." He wasn't sure why, except for knowing that he wanted to write it down and go on from there.

Inspiring words that "just come" from inside or from outside will have something to do with the refinements of a particular poet's poetic language. Words and phrases of this slightly eccentric language are likely to be combining and recombining somewhere in the poet's consciousness. Marianne Moore, asked how a poem started for her, answered that some felicitous phrase came to her; she gave as an example "Katydid-wing subdivided by sun/till the nettings are legion." It's reasonable to imagine that these lines probably wouldn't "come to" very many people. She liked, she said, the light rhymes (*sun/legion*). One may suppose she was mildly looking for such rhymes from time to time, as others might be looking for puns, and that when she found one, a poem might begin. In this case, it would arrive with its violin case under its arm, that is, it would arrive with its music provided for—prosy precise language and almost-unheard rhymes. John Ashbery, in his first book of poems, shows a fondness for certain kinds of words—*canal machinery, fumes, units, cadets, schedule, consult, metal, manual, arctic, sponge, plume,* etc. These are all a little hard to say; one has to do something funny with one's mouth. I imagine his being inspired when one would come to him, especially when combined with another, as in his poem "Illustration":

> A novice was sitting on a cornice
> . . . . .
> We might have soared from earth, watching her glide
> Aloft, in her peplum of bright leaves.
>
> But she, of course, was only an effigy. . . .

The inspiring words that come to poets are to some extent pre-processed, or, rather, the way is left open to some and not to others. "Yippee! she is shooting in the harbour!" the beginning of a beautiful splashy poem by Frank O'Hara, wouldn't be likely to occur to Ashbery or to Moore.

Gerard Manley Hopkins was inspired by another class of words. "Pillow clouds," "tufts," "tossed clouds," from journal entries (1869–71) reappear in a poem (1888) eighteen years later as,

> Cloud-puffball, torn tufts, tossed pillows flaunt forth, then chevy on an air-
> built thoroughfare . . .
>
> ("That Nature Is of a Heraclitean Fire . . .")

If words that come to a poet are in a personal version of the poetic language, inspiring words from outside either are already, by some chance, in that personal poetic dialect or else able to be mistakenly read as if they were, and so to be usable. Elizabeth Bishop, reading a misprint, *manmoth* for *mammoth,* in a newspaper, found a Bishop-friendly word and subject; so Wordsworth found something useful when a young woman said to him that she was "stepping westward"; and Frank O'Hara, hearing on the radio a commercial beginning, "When you're ready to sell your diamonds, it's time to go to the Empire State Building." Williams was with great regularity, it seems, excited and given a nudge into the language of his poetry by both the talk (plain American) he heard around him and the plain prose he read in the paper, and elsewhere. "I haven't shown it/to my mother/yet" says a young girl about her skimpy bathing suit. Williams transforms this into three little lines, with a rhyme of *it* and *yet*—instantaneous poetry. Another poem begins "Our orchestra/is the cat's nuts." It takes special receptors to hear the music of "orchestra" and "cat's nuts." Nor are signs, ads, or menus immune to the process. Williams walks around Rutherford, New Jersey, the way another poet might think of the beloved or read poems:

> The grass thick
> at the post's base
> iris blades unsheathed—
> BUY THIS PROPERTY . . .
> . . .
> I believe
>
> | Spumoni | $1.00 |
> | French Vanilla | .70 |
> | Chocolate | .70 |
> | Strawberry | .70 . . . |
> | Biscuit Tortoni | |
>
> 25¢ per portion . . .
>
> ("Della Primavera
> Trasportata al Morale")

One of the verbal inspirations I have had was from a big wooden box containing life jackets on a transatlantic steamship. There was a lifeboat drill and I ended up standing next to a big box on which was printed the big word BRASSIERES. This was the French word for life jackets—naturally, of course, I thought after a moment, *bra* (arm), something you put your arms through. But, for that moment, I was amazed. Why in the middle of the Atlantic Ocean was I standing, during a lifeboat drill, next to a huge wooden box of brassieres? Something about it seemed part of my poetry, but in fact didn't become so until two years later when (apparently out of nowhere) I thought of a line that combined the two meanings of the word:

Arm in arm we fled the brassiere factory

The poem which I wrote, then, right away, turned out to be about an urgent, and finally satisfied, wish for sexual freedom: with the woman I love, I flee from the factory which is an emblem of physical restraint. This theme and this story hadn't been in my thoughts on the steamship.

Wallace Stevens made up and wrote down titles he thought he might later be inspired by: Cats and Marigolds, The Alp at the End of the Street, Asides on the Oboe, Pax Ajax and the Crocuses, All about the Bride's Grandparents, Still Life with Aspirin. In Stevens's notebooks there are about three hundred and fifty of these.

Fiction and non-fiction are other places poets have found inspiration, either for style, content, or conception. Auden's great poem "1929" owes at least part of its inspiration, I think, to the prose of Henry Green's novel *Living*. Here is Green: "Mr. Bridges in his thinking and in most of his living was all theatre. Words were exciting to him, they made more words in him and wilder thinking. . . ." Auden wrote, a little later,

Coming out of me living is always thinking.
Thinking changing and changing living,
Am feeling as it was seeing—
In city leaning in harbour parapet
To watch a colony of duck below. . . .
(AUDEN, "1929")

James, Hemingway, Austen, and other fiction writers are part of the history of the language of English poetry. Joyce, by his style and his conceptions of content and form, has inspired poets, Sterne by his digressions. Ezra Pound while writing the *Cantos* seems to have been able to find inspiration in a great variety of prose, from Confucian philosophical tracts to other writers' footnotes.

Friends have to be mentioned as a big source of inspiration. They may inspire by example, as Rodin inspired Rilke to work harder—Rodin, always sculpting, had as a motto *Toujours travailler*. The world probably owes him thanks for some marvelous Rilke poems. Poet friends are especially likely to inspire each other. By what they write—one is emulous and envious and can't wait to try something like it oneself. Or by what they say. They can be critics who talk about your poetry in an usually perceptive way, feeling it close to their own.

CHAPTER TWO

Writing

Inspiration may be the beginning of a poem, and it may continue to occur as the poet writes. When it does, the poet is there receiving it and judging it, deciding if it is right for the poem and if so what to do with it. If the inspiration does not keep coming, the poet has to try to incite it or simply to wait for it—that is, to go on writing without it or to stop for a while. All of this may be classified as work. Even if inspiration seems to do almost everything, writing is still work, like the "effortless" leap of the dancer who has been practicing every day for years.

To do this work the poet has not only to remain open to the suggestions offered by sensation, by memory, by thought and feeling, and by the language of poetry—and to judge them as they occur—but also to make the poem into something satisfying and complete. Valéry said a work of art was never finished, it was abandoned. No one would say, however, that Valéry's poems looked lost or incomplete; he knew when it was safe to leave them.

Writing the poem, poets are in an odd kind of state of concentration, meeting the challenge inspiration has given, adventuring into territory not completely known and, it may be, known scarcely at all. The poetry language is with them, and, if it's a lucky day, will keep giving them fresh energy to get through to the end. After which, they may have to start over or throw out part of what is written and try again. The state of mind poets are in when they write of course varies, but it is characteristically an unusual one in which the past plays a part as well as hopes and fears about the future, recollections of what has happened in the past few hours or days as well as memories about ancient Egypt or current events. If you have been reading books about gardening, zinnias and portulacas may be waiting, on call, as well, as may Italian words if you've been to the opera. Every word and every kind of experience is a possible contender for a writing poet's attention, though many are automatically eliminated by that poet's customary way of writing as well as by the theme or subject or mood of the day—and by what has already been written as part of the poem. "No rhyme!" the poet may silently say, "I'm not using it here. And preferably no lines about a bear since this poem I have begun is about sailing in Florida." The bear—tugged in by a sound or a sense association—may arrive in any case: then the poet must decide what to do with it.

The poet's state of mind may seem a little bit like the dream state but the poet isn't asleep and thus passive to whatever arrives but takes an active role in organizing the event. Here! Put that sailboat voyage over here! And the names of the Chinese cities I'll put in the next four lines. The poet also thinks, "I am going to get this said, no matter what!" Or, it may be, not that but "I am going to write this poem, no matter what!" For the poet who says "I'm going to get this said," the no-matter-what may seem a distraction, a vague beauty that has to be struggled through on the way to making a point. The one who says "I'm going to write this poem" may find the no-matter-what more of a help than a hindrance.

Poems may start from very strong and even clearly understood impulses or feelings. On the way to being completed, these encounter two strange collaborators, unlike them and of a different birth: the language of poetry (and the up-till-now history of poetry that's contained in it) and the chance perceptions, whims, and sensations of an August afternoon or of an hour after seeing a friend. Poets learn how to position themselves to be ready to maneuver what they are saying through all this.

It may work best for some poets to write quickly, to get down everything that is there in their thoughts and feelings in as immediate a way as they can. Shakespeare apparently wrote very quickly, "never blotted a line," a contemporary said. It may be the tremendous richness of an overcrowded-to-bursting imagination that leads a poet to do this: with so much there to say, to create, why hold back? Byron and Shelley wrote quickly, too, and often. One critic said that Shelley "never stopped writing." Of Byron, Hazlitt said that he wrote poetry as other men conversed: he wrote while taking a walk, while shaving, while riding in a gondola. Yeats wrote slowly. In fact he often began writing a poem by writing its idea out in prose; then he waited for his splendid lines to come, his "Slouches towards Bethlehem to be born," and "That dolphin-torn, that gong-tormented sea."

Different kinds of poems sometimes seem to result from frequent writing. If one writes every day, one's poems may talk to each other. There's a suggestion of this in the emotional sequences, themes, and variations of Emily Dickinson's poems; in the "I-do-this-I-do-that" poems (and other poems) of Frank O'Hara, a real master of "dailiness" (the sun says to him in one of his poems, "And now that you/are making your own days, so to speak"); in Langston Hughes's *Montage of a Dream Deferred,* in which one aspect of Harlem life suggests another, and another. One gets a similar impression from Elizabethan sonnet sequences, in which the poet-lover writes sonnet after sonnet about his love—Sir Philip Sidney wrote two sonnets about a single kiss he'd been granted, and one sonnet bitterly complaining about the fact that his mistress is letting herself be kissed by her "smellie" dog and not by him. In Wallace Stevens, too, I think, there is often a sense of what Stevens might call "A Thought Revolved": with the productively clashing ideas of reality and imagination the poet has in his head, every day is a good day to write poetry.

Each poet—whether due to character and personal preferences in general or to previous experience of reading poetry—has a particular standard for what a poem is or should be. This standard may change—as a result of the person's experience changing, as a result of age, as a result of discovering a new poet or kind of poetry, but for the time it is there, and discernible. This standard exerts a big influence on any poem the poet may write, irrespective of other factors. The standard affects what kind of inspiration the poet will get, or respond to, and will certainly influence all the maneuvers made in writing the poem. These standards are all to some degree conceptions of truth and of what is worthwhile as well as of what is beautiful and best to be accomplished by writing a poem. Among the standards that pretty clearly are held by the poets included in this book, in the anthology, are those of truth to everyday experience (Williams, Snyder, Wordsworth), truth to wildness, violence, ecstasy, and other heightened emotions (Yeats, in one way, Hopkins in another, in others, Sappho and Césaire), truth to Christian love, humility, and reverence (Herbert), truth to intellectual brilliance (Donne), and so on.

To clarify a little more this idea of standards, it may be helpful to look at two poems written according to two different ones, the first by Gary Snyder and the second by Yeats.

Snyder's "Siwashing it out," his first of "Four Poems for Robin," suggests a standard of poetry that might be called "truth to ordinary experience," a precise rendering of physically and emotionally verifiable details, to be written in plain language that is not far from speech. A poem written according to such a standard could be a detailed account of past events, or, as in this Snyder poem, an emotionally accurate account of a past experience's coming back, with a shock; and for such a poem, few details are better than many: a summer night, shade from leaves, a word or two, the poem as spare and surprising as the moment of remembering—

from FOUR POEMS FOR ROBIN
*Siwashing** it out once in Siuslaw Forest*

I slept under   rhododendron
All night   blossoms fell

Siwashing means camping out, roughing it.

```
Shivering on      a sheet of cardboard
Feet stuck      in my pack
Hands deep      in my pockets
Barely  able  to  sleep.
I remembered      when we were in school
Sleeping together      in a big warm bed
We were      the youngest lovers
When we broke up      we were still nineteen.
Now our      friends are married
You teach      school back east
I don't mind      living this way
Green hills      the long blue beach
But sometimes      sleeping in the open
I think back      when I had you.
```
(GARY SNYDER)

Though the details are few, none of them is made symbolic, and the poem isn't allowed to spin away into words that aren't right on the theme. The woman is Robin, and the forest is Siuslaw. And everything else seems the "way it really was," from the rhododendron and the sheet of cardboard to the big warm bed and their being "the youngest lovers" and to Robin's now being a schoolteacher.

Snyder's poem seems not very different in inspiration from some poems by Yeats about lost love, but what might be called Yeats's standards for admission are quite different: nothing gets in that hasn't undergone a high-intensity transformation into Yeats's language of poetry:

THE COLD HEAVEN

Suddenly I saw the cold and rook-delighting heaven
That seemed as though ice burned and was but the more ice,
And thereupon imagination and heart were driven
So wild that every casual thought of that and this
Vanished, and left but memories, that should be out of season
With the hot blood of youth, of love crossed long ago;
And I took all the blame out of all sense and reason,
Until I cried and trembled and rocked to and fro,
Riddled with light. Ah! When the ghost begins to quicken,
Confusion of the death-bed over, is it sent
Out naked on the roads, as the books say, and stricken
By the injustice of the skies for punishment?

Yeats leaves out the woman, the place, and the time—all the details that make Snyder's poem so affecting. But there is obviously a woman in it (she of the long-ago crossed love), and a place (on earth, beneath the sky), and a time (winter—the sky is cold), but none of these is as important as the violent feeling they cause, a feeling that just about obliterates them from the poem, leaving only itself, and the cruel fantasy of punishment after death that it brings to mind.

Each poet has a conception of what goes into a poem and of what makes it a good one. Obviously, for Yeats, the language has to be charged, intense, and removed from ordinary particulars. The verse has to have a tight organization of rhyme and meter both to suggest, and to hold in, the tension and excitement. "I saw the sky last night" would not get past Yeats's standards for more than a moment: there is not enough in it, it isn't packed with enough poetic dynamite. The line Yeats actually wrote or finally decided on as the best version of those he wrote, to begin this poem, has quite a lot in it: first, there is the drama of "Suddenly"; then the seemingly paradoxical idea of a cold heaven; one is turned, though, away from one's idea of this coldness as bad by being told that it gives delight to birds (rooks). However, Yeats is not a rook; so the fact that rooks delight in it does not give him pleasure but simply makes him feel more alienated. Since Yeats usually began his poems by having an idea and wrote slowly, it would have been (just barely) possible for him to start with something like "I saw the sky last night" or "Last night seeing the heavens." His standard, however, his sense of what the poem should be, would have made him keep making that line denser and richer and perhaps a bit less clear. Whatever inspirations came to him probably would be guided in that direction.

Snyder's first lines go in quite an opposite direction from Yeats's: they are conversational and flat, and only ordinary things happen. A touch of Yeats-like intensity and transformation—like "I lay a-dream beneath the blood-red rhododendron"—would throw the poem off course. What didn't sound "natural" (spoken) wouldn't fit. Any regular rhyme or meter, too, would have to stay out.

It may not be the truth about lost love or any other personal experience that a poet wants to get in a poem but a more general truth. Having such a truth—political, religious, philosophical—predominant in one's thoughts may make for a standard that is limiting, or inspiring, or both. The difficulties are avoiding preachiness, prosiness, and mere intellectuality, and somehow being able to be original while conforming to an idea, as, for example, George Herbert manages to do in any number of poems about God:

I envy no man's nightingale or spring;
Nor let them punish me with loss of rhyme,
Who plainly say, my God, my King.

(GEORGE HERBERT,
"Jordan (I)")

There are such other working standards as wanting the poem to seem like a dream (Breton and other Surrealists); to come from a state of happiness (Keats); to correspond to the pure feelings of a child (Rilke). Imagine Williams's poem about the wheelbarrow, transformed by these standards: "A tornado of tiny red wheelbarrows/At the edge of the announcement by chickens/Forsaken by rain" (dream); "Wheelbarrow-red cakes tinct with cinnamon" (happiness, for Keats in any case); "And the wheelbarrow, next to the chickens/How one's heart goes out to it, and one's hand/In its little sleeve" (childhood).

Another standard poetry may be written by is not making ordinary sense; the hope is to find some extraordinary kind of sense to replace it: if a phrase or a sentence is "too intelligible" it has to be changed:

Oak oak! like like
it then
      cold some wild paddle
so sky then . . .

(JOSEPH CERAVOLO,
"Drunken Winter")

There are many more standards than these, and of course they may be conscious or not, or partially one standard and partially another. Whatever standard a poet has, the standard won't write the poem. Rather, it is there as a steadying (or unsteadying) influence on whatever is given by inspiration—thoughts, feelings, and the excitement of the poetic language—somewhat as an ethical standard might be, a sense of fairness, though in this case more a sense of beauty or measure or rightness. If, after writing "I slept under rhododendron," Gary Snyder had felt the appeal of a sort of rhyme and the line had come to him "Thought of being in your bedroom," I can imagine his being entertained by it for a moment but not his accepting it into the poem. What the poetry language, with its wild predilection for music, proposes is always sooner or later subject to some kind of judgment. The reverse is also true: a good "idea" will either be taken up by the poetry language—transformed by it—or it won't be much use in the poem.

With these aspects of writing in mind, it may be helpful to set up a trial poetry-writing model and to see how a poem might proceed, on the one side buffeted by inspirations and on the other judged and controlled by the poet's idea of what he or she wants to write.

Let us suppose that a line "comes" to you: "It was good to be in Chicago." Once this line is written down as poetry or thought of as poetry, it begins to suggest other lines, other words, other ideas, as anything in the language of poetry tends to do. Said in conversation, it would probably simply connect with other words in a "sensible" way: "It was good to be in Chicago. I liked the climate. Let's go there again." You're not likely to think, then, or to say, "It was good to be in Chicago/On the way to Santiago" or "It was good to be in Chicago/Five hundred years ago," as you might in writing poetry, when you are thinking about it, sinking into it, and hearing its music.

Having written "It was good to be in Chicago," what may come to mind is a contrast, "But bad to be in New York," which you had no intention of writing when you started; or, transported to Chicago by the sound of its name, you may feel the cold lake wind and write about that:

> It was good to be in Chicago
> In the wind

(or, somewhat more grandly)

> With its lake and its wind

Taste here may lead you to change "its lake" to "the lake."

The elevated train may come to mind, or the World's Fair of 1933, or a friend or a lover:

> It was good to be in Chicago
> With you. It was cold.

Suddenly the poem has suggestions of love, which the poet may welcome or not.

The word *Chicago* may at the same time, or separately, be suggesting quite other things by its physical aspects—its sound and its rhythm. If the writer is feeling open to rhymed sounds, Chicago may suggest *embargo, tobacco,* or *cargo,* which are unrelated to it, as far as meaning goes, but are close physically:

> It was good to be in Chicago
> At the time of the embargo

(or, more fancifully)

At the time of the love embargo.

The rhythm of the line "It was *GOOD* to *BE* in ChiCAgo" may inspire lines with the same rhythm or with a contrasting rhythm:

> And to go to the Field Museum
> And to read the Chicago *Tribune*

or

> It was good to be in Chicago
> For the first time . . .

Once the rather energetic rhythm of the first line is there, you may have the impulse to write a calmer line—"For the first time." There is nothing poetically effective about this line in itself, but after "It was good to be in Chicago," it's a pleasant contrast, with its sound of quietness and seriousness, and a suggestion of something lost.

Responding to both the sense and the sound of *Chicago*, you may—as suggested before—think of *Santiago*, which is both a city, like Chicago, and also rhymes with it:

> It was good to be in Chicago
> On the way to Santiago . . .

This product of an accident of sound and sense, may, in turn suggest a whole series of "on the way" couplets—even if "on the way" was put in only to connect the rhymes—with variations that could take it far from its original theme of the satisfyingness of being in Chicago:

> It was good to be in Chicago
> On the way to Santiago
>
> It was good to understand
> On the way to being ignorant again

As interesting as the "on the way" theme might be, though, the poet may find it goes too far from the original intention, from the main thing he or she wanted to say—about being in Chicago. If the experience the poet "has to" get is something about Chicago or about loving someone in Chicago, even the word "Santiago" may also have to go: it may seem distant and overexotic, bad for the sincerity and the concentration. *Santiago,* rhyming with *Chicago,* is playful and indicative of the power to move around quickly, which doesn't go with the close depiction of a single moving experience, which may be what the poet wants.

Now in fact the "on the way" couplets might get into a deeper truth about love than would sticking closer to a particular experience in Chicago. Everything in life may be seen to be "on the way." And if the poem took this "on the way" direction, the poet could end up finding his or her feelings about Chicago being illuminated by a truth coming from a surprising quarter, a quarter itself the chance result of the matching sounds of two words—*Chicago* and *Santiago.* In order to get to this truth, the poet would need a trusting and permissive attitude toward where the poetry language leads. With a stricter and more decided-in-advance attitude, the "on the way," and the poetic promise that goes with it, would probably be immediately dismissed.

Among the many other things that might happen in the writing of this poem with the "given" line about Chicago, is that *Santiago* itself, though a mere phonetic result of *Chicago,* may, once it is there, with a life of its own as strong as *Chicago*'s, in fact take over the poem: the poem may now be turned decisively to details of Chilean experience:

> It was good to be in Chicago
> On the way to Santiago
> With its rock wall of mountains
> And its gardens high above streets
> That are rocketing with bone-colored taxis

Encouraging such possibilities and judging and controlling them are part of the work of writing a poem, and if it seems like being a one-man band, it is. Probably if one had to do it all consciously it couldn't be done. Even stern Paul Valéry admitted into the process some element of the unknown.

Even this, however, is not all the work. Lines may be poetic, exciting, and interesting, but unless they are put together in the proper way they tend to lose their energy, like disconnected wires, and not to amount to much. "Bright star! would I were steadfast as thou art" gets its energy from being the first line of a splendidly structured sonnet, and "So much depends/upon/a red wheel/barrow" needs its rainwater and its chickens. Poets do feel the pleasure of the individual lines and it is one thing that keeps them going; another is their sense of the whole thing, of what these lines are going to be put together to make. This will be the idea of a form, which may be either technical—having to do with line length, meter, rhyme scheme, and so on—or rhetorical, or both. By "rhetorical form" I mean the emotional and intellectual shape of a poem. In regard to this kind of form, a poem may be cumulative, like many of Whitman's, and like Williams's "Della Primavera

Trasportata al Morale: April," and come to an end when it has amassed a sufficient number of details. Or, rather than being an accumulation, a poem may be based on contrast, like Yeats's "A Deep-Sworn Vow" or on an illuminating juxtaposition, like Hopkins's "The Windhover." The movement of thought and feeling may be circular, as in Keats's "Bright Star," which comes around to the same high place in which it began. Poems may also, of course, be narrative, like Herrick's "The Vision" and Rimbaud's "Dawn"; or dramatic, like Marvell's "Ametas and Thestylis Making Hay-Ropes" and Yeats's "Crazy Jane Talks with the Bishop." The dominant mode may be descriptive, as in Rilke's "Archaic Torso of Apollo" (when the description is done the poem is done, though there may be, as here, a brief comment at the end); or it can be variations on a theme, as in Stevens's "Thirteen Ways of Looking at a Blackbird." Of course there are more. Each of these formal conceptions provides a place for inspirations and ideas to fit in and be part of what makes them even better than they are alone. Each offers the prospect of a way to end. This form may not be known at the beginning, or it may in any case be a little hazy. Concluding the poem may be difficult before some sense of the form becomes clear.

As an example of form's being a little hazy, Snyder's "Siwashing it out" might seem at first to be narrative in form, or anecdotal, but the determinant form in it actually is contrast: that is where the drama and the feeling are—in "shivering on a sheet of cardboard" contrasted with the "big warm bed," "living this way" with "when I had you." Conceivably, writing such a poem, and thinking of it as a narrative, the poet could go on putting in details he remembered about the time he was with Robin. It might, then, however, begin to seem thin, and merely nostalgic; he would have to find in it, or feel for it, a different "form." This is a painful part of writing, or can be, when things start out well and then the work seems, unaccountably, to be going nowhere. The inspiration needed is a fresh thought about what to do in relation to what is already there. One may get this idea from staying with the poem or from setting it aside, then looking at it again. A change to another form may appear to poets merely as an impulse, an interesting idea, some pleasure they discover as they go on writing. Eliot wrote the first part of "Ash Wednesday" as a separate, discursive poem; it occurred to him only much later to make it one part of a poem in the form of variations on a theme. Cowper, challenged by a lady friend to write a poem about a sofa, began to write an anecdote but ended up writing his vast meditative and descriptive poem *The Task*.

There are connections between the technical forms of poems and these rhetorical ones. Some technical forms have rhetorical forms more or less built into them: the sonnet, for example, as Shakespeare wrote it, is divided into three parts (quatrains) of four lines each and one concluding rhyming couplet. Writing it, a poet is strongly invited to divide up thoughts and inspirations in the same way, to fit the form. One idea in the first four lines—shall I compare thee to a summer's day? No! you're more beautiful; a variation on or continuation of it in the next four—summer is too changeable, uncertain, and doomed to die; another in the third quatrain—though summer dies, you will never die; and in the final two rhyming lines, a strong conclusion: you will live forever in this poem. Writing such a work, with its simply, compactly orchestrated form, a poet's thoughts may be well organized in advance of even setting down a word; with practice, a poet may be able to "think" in sonnets as well as he or she can think in blank verse. The inspirations, the leadings of the poetic language, take directions as clear for the poet as might for a composer the inspirations while composing a fugue.

Even with a sense of what the end is, or of where it should come, it may be a difficult part of the poem to write. The end may be even more important to the poet than it is to the reader. To the poet a successful conclusion means "I have done enough, the poem is a good poem, it is over, and that is that. I am happy." This may be followed by doubts: "But am I happy? Let me read over the last part again." Often, then, the poet finds he or she is not so happy and that the wish to end the poem was the main thing that caused an end, not its quality. Then one has to reconsider, to open up the poem again—one may read through attempting to see if a new ending will spontaneously appear. If not, there are other kinds of work that may have to be done: if there is something wrong with the end, that may well mean there is something else wrong with the poem. Dissatisfaction with the end may bring the illumination (and the distress) needed in order to make the poem better altogether.

Sometimes no conclusion will be good because it isn't appropriate for the poem to end there: it should end either sooner or later. One sign of a bad ending may be that it looks a bit more awkward or more "sensible" or more rhetorical or more formal than the lines before it. This may be the sign of a tacked-on ending, a result of the feeling "I've got to conclude." Or the poet may have had a change of heart, wanting the poem to be more accessible, more rational, more passionate, or more poetic than it had so far been. This can't be accomplished, however, by an ending alone, any more than one can alter a raggedy evening by a noble farewell! The poem can be only what it has been so far, but a little better, if the proper turn can be made to bring it to a close.

Some poets like to sneak out of their poems unnoticed (John Ashbery long ago told me this was his preference), whereas others like to end them with a bang. Also, at the end one may begin a new subject, a new point of view; Yeats often ended his poems with a question, Hopkins with an ecstatic affirmation.

Poets get "stuck" at places other than the ending. After starting the poem, one may suddenly come to a halt. For some reason, neither the sound nor the meaning of what one writes is suggesting anything else that one likes as well. This may be due to lack of energy (the poet is tired), to anxiety (the poem touched on something disturbing), to distraction (honking in the street), or to "bad" associations that block the good ones—"Chicago" keeps making you think of gangsters and you can't or don't want to write about gangsters. Obviously, the mind needs refreshment so it can come back to the poem. Tea, coffee, or a short walk may be effective. Yeats, in his later years, when "stuck," read a detective novel for half an hour, then went back to work. John Ashbery told me that at such moments he sometimes read Wallace Stevens. Yeats's method was to opt out of poetry, Ashbery's to opt into it, as it were, at another station. After a brief pause, the poet may read the poem over, fold over the page where the poem seems to be starting to diminish and go on. Or go back to the desk and write another poem (Frank O'Hara did this. I think D. H. Lawrence did, too.) Sometimes poets give up temporarily, then, with the eagle eye of the following morning, can see what has to be done, especially if a clean copy was made the night before, which Mayakovsky said was the most essential thing for a poet to have.

When reading a poem over, a good test is that each time it should be new. The ordinary self, the one reading it, who is not quite the one who wrote it, should be pleasantly surprised. If this doesn't happen, more work may be needed. Some poets revise a lot, others revise very little. Poets revise phrases, lines, and stanzas, or whole poems. Revising is conscious in intention, but in order to be effective it needs inspiration as much as any other stage of writing. Looking at a poem again, a poet may see something that hadn't been—or couldn't have been—seen before. Some time had to pass in between. Then a desirable cut may become obvious, or a place where something good can be added.

Valéry said inspiration should be felt by the reader not by the writer; that at least it didn't matter if the writer felt it or not. All the same, most poets, I think, would say that when writing they did feel it, or something like it. In revising, in any case, the poet is both reader and writer, and the inspiration obtained from reading can help the rewriting.

One may see, for example, something that seemed good before but now seems less so and as if it would be better replaced by something else. Here are the last four lines of Keats's first version of his sonnet "On First Looking into Chapman's Homer":

> Or like stout Cortez, when with wond'ring eyes
> He star'd at the Pacific, and all his men
> Look'd at each other with wild surmise—
> Silent, upon a peak in Darien—

In looking at this again, Keats changed *wond'ring* to *eagle:*

> Or like stout Cortez, when with eagle eyes
> He star'd at the Pacific . . .

When Keats wrote the lines first, he must have been thinking of how amazing that sight of the Pacific seemed—worthy of wond'ring at—and that is how Cortez would have felt when he looked at it. Keats himself must have been feeling that "wonder" as he wrote, and the feeling stayed with him as he wrote about Cortez's men looking at each other "with a wild surmise." But once he had written this last phrase, he must have seen, on reading over the lines, that his poem no longer needed "wond'ring": "wild surmise" said the same thing but said it better; and to have them both makes for a weak repetition. Noticing this and no longer excited by "wond'ring," Keats may have been a little dissatisfied, too, by the phrase "wond'ring eyes"—for two reasons: it sounds a little too close to "wandering eyes," and eyes, in fact, don't wonder—people do, but eyes don't. "Eagle eyes"* is much better: it characterizes the great explorer/conqueror Cortez and suggests as well a kind of eyes—those of an eagle—that might look grandly down from a high place. And, besides all this, *eagle* makes a tune with *peak* in the last line. It's not possible to know which of these reasons for change came first; Keats might have changed *wond'ring* to *eagle* because of the rhyme with *peak* and then later seen the rest. It seems, in any case, a good example of inspiring and inspired revision.

Shelley, reading over "Ode to the West Wind," may, for a while, have been sufficiently enchanted by it to just glide over its awkward original last line—"When winter comes, spring lags not far behind"—but finally he had to rewrite it. I don't know whether it was the need to do so that inspired him, but something gave him a much better one: "If Winter comes, can Spring be far behind?"

There may be a whole section of a poem in which a poet can see, when looking at it again, a decrease in energy and excitement. It's hard to change that, but it can be done if one "gets back into" the poem (and I don't quite know how), as Frank O'Hara did in revising the last three stanzas of "A Terrestrial Cuckoo." I give the changes here as he made them in manuscript—it may give hope to poets who want to give up after a first version, and a new conception to anyone who thinks of "revision" as only a matter of tiny changes—putting in a comma here and there, cutting a line or changing one word:

---

* *Eagle eye* was not a cliché when Keats wrote it.

What a hot day it is! for
Jane and I, above the scorch
of sun on jungle waters to be
paddling up and down the Essequibo
in our canoe of war-surplus gondola parts.

We enjoy it, though: the bats squeak
in our wrestling hair, parakeets
bungle lightly into gorges of blossom,
the water's full of gunk and
what you might call waterlilies if you're

silly as we. Our intuitive craft
our striped sweatshirts and shorts
cry out to vines that are feasting
on flies to make straight the way
of tropical art. "I'd give a lempira or two

to have it all slapped onto a
canvas" says Jane. "How like
lazy flamingos look the floating
weeds! and the infundibuliform
corolla on our right's a harmless Charybdis!

or am I seduced by its ambient
mauve?" The nose of our vessel ~~pushes~~ smells
into a bundle of amaryllis, quite
artificially tied with ribbon.
Are there people near by? and postcards?

We, essentially travellers, frown
and backwater. What will the savages
think if our friends turn up? with
sunglasses and cuneiform decoders!
probably. Oh Jane, is there no more frontier?

```
We strip off our pretty blazers

of tapa and dive like salamanders          vernal
into the muddy stream. Alas! they

have left the jungle aflame, and in

friendly chatter of Kotzebue and Salonica our
                              swiftly retreat downstream
friends drift down the stream

on a flowery float. We strike through
                              tigers hotly
the tongues and mosquitoes towards
                       Black taboos, dada!
orange mountains, dark exoticism,

and clouds. To return with absolute treasure!

our only penchant, that. And a redbilled
                               +aurora highlands
taste must be deserted for snowy
highlands, and caravanserais of dust, cries out

"New York is everywhere like Paris!

we'll go back when we're rich, behung with lice!"
```

toucan, pointing

The rationale of the revisions, clear in all of them, may be especially so in the change from "dark exoticism" to "Black taboos, dada!": to bring in more life, and not to describe, but to present.

Sometimes it is a whole poem a poet looks at and wants to revise, even after it has been published. Williams did this kind of revision a number of times—one example is "The Locust Tree in Flower" (see anthology, p. 247). In revising the poem, Williams cut it down to the barest essentials, leaving only one word in each line. In the other, published version, he said there was too much—you "couldn't see the tree." Yeats, after publishing his first version of "The Wild Swans at Coole," reversed the order of the last two stanzas; when he did this, the swans seemed to represent sexual and creative power in a way they hadn't before. The original order of the stanzas was more logical; the reverse order was better poetry.

Revision may be a help to poets even if it fails of its first objective. The work done revising one poem may help with the next. Revising, a poet is doing work that involves trying this, trying that, exhilarations, despair, new starts, getting into the poem very consciously, more than ordinarily, questioning its assumptions and its connections, even being bold enough to go in and change the "inspired" music. For some poets this is their favorite part of writing. It gives an experience "inside poetry." When one has successfully revised a poem, one knows who made it. Auden said that, for other people, one was a poet if one had written one poem, whereas the poet himself felt like a poet only when he had just finished revising a new one.

Revising may work best when poets find a way to make it as open to the unexpected as writing a poem in the first place. This may mean shaking the poem up—giving it a new form, for example, changing its order, making it longer. Bold cutting may result in suggestive transitions and wonderful spaces. Making a poem longer may bring it to its proper length and may also often help with cutting it: with twenty more lines it may be easier to leave some out.

Some poets and some who think about poetry and many who don't think about it are "opposed" to revision. Poetry, they believe, should come full-fledged like an angel from the Imagination. Anything else is tainted. What can the intellect do that would favorably affect this angel? Well, everyone likes the angel, but why limit the angel to one flight? The angel not only arrives but also may be there during the writing, may disappear and may return for revision. "If Winter comes, can Spring be far behind" is not an example of "First thought, best thought," and neither is Williams's "Among/of/green//stiff/old/bright//broken/branch." The enemy is not revision but the absence of the angel. By the right kind of work, one can have it there at every stage.

Of course revision can turn out poorly. Wordsworth, Whitman, and Auden, when they revised, sometimes made their poems in one way or another more conventional. There are some things about a poem that are hard to change; these probably include the spirit it was written in in the first place, and the kind of energy it had.

What this knowledge of writing—and I have given only the briefest and sketchiest account of it—can do for readers, I hope, is to help them to know what they are reading when they are reading a poem. They are looking at a curiously motivated kind of communication that is not entirely the result of rational or conscious work. It is no wonder if everything isn't clear from the first moment. Or even after reading several times. One reads poetry for its intellectual meanings, but also for something else.

CHAPTER THREE

Reading

Reading poetry gives experiences there is no other way to have. It gives them quickly, suddenly, just about whenever we want. John Donne is with his mistress and talking when the morning sun comes in the window. The whole situation is there the moment I open the book:

> Busy old fool, unruly sun,
> Why dost thou thus
> Through windows and through curtains call on us?
>
> ("The Sun Rising")

In the ordinary course of things I could never get to meet John Donne; this privilege was reserved to a few people who lived in the early seventeenth century. However, I can find him in his poems, talking brilliantly about his strongest thoughts and feelings. Even if I did know him, I'd be unlikely to hear him speak as he does here, so intimately, and so fancifully (addressing the sun), and making music of what he says as well, with meter, alliteration, and rhyme. Such experiences are there in books that are waiting for us to pick them up. Many people don't pick them up because they are afraid they will be difficult—difficult to understand, difficult to judge. How are we to know what a poem means, what those brilliant people are actually saying, or singing, to us? And how can we be sure it is really poetry? With a little knowledge of what poetry is like, a reader can start to enjoy a poem even without a knowledge of exactly what, in a prose sense, it is saying. What seems nonsense at first may after all have something in it if one knows how to read it. It may take a little knowledge and also a little courage to feel this enjoyment, since in ordinary prose and conversation words are used in such a different way: their intellectual meaning, their prose sense is the main and even the only point: Get that dog out of there! It's raining. Mix two cups of sugar with one cup of milk. The President today announced a price freeze. Accustomed to such uses of language, a person might well be made a little dizzy by reading, for example, "Tyger! Tyger! burning bright/In the forests of the night" (Blake) or "anyone lived in a pretty how town" (Cummings). What's wrong with the tyger? Is he on fire? What is a "how town"? And who did you say lived there? Not knowing what poetry is like, unfamiliarity with its particular language is one thing that makes it hard to enjoy the bright burning tyger and the slightly out-of-synch anyone and pretty how. Once you can enjoy them, understanding is on the way, for pleasure, in reading a poem, is the first sign of it. The same is true of music—listening to a Mozart concerto without pleasure suggests strongly you're not catching on to it, and the same goes for staring unfeelingly at a painting by Titian or Matisse. Art seems to be constructed so as to give us experiences, and understanding, by means of the pleasure it gives us. Intellectual understanding is one of the pleasures, but, in a poem, for example, so are the repeated sounds of "Tyger! Tyger!," the very fact of talking to a tyger, the fact that night is turned into a forest, and so on. In the Cummings poem there is, immediately, the pleasure of the turned-about words. All the pleasure-giving parts in a poem may not come to us at once; the ones we get make us eager to have the others, and so we go on reading (and re-reading).

Different poems offer different immediate satisfactions. Yeats's lines "The intellect of man is forced to choose/Perfection of the life, or of the work" ("The Choice") give a sharp, intellectual sort of pleasure right away—I get from them the sensation of strong, clear thinking, even if I don't quite know the exact nature of "the intellect of man" and exactly how or why it is "forced to choose" and what "perfection of the life" is. An experienced reader of poems reads the lines for their sharpness and their intensity, and knows that whatever intellectual clarity there is in them will come when it comes. But the poem more or less tells its readers how to read it: think hard and stay tensed. A very different suggestion is given by the first lines of Wallace Stevens's "Disillusionment of Ten O'Clock":

> The houses are haunted
> By white nightgowns

The close-together alliteration (*Houses/haunted*) and the internal rhyme (*white/night*) make a bouncy music that precludes immediate intellectual understanding; so does the apparent absurdity of what's being said. Both say: take in these details and enjoy them; you may be searching for another meaning, but since this search is so interrupted by the bounce, the bounciness must be part of whatever meaning there is; so you might as well go along with the crazy ghost story. The poem turns out to be, among other things, a critical commentary on the lack of imagination in puritanical America, but the only way to get to that meaning is to go along with the (imaginative) nonsense.

Much of the difficulty of reading poetry comes from unfamiliarity, from not being able to take the suggestions the poem gives as to how to read it. It's possible, too, to be misdirected by teachers and critics, so that poems are read in an unprofitable way. Common mistaken ideas about how to read poetry include the Hidden Meaning assumption, which directs one to more or less ignore the surface of the poem in a quest for some elusive and momentous significance that the poet has buried amid the words and music. This idea probably comes from the fact that, being moved by a poem, one assumes an important religious, philosophical, or historical cause for being moved and tries to find it hidden someplace in the poem; whereas in fact a few words rightly placed can be moving if they catch a moment of life—almost any moment; if, amidst all the blather and babble of imprecise, uncertain language in which we live, there is something better, some undeniable little beautiful bit of light. This is given to us, of course, by the music and the words, not something that they conceal. Important, and at first unseeable, meanings may be in poems as they may be in other experiences, but there is no way to find them except by having the experiences. It's not the nature of poems to be clues, or collections of clues, so to read them as if they were is not to properly experience them, thus to be lost. Many people talking about poetry are lost, and even more people have given up reading poetry because they knew they were lost and didn't like it. A poem may turn out to be a deep and complex experience, but the experience begins by responding to the language of poetry in front of you, not by detective work that puts that response aside.

Other ideas, possibly even more deleterious, are that poetry is of interest mainly as some sort of mechanism that has to be taken apart (and this may be to look for meanings that not even the author was aware of), or that poetry is important mainly in relation to its historical context: one might read, then, for example, Shakespeare's sonnets as reflections of Renaissance dual sexuality. The trouble with such approaches to reading is that they concentrate on what is not there at the expense of what is. It is true that poetry, like painting or music, is interesting from many points of view; and it is also true that one can find out valuable information about past times from a poem, just as one may find out something of what a place is like, or a person. Before one can do this, however, one has to see the poem for what it is, for the combination of words it is, with the music it has, and for the experience it gives. Poems don't constitute good evidence for something else until they're first read for themselves.

Read in the right way, poetry is a rich source of pleasure, knowledge, and experience. Not knowing poetry is an impoverishment of life such as not knowing music or painting would be, or not traveling.

Even when one knows how to read it, poetry may be difficult. These difficulties can be resolved, though, by persistence and by familiarity. Since good poems can be enjoyed before they are understood, persistence on the way to familiarity (and understanding) is a pleasure, as in getting to know a friend, say, or a city.

Knowing the language of poetry, how poetry is inspired, how poets go about writing it, takes away some of the unfamiliarity and helps a reader to know what to expect in reading it. Knowing, for example, the importance of sound in poetry, the way its language is led along musically from one word to another, that it is inclined toward personification and apostrophe and exaggeration, readers should have little trouble with "O wild West Wind, thou breath of autumn's being" or "When to the sessions of sweet silent thought/I summon up remembrance of things past. . . ." These will be comprised of recognizable notes. Knowing that first lines may come from anywhere, readers will be more comfortable just letting them happen, and also in following them, to whatever further expectable or quite unforeseen places they may lead, not bothered that at first they may not know where they are or know what the poet is talking about, looking at a page that begins "We need not visit this big metal archway" (John Hollander, "Powers of Thirteen") or "At Woodlawn I heard the dead cry" (Theodore Roethke, "The Lost Son") or "On the borders of the illusion" (David Shapiro, "Unwritten"). The sensation of immediately being "elsewhere" may be followed by that of a sudden and unexpected turning: "On the borders of the illusion/Phaedo condemned the death of Socrates." For some turnings, a reader may have to hold on tight, confident that eventually the understanding will match the excitement—

> Lord, how can man teach thy eternal word?
> He is a brittle crazy glass . . .
> (George Herbert, "The Windows")

And knowing how poems are written, the reader can be happy with the success of a poem's "sounding right," whether it is clear yet or not. In these ways the reader shares the experience the poet has writing the poem and has as well the quite different experience of coming on it unexpectedly, already written by someone else.

Knowing the poetry language won't immediately resolve all problems, but it can help make the "difficulties" enjoyable—difficulties that may turn out to be essential to what's best about the poem, difficulties connected to intensity, surprise, musicality, precision. Yeats's question: "Why should I blame her that she filled my days/With misery?" ("No Second Troy") is suspenseful and dramatic before it is clear—you can't know who *she* is nor what she has done. Even the music can make a poem unclear; distracted by it, a reader may hear scarcely anything else:

> No wonder of it! Sheer plod makes plough down sillion
> Shine!
>> (HOPKINS, "The Windhover")

The poetry-language connectedness of *plod* and *plough, sheer* and *shine*
which causes Hopkins's statement to "make sense" as poetry is also the
connectedness that makes it seem to not make sense as ordinary prose. You
get the music first, which is a promise of meaning but is also for the
moment a distraction that partly drowns it out. Another kind of poem
may bewilder by saying so little, like certain poems of Williams that are
over almost before you may have any idea of what is being said; their precision is a pleasure, but what they are precise about may not be evident till
later. The secret is to keep reading and to take whatever a poem gives first as
what it gives first, and stick with that, and see if there is more.

Certainly you don't have to be embarrassed by not understanding a
poem right away. If teachers have taught you to be, they have done a disser-
vice, and in fact many people, because of such teachers, have been scared
away from poetry. The cure is simply to forget the bad instruction and to
read some poems. If one poet doesn't please, read another.

Poetry isn't, characteristically, a statement that proceeds logically and it
hardly ever offers proof for what it says, nor any explanation. It won't, like
a newspaper article, identify the who, what, where, and why of its subject:
"She walks in beauty, like the night" (Byron). We don't know who is walking. "So much depends/upon/a red wheel/barrow" (Williams). We don't
know what. "I placed a jar in Tennessee" (Stevens). We don't know why.
None of this matters in poetry, which is a different sort of channel, that
broadcasts a different kind of news. Frank O'Hara wrote in a poem that
when he wanted to know the news he read Byron. He didn't mean the news
of Byron's time but of his own: the urgency of what Byron had to say was
still there. All the "non-newsworthy" lines I just quoted communicate news
while not giving essential facts. The news is experiential and emotional.

This doesn't mean that a reader stops thinking. Reading a poem always
involves the intellect, since words have meanings. However the intellect rarely
is the first one there. Usually, pleasure quickly goes ahead—pleasure in
words, in the music they make, in their atmosphere and their suggestiveness.

> Bright star! would I were steadfast as thou art—

It's hard to say what might first give pleasure in this line—but "Bright
star!" is attractive in itself, and then the fact that Keats is talking to a star is
something grand—how wonderful to be talking to a star! How unlike our
usual situation! There are also the pleasures of those sounds *bright, star,*

steadfast, art; the expression of so lofty a wish (to be steadfast as a star); and the somewhat loftily archaic "thou art." This is already quite a good time a reader is having with the beginning of this poem without being sure what it's about, without knowing for example why the poet is talking to a star or what it is exactly that he wants. There is, so far, the experience of being there, talking. To get more, the reader goes on with the poem.

> Bright star! would I were steadfast as thou art—
> Not in lone splendour hung aloft the night
> And watching, with eternal lids apart,
> Like nature's patient, sleepless Eremite,*
> The moving waters at their priestlike task
> Of pure ablution round earth's human shores. . . .

As soon as Keats says "not," the situation becomes more complicated: he wants to be like the star but not in certain ways. Even before the understanding of which ways, there is the pleasure of "lone splendour" and then of the star's being "hung" as if it were a paper lantern: "aloft the night" is pretty, though confusing—it may take a while to realize it means hung up there high in the night sky. Meanwhile, there's the pleasure of the contrasting tones of the words—the very physical and plain *hung*—and the grand and vague *aloft,* and *lone splendour*—and *the night,* which is both plain and grand. And the music of the line is given something extra by the natural, rich stresses that give it two tunes at once—that of the iambic pentameter:

Not *IN* lone *SPLEN*dour *HUNG* a*LOFT* the *NIGHT*

and that of the natural speech stresses

NOT in *LONE SPLEN*dour hung a*LOFT* the *NIGHT*

These balancing tunes keep the poem aloft there, in poetry language, remaining rich and a little uncertain. There's a similar situation in regard to the sense. Keats says *not,* he doesn't want to be like the star in this particular way; but his line makes the star's situation seem irresistibly wonderful; so even the most attentive and experienced reader is getting contrasting experiences while reading the line. Another thing that's happening is that the pleasure of the rhymes, the desire to enjoy them by quickly getting from one to another results in one's "reading too fast," being drawn on by the music without stopping long enough in between to figure everything

*Eremite is an old word for *hermit.*

out. And if one did stop, one might miss the musical connection lines three and four have with the first two and thus miss the continuing sense of what is going on. Getting to *apart* and its rhyme with *art* and to *Eremite* and its rhyme with *night* the reader is pulled happily forward. Some concentration on the meaning, however, is necessary even if you are reading mainly for the music; for otherwise there is less of the music—without an idea of the meaning you can't "say" the lines right. So the poem is something of a trick from beginning to end, seeming to tease with pleasures that interfere with the pleasure one really wants, which is understanding it all right away.

Of course, the poem is really understood by having the experiences it gives, which may distract from its intellectual content and add to its poetic content, what it really does "say." This content is what has happened to you as you have been reading it. A poem is an experience and not a description of an experience—a communication of a lively, sometimes even of a rambunctious kind.

Keats's sonnet concludes,

> Or gazing on the new soft-fallen mask
> Of snow upon the mountains and the moors—
> No—yet still steadfast, still unchangeable,
> Pillowed upon my fair love's ripening breast,
> To feel forever its soft fall and swell,
> Awake forever in a sweet unrest,
> Still, still to hear her tender-taken breath,
> And so live ever—or else swoon to death.

The meaning of this poem is not Keats's wish to be steadfastly pillowed on the breast of his beloved, although that's part of it; it's everything that has gone on in the poem, whether in what the words depict (for example, that wish and the fact of the poet's speaking to the star) or in what the words are (with their music of *bright star* and *steadfast, breast* and *rest,* etc.).

The intellect can catch on to all this when the experience is complete; it's hard to see how it could do so before. But even after the main experiences of the poem have been taken in, the same teasing back-and-forth between sensation and understanding that was at first confusing will still be there to make the poem an experience and not a treatise. One will be "fooled every time," or pleasantly surprised.

The knowledge communicated by poetry is knowledge based on experience—here, of talking to a star; of imagining what it is like to be a star, up there alone with a view of the whole world with its oceans, mountains, and snow; of having the sweet erotic fantasy of lying pillowed forever on the beloved's breast. All this becomes part of what the reader knows, as it would be known from experience, not from being told about it. The convincingness of it is inside, in nerves and feelings that have been affected by the impact of the words as they might have been by the impact of the soft night itself, of the mountains, of the snow, of desire.

Poetry less Romantic, and based more strictly on intellectual or philosophical concepts, also communicates in this way, giving experience that ends up as knowledge—this quatrain of a Shakespeare sonnet about the destructions of time, for example:

> O, how shall summer's honey breath hold out
> Against the wreckful siege of battering days,
> When rocks impregnable are not so stout,
> Nor gates of steel so strong, but Time decays?
>
> (SHAKESPEARE, Sonnet 65)

Among the experiences these lines give the reader are "summer," "honey breath," "wreckful siege," "battering days," "rocks impregnable," and "gates of steel." The reader is assaulted by the violent words—*wreckful, battering,* etc.— and caressed by the soft, sweet ones—"summer's honey breath," and has, from this experience, a sense of time's destructiveness not likely to be felt in ordinary circumstances. Shakespeare does the work of hard feeling and thinking and gives it to his readers as experience, so that reading him they have it and know it. People who don't read philosophy or history, for example, may know a good deal about them from poetry, which transmits them in the form of experiences, not as something looked at from the outside.

In Williams's famously puzzling "The Red Wheelbarrow,"

> So much depends
> upon
>
> a red wheel
> barrow
>
> glazed with rain
> water
>
> beside the white
> chickens

the experience/knowledge equivalence is the key to its mystery. Reading— because of the way the lines are divided—we have the experience of looking intently at a red wheel, a red wheelbarrow, rain, rainwater, white, and chickens, all the while conscious of Williams's opening statement that these things are important and that a lot depends on them. So we've looked at them all as if they were important—and in doing so we find out that what is important is our doing exactly this. If we hadn't seen these things, if we didn't feel the sense of immediacy, and even of urgency about them and other ordinary things, something would be missing from our lives.

Keats's poem is on first reading difficult because of its richness, Shakespeare's because of its intense compactness, Williams's because of its laconic brevity. There is another kind of difficulty in a poem like Stevens's "Anecdote of the Jar," which is teasing and ambiguous. The story it's telling seems unlikely to be the real story—but that is the only story it tells.

ANECDOTE OF THE JAR

I placed a jar in Tennessee,
And round it was, upon a hill.
It made the slovenly wilderness
Surround that hill.

The wilderness rose up to it,
And sprawled around, no longer wild.
The jar was round upon the ground
And tall and of a port in air.

It took dominion everywhere.
The jar was gray and bare.
It did not give of bird or bush,
Like nothing else in Tennessee.

In the first stanza, even without understanding much, a reader may be pleased by the absurd, very funny first line, absurd because of the difference in scale between the jar and Tennessee (I bought a cigarette in Oklahoma, I returned a safety pin to Austria); also by the folksy (folk-tuney) sound of "round it was"; and by the surprising word *slovenly*, denoting the messy-haired, messily dressed wilderness; and by the surprise repetition of *hill* instead of the rhyme one might expect in the guitar-song rhythm of this poem. A pleasure of the whole stanza is its sounding like a country-and-western or folk song. The title is also amusing: "Anecdote" doesn't sound as though it belonged in the title of a poem. There is a narrative thrill in the first stanza, in the tale of an object with magical powers. The little jar has an astounding effect on its surroundings. There are similar pleasures in the rest of the poem. The slovenly wilderness becomes even more personified: it sprawls around. Rhymes occur in unexpected places: round upon the ground; *air/everywhere/bare*. There's also the odd use of the word *port*, and the simultaneously archaic and playful "give of bird or bush."

Then there's the sudden turning of the plot: the victorious jar turns out to be the villain—it's gray, bare, and ungiving; rather a scary thing to be dominating Tennessee. In the last line there is the country-music-song sound again, that echoes the first line—"Like nothing else in Tennessee."

If you have gotten these pleasures, you have a good experience of the poem as a song and as a story: the jar's triumph and its failure; the slovenly wilderness of Tennessee; the modernist variations on country music. The jar's bad qualities are talked about directly (its grayness, bareness, and sterility) but are also suggested by the dull mechanical kind of music used to speak of it: the flat, repetitious too-soon-arriving rhyming of "the jar was round upon the ground," and the too-close-together *air/bare/where* rhymes; even the exaggeratedly iambic beat of "The *JAR* was *GRAY* and *BARE*." An unfavorable impression of the jar is given by the music alone. Contrasting with it is the livelier music of "slovenly wilderness," "bird or bush," and "Like nothing else in Tennessee." The music of the poem is making its point even while the exact intellectual import of the words may not yet be understood.

As always, the poem has to be experienced as language and as a work of art for understanding to come about. One difficulty, even if it is read just right, is that Stevens's poem, like Keats's "Bright Star," isn't a simple but a complex experience, containing apparent contradictions. If the "theme" is that the jar is bad, then why is the tone so jolly? Maybe the badness of the jar is only part of the theme. Why not be jolly about perceiving a mistake you've made, about a surprising turn of events that brought you a new understanding? This complexity improves the story. The reader gets to cheer the taming of the wilderness in the first stanza and later in the poem have doubts about it. Understanding comes from going through it all.

Of course there are further stages to understanding all that may be in a poem; there are thoughts it can provoke without specifically mentioning them. After experiencing Stevens's strange story of the powerful jar, a reader is likely to go on thinking about it and seeing if there's not some way in which it does make sense. How can a jar dominate a landscape? Well, if you put a jar in an empty room, it becomes the center of attention: it divides the spaces of the room and it is the first thing seen. And so a château dominates a hillside or a plain. An idea, or a work of art, might similarly come to dominate the "idea landscape" around it. Such domination could rigidify the ways we live and think.

This last thought is more likely to occur to a reader who has read other poems by Stevens. As always, a great help in understanding a poem is knowing more poems by the same poet. A main subject of Stevens's poetry is the relation between the world, the imagination, and poetry. A frequent theme is that poetry should be always changing; otherwise it will tend to be fixed, and false to an everchanging reality. His poem "Thirteen Ways of Looking at a Blackbird" is an example of poetry's constantly changing, even when it is describing the same thing.

The fact that the poem is rich and suggestive doesn't make it forbiddingly difficult—though it may seem so, even incomprehensible, if its complexity is the first thing a reader pays attention to. The pleasures of reading a poem come naturally in a certain order: laughter at the small jar placed in big Tennessee, then enjoyment of the jar's power before its bad qualities are noticed; and these pleasures are likely to come along before those of speculating about what the "jar" and its effects might mean in a larger context. Of course there are exceptions. A flash of intellectual understanding may come at any time. Even if it does, the verbal and emotional events of the poem can't be skipped; if they are, the reader may have an idea but not have the poem.

The ability to read poetry the way I'm suggesting—having one experience after another—isn't automatic; bad poetry education may interfere, and not having read much poetry may interfere. This way of reading may seem too "easy," too unintellectual. In fact, of course, it isn't; it is just easy and unintellectual enough to give the best chance of understanding poetry. I recommend it; if it doesn't work, you can always go back to another way of reading.

Aside from the problem of being unsure about how to read poetry, there may be, in any poem, minor difficulties, such as an unfamiliar word, like Keats's *Eremite*, or unfamiliar syntax, like Shakespeare's when he writes "are not so stout . . . but Time decays" (in Sonnet 65; see p. 116). Other syntactical confusions can occur when the music distracts from the sense the way it does in this Shakespeare song:

> Orpheus with his lute made trees,
> And the mountain tops that freeze,
> Bow themselves when he did sing . . .

The strong and delightful rhyme of *trees* and *freeze* makes a reader want to emphasize both words and linger over them—the rhyming sound of *freeze* brings everything to a stop. When the poem starts up again, with "Bow themselves" it's almost as if it's starting all over. So the first sense one gets is that Orpheus with his lute created trees. This is a stirring conception, but a few more readings make it clear that instead of creating trees, what Orpheus did in fact do was to make them bow down; so there is now a new poem to read that is more coherent than the poem at first imagined.

Syntactical uncertainties that are at first discouraging may later turn out to add something of value to the experience. In some of Emily Dickinson's lines readers' minds may be put in a slight blur by the apparent uncertainty of what goes with what in a sentence. Once figured out, what was formerly blurred is now clear but also blurred in a way that adds to the experience; so the figuring out is worthwhile. For example, in these lines:

> There's a certain Slant of light,
> Winter Afternoons—
> That oppresses, like the Heft
> Of Cathedral Tunes—
>
> ("There's a Certain Slant of Light")

it's hard not to be confused at first, a little confused anyway, by Winter Afternoons. Are Slant of light and Winter Afternoons the same thing? or does this slant of light come on winter afternoons? One reads the poem—with one's mind—as "There's a certain Slant of light, [On] Winter Afternoons," which is what makes sense; and one reads it, with one's poetry sense, or one could say "experientially," as "There's a certain Slant of light/[*PAUSE*] Winter Afternoons," where one gets to enjoy the winter afternoons as simply making an appearance in the poem.

When Yeats, at the beginning of a poem, says,

> I made my song a coat
> Covered with embroideries

it's hard to tell whether he made his song (presumably his poetry) *into* an embroidered coat or whether he made an embroidered coat for his song to wear. To find the answer one has to read attentively to the last lines:

> Song, let them take it,
> For there's more enterprise
> In walking naked.
>
> ("A Coat")

Apparently, the song is personified and thus *wore* the coat. Once this is clear, everything else in the poem is clear, and more exciting for having been so quickly and sparely stated.

There are some poems in which the difficulty is so much a part of the meaning that the two can't be separated: the poem can't be "understood" without its coming close to seeming incomprehensible. This is true of a number of poems by Gerard Manley Hopkins, in which the music and the language seem intended to reproduce the intensity of Hopkins's own responses to the concealed/revealed divinity in nature. This divinity is to some extent "beyond him," except in the instant of his realization, as in this vision of the diving windhover and the crucified Christ as one being:

> Brute beauty and valour and act, oh, air, pride, plume, here
> Buckle! AND the fire that breaks from thee then, a billion
> Times told lovelier, more dangerous, O my chevalier!
> (HOPKINS, "The Windhover")

The pounding (and confusing) repetition of beats and sounds creates the excited state in which the identity can for a moment be felt. A whole poem can be difficult in this way, or just a part of it. In Shakespeare's sonnets, often, after relatively calm sailing for four or eight lines, one comes on a difficult part that demands complete intellectual attention—in vain; it seems too much for the mind to handle at one time:

> Love's not Time's fool though rosy lips and cheeks
> Within his bending sickle's compass come
> (SHAKESPEARE, Sonnet 116)

The struggle to understand to some extent produces in oneself the violent intensity of what's being said. It isn't easy to think of love and death together, to think of the beauty of a loved person being cut away by Time's sickle (Death's scythe), and yet to feel the power of love enduring in spite of that. No matter how well that speaks for love, it's a horrible sort of carnage for love to have to survive. If talked about calmly, it would lack an emotional truth. (Compare, "No matter how old and ugly you become, I'll keep on loving you.") Shakespeare jams everything together so we can't take it in—or, rather, so we get some experience of it but don't at first quite know what the experience is. We see Love, as a person, being *not* the fool or jester of King Time; then King Time becomes the destroyer of youthful beauty. This destruction feels as if it were the main, conclusive thing, since it comes last in the sentence; we suffer it before we find out, on second or third reading, that it is (in a way) not so disastrous: love can endure in spite of it.

There is another kind of "necessary difficulty" in Yeats's poem, "A Deep-Sworn Vow":

A DEEP-SWORN VOW

> Others because you did not keep
> That deep-sworn vow have been friends of mine;
> Yet always when I look death in the face,
> When I clamber to the heights of sleep,

Or when I grow excited with wine,
Suddenly I meet your face.

If the reader knew right away what Yeats was talking about, the poem might have no more dramatic effect than the mild one furnished by the old popular song "I've Got You Under My Skin." In the song, the situation is immediately clear: one person is obsessed by love for another person and can do nothing about it. The strongest response to this song may be "Yes! I feel—or have felt—that way, too!" (or maybe, "I wish I felt that way!"). This is not so with the Yeats poem. First there is a bit of history: you didn't keep your promise to me so I've had other friends. It's not entirely clear what the vow was or what "friends" means exactly. However, both meanings do suddenly seem clear at the end of the poem. Before that time, however, there are three more lines that mention apparently unrelated incidents in the narrator's life since the time of the breakup: sometimes he becomes aware of death; sometimes he has deep dreams; sometimes he gets a little high on wine. It is hard to see, reading along, the connection between these three. Death and sleep are similar, but Yeats doesn't talk about death but about the awareness of death, which doesn't resemble sleep; nor does "growing excited" with wine resemble either sleep or death or the awareness of death. Some of these states seem life-deadening, some life-heightening. The only way to understand their connections is to experience the last line: "Suddenly I meet your face." This immediately connects the reader to line three, "Yet always when I look death in the face," so the connection is at first confusing, since it isn't death he is seeing there at the end. It is, rather, something as strong—and as upsetting—as death: it must be the lost loved woman. "Your face" must be her face; it must have been a vow of love—what other face but that of such a one could he be so affected by? And his other "friends" must be lovers, since other lovers would be the most logical consequence of the broken vow—and certainly the only meaning of the word that would explain the word *yet;* which, one now can see, means "I've been intimate with other women, *yet*—yet it is you I see when I am afraid of death." But what about dreaming and drinking wine, which still seem unconnected? There is a way, though, in which they are not; and if, reading the poem, you have felt the shock of suddenly seeing the loved one's face without at all wanting to, you will have the connection: sudden awareness of death, dreaming, and intoxication by wine are all states in which we are not ourselves, and no longer in control of our feelings. All it takes, the reader realizes finally, is such a loss of control to destroy the "sensible" resolution and to reveal the true state of things: the love still there beneath the surface, and still powerful. Understanding this poem depends on the uncertainty gone through as it's being read; without that, there is no shock at the end, thus not the experience.

Reading a poem includes knowing and not knowing. Uncertainty, shock, and surprise, as well as music and knowledge, may be a part of what the reader gets.

There are, it should be added, poems that are deliberately and perhaps permanently unclear—see, for example, those of Ashbery and Ceravolo in the anthology. Poets may wish to give, and readers be interested in the experience of getting, shocks of intellect, emotion, and sensation without entirely knowing where they are coming from.

LONG POEMS

Long poems offer many things at once; if they are stories, there is time for landscapes, cities, sub-plots which are other stories, and comments by the author. The reader can experience history, travel, philosophy, and theology, and be present in many different characters' lives. These experiences are available in novels, too, but poetry offers along with them certain specific pleasures of language and of music.*

Though they may look "harder," long narrative poems are often easier to understand than lyrics: the reader of a lyric is in a state of suspense about meaning while the impact of the different parts of the poem come together and have their effect. This suspense, a pleasure in reading lyrics, could be daunting in a long work. There, however, the story carries one along; whatever other beauties there are will be subordinate to that—they won't interfere with it. The sky over the battlefield may be blue, azure, robin's egg, or navy—it is its signifying clear weather and victory for the Achaeans that matters most.

The incidental details of long poems are enjoyed not so much as a tourist would but as might a traveler with a purpose—busy, and dramatically engaged.

Probably the greatest appeal—to both readers and writers—of a long poem is its promise of going further than any short poem could, of taking in more of the world, and of finding the music to render it all the more vivid and complete by re-creating it in the language of poetry. If poetry can do so much with a small theme like sending flowers, or waking up to find it has snowed, or looking at a locust tree (see anthology, pp. 174, 247, 292), what might it not be able to do with a city, a civilization, history, a story in which the great themes of our lives are there together?

For the writer, a specific attraction is the prospect of being able to go on

---

* For examples of long narrative poems, see anthology pp. 141, 146, 163, 180, 189, 190, 202.

indefinitely. Another is of escaping from the "lyrical trap," of being able to be many characters and to be in many places, to transcend the personal and find the excitement of the personal in what before was impersonal and distant. It's a pleasure to write a lyric poem as oneself—but what a pleasure, also, to be able to speak from the heart of Achilles, of Penelope, of Satan—and to be in other places, and in other times. Writing a long poem, one may do what, from an ordinary poetic point of view, seemed impossible.

As grand as long narrative poems may be, they have been out of fashion for hundreds of years. In ancient Greece and Rome, as in Renaissance Europe, one great thing a writer might aspire to was to write an "epic," a long narrative poem on some high and noble, usually historical subject. By the eighteenth century, however, long narrative poems had been replaced as the main storytelling medium by novels; as novels, now, are threatened by films. The great long poems of the past, however, are still there to read. There are also some recent long poems, very different from these.*

The difficulties of past long poems come partly from their pastness—obscure references, old-fashioned language, unfamiliar ideas—and also from our lack of experience in reading them; in fact, a reader may have to concentrate quite a lot for five or ten pages—then it's easier. This was my experience with *Paradise Lost* and *The Faerie Queene*, though not with *Don Juan*, which I was able to start liking immediately. This point of liking may come on page one or on page five or ten; once there, it is likely to be definitive. Long poems are like roads that begin in the mountains and end up on the plain: they become easier as they go along. The poetry language of a long poem tends to stay the same throughout, and, reading, one gets more and more used to it, as one does, for example, to the blank-verse speeches of Shakespeare's plays, which end up sounding much like ordinary (if unusually brilliant) conversation.

In the past (before the end of the eighteenth century) long poems were almost always narrative and they usually told heroic or otherwise momentous stories—stories that, like Dante's travel to hell, purgatory, and heaven, were at the very center of life. Wordsworth's *The Prelude*, written in 1798, was no exception, but Wordsworth had a new idea of what the world's most important subject was: the growth and development of a poet's mind. The next revolutionary epic poem centered on an individual was Whitman's "Song of Myself," which gives up the narrative part of the long poem in favor of a vast collection of individual experiences connected by a few main ideas: that all persons are one, with each other and with nature, that life at every instant is pricelessly meaningful and exciting, that the physical and the spiritual are one.

* For examples of modern long poems see anthology, pp. 222, 232, 253, and 302.

As good an experience as it can be to read straight through a great poem like *The Prelude, The Odyssey, The Divine Comedy,* or *Paradise Lost,* readers aren't obliged to do so. There are no daily quizzes. Nor do they need to begin at the beginning. If the first page is off-putting, a non-off-putting passage anywhere in the poem is a place to begin. Catching on to the style of a long poem from some part of its middle, one may then go back and read, with pleasure, the beginning, which may at first have seemed unfriendly.

The authors didn't necessarily begin at the beginning, end with the ending, or write their works consecutively. True, with their final judgment, they revised and ordered them; but there is no impropriety in readers' taking a while to get to that stage. It's all right to like parts until this liking leads to a wish to have it all.

It is helpful to assume, with a long poem as with any other, that what you are getting from it at first is, for the moment, good enough—later there will be more. If in Milton's passage about the earth's most beautiful gardens (see anthology, p. 180), what you enjoy are the names of places and persons, that's a good start—it must have been something that made Milton happy as he wrote it; to "understand its meaning" and not get that pleasure of the names would be to misunderstand it. When I taught poetry writing in an elementary school, I read aloud the beginning of *Paradise Lost* to some fifth-grade students and asked them what they thought of it. Its intellectual content, as I had imagined, was too dense with unfamiliar things—"forbidden tree," "mortal taste," "all that woe," "Sion," etc.—for them to catch on to, but, as I also had imagined, they did get something. "It sounds like the preacher," one little girl said. She had made a start toward understanding the poem. She might, if she were a bit older, want to read more, to enjoy that sound.

DRAMATIC POETRY

> In the poetry of plays words are more lively words than in any other kind of poetry and if one naturally liked lively words and I naturally did one likes to read plays in poetry.
>
> —GERTRUDE STEIN

The theater is poetry opened up, given more voices, put into a three-dimensional place, and provided with people to say it aloud. With this kind of physical reality and room it can become dramatic in new ways. Romeo says "I love you" to a woman in a lighted room that gives onto a balcony, not to nothingness or to "all eternity" or "posterity" on a blank page. And she to whom he says it is out on the balcony then and speaks:

She doesn't know yet that Romeo is there, but the audience does. This is called "dramatic irony": the audience knows something the characters on-stage don't know. The classic example is Sophocles' Oedipus crying "I'll find and kill the man who murdered my father!" The audience is wrenched by feeling; they want to interfere. They know, but Oedipus doesn't, that he himself is the man he is threatening to kill. And, even here, in the much milder balcony scene, the reader or spectator is hearing Juliet's speech in two ways at once: as it sounds to her, not knowing that Romeo is there; and as it sounds to Romeo, secretly listening. This arouses emotion; one wants to interfere, to tell Juliet to look down into the courtyard; the spoken poetry affects one like an action of which one is a part. The poetic effect of Hotspur's cry as Prince Hal kills him in battle—"O Harry, thou hast robbed me of my youth!"—would be minimal without what has come before and the action now. You have only to imagine this as the first line of a lyric poem to see how much its effect is dependent on what is happening.

This connection between the action and the poetry doesn't mean that a reader can get nothing from individual passages. These simply have to be passages of a certain kind—discursive like Tamburlaine's speech to Zenocrate (see anthology, p. 167) or those in which there's enough action to give a full dramatic effect like the entire "balcony scene" from *Romeo and Juliet*, for example, or the scene of the two lovers parting at dawn in Act III (see anthology, p. 168). These give a sense of dramatic poetry, even when the rest of the play isn't there.

The poet/playwright has a whole new set of conventions in addition to those of poetic language, conventions just as exciting as the linguistic ones. The "theater language," with its added dimensions of space, characters, and action, provides new inspirations. For the line "My luve's like a red, red rose," it may be the poetry language which has given the poet the repeated *red* and the alliterative *rose*. The "theater language" at this point may lead him to have the character pluck a rose, or to have the beloved so spoken of come onstage, to wear a red blouse, to show her rosiness, and perhaps also to reply "I'm glad you think so!" This is a conservative sketch of what can happen. A chorus of roses may appear, to approve or to protest. Time may appear in a mask, to tell the lover that roses fade; his rival may enter and challenge him to a fight. The suggestive possibilities of every word (and every action) are considerably increased: words can suggest other words or actions; actions, other actions or words.

Reading a poem, we're ready to be surprised, pleased, and given more information by the next line. "Bright star! would I were steadfast as thou art" expresses a wish which then the next line will modify—yes, I'd like to be like you but "Not in lone splendour hung aloft the night." Steadfast but not that way, Keats says. In a play we may be as ready to respond to what happens next, in front of us, as it were, in three dimensions, as to what is next said. Once the YOUNG MAN speaks the line, "Bright star! would I were steadfast as thou art—" we are ready for the next line, but also for the entrance of the YOUNG WOMAN ("What's this? a young man talking to a star?") followed by the young man's response ("Fanny! It's you!"). Or for the entrance of her angry father. Or, if it's a poetic play that turns that way, for the Star itself to reply ("It's lonely here, my friend, and all the splendour/You think you see is only in your seeing. . . ."). The Star might, if it is a masquelike, fanciful play, fall to the stage (to earth) then get up and dance.

Poets can be as free with these theatrical possibilities as they like, keeping them strictly under control so the play goes according to plan, or letting them suggest new directions and new scenes. Poetic plays may be realistic, "political," dreamy, fantastic. They can be tightly put together or be permitted like some out-of-synch circus to run wild. They can be conventional or "experimental." Twentieth-century poets have been particularly interested in the possibility of redeeming poetic drama from its neo-Shakespearean trance; they have borrowed traditional elements, such as choruses and masks, from all kinds of theater—puppet shows, religious rituals, Noh plays, music-hall comedy routines—in order to liven theater up to the point of poetry.*

Plays of course have the theatrical attractions of space, action, and characters without being written in poetry. If theater adds these possibilities to poetry, what does poetry add to a play? It lifts up its conversation, for one thing, its dialogue, so that the slightest, most casual remarks may take on a lyrical importance (as they do in a more exaggerated way in opera). All that's needed are slight pauses at the ends of lines, and usually some other kind of regularly recurring rhythm to go with them, and everything that's said, as in a lyric poem, seems to mean more than it ordinarily would:

> Last evening I met him on the road.
> He asked me to walk with him
> To the top of the hill . . .
> (WALLACE STEVENS,
> "Three Travelers Watch a Sunrise")

For the writer, this elevation caused by poetry may inspire greater subtlety of perception and more beautiful language than would otherwise be used in a play:

* For modern dramatic poetry, see anthology pp. 218, 260, 283.

Upon such sacrifices, my Cordelia,
The gods themselves throw incense. Have I caught thee?
He that parts us shall bring a brand from heaven,
And fire us hence like foxes. . . .

(SHAKESPEARE, *King Lear*)

Situations and scenes may be suggested by the confidence the poet/play-wright has that this kind of language is there to be used. In addition, the inclinations of poetry—such as comparison, personification, exaggeration, etc.—may inspire not only dialogue but also the creation of characters, as, in Lorca's *Blood Wedding*, the three-dimensional personification of The Moon—

LA LUNA. Open roofs, open breasts
Where I may warm myself!
I'm cold! my ashes
of somnolent metals
seek the fire's crest
on mountains and streets
. . . . . .
I will light up the horse
with a fever bright as diamonds . . .

(LORCA,
Bodas de sangre
[*Blood Wedding*])

Poetry can give the kinds of depth and variety to what happens onstage that it can give to what is written in a book.

Poetic drama is relatively hard to get to know. Ideally, plays should be seen (as well as read); but good productions—in fact any productions—of poetic drama (aside from the plays of Shakespeare) are rare. In college, if taught at all, poetic plays are part of a drama course, with not much time for poetry. Plays are too long for poetry anthologies, and excerpting from them seems, to most editors, a somewhat dubious thing to do. I think excerpts are a good idea: the poetry of plays is good, and may not otherwise be found by many readers; it's a part of the history (and variety) of poetry and clarifies that history by being considered with the rest of poetry; reading short passages invites one to read, and even to go to see, when one can, the whole plays.

POETRY IN OTHER LANGUAGES
AND IN TRANSLATION

The reason for reading poetry in other languages is to not miss the great things that are in it. These are comparable to what you might miss if you were never to travel: reading Dante, for example, and hearing that voice from a place not your own (Florence) and a time you couldn't have lived in (the thirteenth century), and the voice of a towering genius who lived only once, and it was then, and there:

> In the middle of the journey of our life
> I found myself in a dark wood
> Where the straight path was lost

Or, reading Rimbaud, and knowing a twenty-year-old genius of a boy in France a hundred and twenty-five years ago, who has "seated Beauty on his knees and found her bitter and cursed her," who has "kissed the summer dawn," who wants to walk (ecstatically) on "blue summer evenings":

> On blue summer evenings I'll go down the pathways
> Pricked by the wheat, crushing the tender grass—
> Dreaming, I'll feel its coolness on my feet.
> I'll let the wind bathe my bare head.
>
> I won't talk at all, I won't think about anything.
> But infinite love will rise in my soul,
> And I'll go far, very far, like a gypsy,
> Into Nature, as if with a woman.
>
> (RIMBAUD, "Sensation," tr. KENNETH KOCH)

These are voices not heard in poetry written in English. Our own poetry may seem to include everything, at least what is important to us—until we read foreign poetry, and find out that there is more:

> Of course, it is strange to inhabit the earth no longer
> to give up customs one barely had time to learn
> not to see roses and other promising things
> in terms of a human future . . .
>
> (RILKE, "Duino Elegy, I," tr. STEPHEN MITCHELL)

No one would think of looking only at paintings by artists in English-speaking countries, or of listening only to English and American music.

Imagine no Titian, no Mozart, no Beethoven, no Stravinsky, no Matisse. French painting can be seen with English eyes, Mozart listened to with American ears; but for poetry one needs to know the language. When lacking such knowledge, one reads translations.

Translators have the difficult task not only of bringing over the meaning from one language to another but also of bringing over the "poetry" (that is to say, to find a poetry-language version in English equivalent to the poetry-language version of the original). Differences between, say, French and English poetry language are greater than the differences between ordinary French and English, largely due to the greatly increased role of music. *Amour* can be translated as *love*, but what are we to do about the sounds? And there is not only the mismatching of individual words but that of the whole languages. The French language doesn't sound like the English language—its vowels aren't pronounced the same way; there's a different rhythm to its phrases and sentences—they usually go, and end, *UP*; the stresses, which account for meter, aren't as strong. This being true, a translator really has to give up any idea of "getting the music"—an equivalent music is possible but not the same music. That's why it's foolish for translators to concentrate on reproducing meter and rhyme scheme: getting these details, they will almost certainly miss an appropriate music for the whole poem, and end up holding a coat that the poem has slipped out of.

The nuances of words also differ in different languages. In Rimbaud's "Sensation," *soirs*—which I translated as *evenings*—has in French some afternoon in it as well. *Nature* is one thing in English and *la nature* in French another. What a good translator can hope to get is most of the meaning (the prose meaning) and the tone. The tone, for example, may be that of a dreamy young poet talking about a fantasy he thinks will come true ("Sensation"), or that of a level-headed, experienced, passionate man speaking about matters of the greatest urgency (*The Divine Comedy*).

For poems in a language one doesn't know, and especially those that use entirely different alphabets—like Hebrew, Greek, Turkish, Russian—or no alphabets at all but characters—like Chinese—one depends on finding the best available translations. These will be recognizable aesthetically by their being a pleasure to read. As far as accuracy goes, it may be good to check them against other translations, particularly translations into prose, or, for Chinese and Japanese, translations of each separate character. Even an imperfect translation can help a reader to "read through" to get a sense of the original. This is an odd thing to do in reading poetry, which usually is read the way music is listened to: a false note is a serious disturbance. Poetry depends on the accumulation of good experiences—on going, in Keats's sonnet, from "Bright Star" to "steadfast" to "thou art" and sailing on from there. If I read "Bright star! would I were faithful as thou art," I think

I would stop reading; there would seem to be no reason to have confidence that someone who could write such a line could give me an experience of the kind I want in poetry. Reading a translation of Li Bai, however, I find:

> Moonlight in front of my bed—
> I take it for frost on the ground!
> I raise my eyes to watch the shining moon,
> I lower them and dream of home.

"Moonlight in front of my bed" seems unclear: What is "in front of" a bed? In this case, however, I don't stop but go on reading. I believe Li Bai is a great poet, his poems have made me happy before, so I want to do my best to "read through" the translation to find the true poem that the translation is simultaneously hiding and revealing. The next line is "I take it for frost on the ground"; this colloquial "take it" is a bit confusing, but the next two lines make clearer what it means:

> I raise my eyes to watch the shining moon,
> I lower them and dream of home.

I really can see (or imagine) the wonderful poem in back of this translation/screen. Waking up, the poet imagines he sees frost on the ground, which makes him think he is back home, where it is winter. He realizes, then, that it's not frost but moonlight. He looks up at the moon that is the real cause of the whiteness of the ground, then looks back down at the whiteness and lets it help him dream that he is home.

I don't think I could so easily get an idea of the beauty of the original poem if the translation were in prose. My good reading is assisted by the few simple features of the poetry language the translator uses: the division into lines, and the parallel phrases "I raise my eyes to watch" and "I lower them and dream." These provide enough music (even though the phrasing is a little awkward) to put me in the suggestive world of poetry, where I am open to emotions and sensations. A better translation of course helps me see the poem more clearly:

> Before my bed . . . bright moonlight!
> I thought it was frost!
> I look up to watch the bright moon
> I look down and think of home.

This version is clearer, more colloquial, and has a pleasanter, sharper parallelism in lines three and four, as well as all the agreeably chiming *b* sounds, the repeated word "bright," and the sound similarities of "moon," "down," and "home."

Reading several translations of a poem and reading other poems by the same poet can give a better idea of what is there and to be looked for.

With a language closer to English—like French, say, or Spanish—you can learn the sounds of words and the rhythm of phrases and be able to enjoy these to some extent even before being sure of the meaning. Baudelaire's sonnet "La Beauté" ("Beauty") (see anthology, p. 206) begins:

> Je suis belle, ô mortels! comme un rêve de pierre
> (Zhe sooee bell oh more tell calm uh rev uh duh pyair)

If you know how the words are pronounced, you can enjoy *bell* and mor-*TEL*, as well as the iambic da *DUM* da *DUM* beat. Certain words are the same as English words, or close to the same—like *ô* and *mortels*—others may be recognized for other reasons—*belle* as *beautiful*, and *rêve* as *dream*. You could make a good guess about *rêve*, for one thing, from the English word *reverie*. You could also make wrong associations, of course, and take the line to mean "I am a bell, oh mortals, like a dream of Pierre!" The best solution, if you know a little of the language, is to have the original poem with the translation on a facing page. Given a fairly exact translation such as,

> I am beautiful O mortals like a dream of stone

the reader won't make serious mistakes. *Belle* will be guided back where it belongs, not to *bell* but to *beautiful*; and *pierre* to *stone*.

Even with no knowledge of French, it's worth "reading through" a translation to get Baudelaire's vision of an arrogant and heartless stone-hard goddess of beauty who delights in the pain and despair of those who desire her.

There are translations that are good or great in themselves—Pound's, for example, of Chinese poetry. Readers, if they find dull translations of someone they have reason to believe is a good poet, should immediately try other translations.

There are some very good translations of narrative poems. Here the translator has more chance of success, since the emphasis is on the story; the main problem is finding a stanza or line that will keep the poem going with the kind of momentum it has in the original and that offers the same chance for pictures, asides, and other beauties the narrative carries along with it. Ovid wrote the *Metamorphoses* in unrhymed dactylic hexameters and Golding translated them in rhyming "fourteeners" (see anthology, p. 146). The meters are quite unlike, but Golding's keeps the action going and the most important part of the "poetic content" is there: stories and characters, given added life by music. Galatea is transformed and one believes it and is excited; Io is changed to and then back from a cow and one is horrified, compassionate, relieved, amused; and so with a hundred other transformations.

Translation is an uncertain and irregular vehicle for transporting poetry, but when it works well—and sometimes even when it works not quite so well—it brings us marvelous things that there is no other way we could have. There is a philosophical view—Walter Benjamin talks about it—that all poetry is in fact a translation of feelings and perceptions that are in some ways unsayable. Acquaintance with the poetry language can help us to know if the translation we are reading is a poem or only a somewhat distant report of a poem; we get from it what we can. I have enough confidence in what does come across in translations to devote a good deal of space to them in the anthology. Otherwise, there would be no Homer here, no Sappho, no Dante, no Baudelaire, no Li Bai.

PART III

An Anthology of Poems

HOMER

GREEK (LATE EIGHTH CENTURY B.C.)

from *The Iliad,* Book Eighteen

As thus his troubled mind discours'd, Antilochus appear'd,
And told with tears the sad news thus: "My lord, that must be heard
Which would to heaven I might not tell! Menœtius' son lies dead,
And for his naked corse (his arms already forfeited,
And worn by Hector) the debate is now most vehement."
    This said, grief darken'd all his pow'rs.   With both his hands he rent
The black mould from the forced earth, and pour'd it on his head,
Smear'd all his lovely face, his weeds, divinely fashioned,
All fil'd and mangled, and himself he threw upon the shore,
Lay, as laid out for funeral, then tumbled round, and tore
His gracious curls.   His ecstasy he did so far extend,
That all the ladies won by him and his now slaughter'd friend,
Afflicted strangely for his plight, came shrieking from the tents,
And fell about him, beat their breasts, their tender lineaments
Dissolv'd with sorrow.   And with them wept Nestor's warlike son,
Fell by him, holding his fair hands, in fear he would have done
His person violence; his heart, extremely straiten'd, burn'd,
Beat, swell'd, and sigh'd as it would burst.   So terribly he mourn'd,
That Thetis, sitting in the deeps of her old father's seas,
Heard, and lamented.   To her plaints the bright Nereides
Flock'd all, how many those dark gulfs soever comprehend.
There Glauce, and Cymodoce, and Spio, did attend,
Nesæa, and Cymothoe, and calm Amphithoe,
Thalia, Thoa, Panope, and swift Dyanmene
Actæa, and Limnoria, and Halia the fair
Fam'd for the beauty of her eyes, Amathia for her hair . . .

(TR. GEORGE CHAPMAN)

This passage describes Achilles' violent grief on hearing of the death of his best-loved friend Patroclus. Chapman's translation is in fourteener couplets: seven-foot iambic lines rhyming in pairs. Fourteeners turned out to be a good form for translators of long poems. The long line gives the translator the space to tell the events of the story in a variety of ways, and space, too, to add whatever may dramatize or otherwise enhance it. These lines of

Chapman's translation are rushed, violent, and full of action; the music races from one line to the next in a way that makes the reader somewhat breathless, as if in the presence of what is going on. E. V. Rieu's prose version (of lines 23–27) is much calmer:

> The maidservants whom he and Patroclus had captured caught the alarm and all ran screaming out of doors. They beat their breasts with their hands and sank to the ground beside their royal master.

These are translations almost into two different languages, that of ordinary English and that of the Renaissance-English language of poetry. The translator's choice as to how to render the *Iliad* may largely depend on how the original text seems and feels to him—if he feels it with a crashing sort of music, he tries to find an equivalent music in English. It should be said that to some extent, too, the translators' choices depend on the tastes and fashions of their times. Translating a heroic poem into heroic English verse was certainly a main choice of Chapman's time—the early seventeeth century—just as translating it into quiet, precise prose is one of the choices of our own. Another is Lattimore's, which is an attempt to have the best of both—violence and precision:

> Now as he was pondering this in his heart and his spirit,
> meanwhile the son of stately Nestor was drawing near him
> and wept warm tears, and gave Achilleus his sorrowful message:
> "Ah me, son of valiant Peleus; you must hear from me
> the ghastly message of a thing I wish never had happened.
> Patroklos has fallen, and now they are fighting over his body
> which is naked. Hektor of the shining helm has taken his armour."
> He spoke, and the black cloud of sorrow closed on Achilleus.
> In both hands he caught up the grimy dust, and poured it
> over his head and face, and fouled his handsome countenance,
> and the black ashes were scattered over his immortal tunic.
> And he himself, mightily in his might, in the dust lay
> at length, and took and tore at his hair with his hands, and defiled it.
> And the handmaidens Achilleus and Patroklos had taken
> captive, stricken at heart cried out aloud, and came running
> out of doors about valiant Achilleus, and all of them
> beat their breasts with their hands, and the limbs went slack in each of
>   them.
> On the other side Antilochos mourned with him, letting the tears fall,
> and held the hands of Achilleus as he grieved in his proud heart,
> fearing Achilleus might cut his throat with the iron. He cried out

terribly, aloud, and the lady his mother heard him
as she sat in the depths of the sea at the side of her aged father,
and she cried shrill in turn, and the goddesses gathered about her,
all who along the depth of the sea were daughters of Nereus.
For Glauke was there, Kymodoke and Thaleia,
Nesaie and Speio and Thoë, and ox-eyed Halia . . .

SAPPHO

(SEVENTH–SIXTH CENTURY B.C.)

That man is peer of the gods, who
face to face sits listening
to your sweet speech and lovely
    laughter.

It is this that rouses a tumult
in my breast. At mere sight of you
my voice falters, my tongue
    is broken.

Straightaway, a delicate fire runs in
my limbs; my eyes
are blinded and my ears
    thunder.

Sweat pours out: a trembling hunts
me down. I grow
paler than grass and lack little
    of dying.

(TR. WILLIS BARNSTONE)

To me he seems like a god
as he sits facing you and
hears you near as you speak
softly and laugh

in a sweet echo that jolts
the heart in my ribs. For now
as I look at you my voice
is empty and

can say nothing as my tongue
cracks and slender fire is quick
under my skin. My eyes are dead
to light, my ears

pound, and sweat pours over me.
I convulse, paler than grass,
and feel my mind slip as I
go close to death

(TR. W.C. WILLIAMS)

This is a lyric poem of extreme feelings: the poet's jealous, helpless passion
for the one she loves is the only thing that exists. This kind of fiery concentration of feeling in a few lines is a sort of poetic absolute that has inspired
many poets to try to do something like it. (Readers can decide which translation they prefer—it's also possible, since neither is the original poem, to
like having both.)

SEXTUS PROPERTIUS

ROMAN (FIRST CENTURY B.C.)

From *Homage to Sextus Propertius*

Yet you ask on what account I write so many love-lyrics
And whence this soft book comes into my mouth.
Neither Calliope nor Apollo sung these things into my ear,
    My genius is no more than a girl.

If she with ivory fingers drive a tune through the lyre,
    We look at the process.
How easy the moving fingers; if hair is mussed on her forehead,
If she goes in a gleam of Cos, in a slither of dyed stuff,
There is a volume in the matter; if her eyelids sink into sleep,
There are new jobs for the author;
And if she plays with me with her shirt off,
    We shall construct many Iliads.
And whatever she does or says
    We shall spin long yarns out of nothing.

Thus much the fates have allotted me, and if, Maecenas,
I were able to lead heroes into armour, I would not,
Neither would I warble of Titans, nor of Ossa
                spiked onto Olympus, . . .

(TR. EZRA POUND)

This passage—a very freely translated version of a passage in Sextus Propertius—exemplifies Pound's idea that a good translation should make a
poem fresh and new, while at the same time keeping characteristic qualities
of its original time and place. The mixture of literary and colloquial language makes the poem immediate, contemporary, and "Roman" at the
same time.

    Calliope is a muse, Apollo is the god of poetry, Cos was famous for its
silks.

OVID

ROMAN (43 B.C.–17 A.D.)

from *Metamorphoses,* Book I (Apollo and Daphne)

Hir haire unkembd about hir necke downe flaring did he see,
O Lord and were they trimd (quoth he) how seemly would she bee?
He sees hir eyes as bright as fire the starres to represent,
He sees hir mouth which to have seene he holdes him not content.
Hir lillie armes mid part and more above the elbow bare,
Hir handes, hir fingers and hir wrystes, him thought of beautie rare.
And sure he thought such other parts as garments then did hyde,
Excelled greatly all the rest the which he had espyde.
But swifter than the whyrling winde shee flees and will not stay,
To give the hearing to these wordes the which he had to say:
    I pray thee Nymph Penaeis stay, I chase not as a fo:
    Stay Nymph: the Lambes so flee the Wolves, the Stags the
                                        Lions so.
With flittring feathers sielie Doves so from the Gossehauke flie,
And every creature from his foe. Love is the cause that I
Do followe thee: alas alas how would it grieve my heart,
To see thee fall among the briers, and that the bloud should start
Out of thy tender legges, I, wretch, the causer of thy smart.
The place is rough to which thou runst, take leysure I thee pray,
Abate thy flight, and I my selfe my running pace will stay.
Yet would I wishe thee take advise, and wisely for to viewe
What one he is that for thy grace in humble wise doth sewe.
I am not one that dwelles among the hilles and stonie rockes,
I am no sheepehearde with a Curre, attending on the flockes:
I am no Carle nor countrie Clowne, nor neathearde taking charge
Of cattle grazing here and there within this Forrest large.
Thou doest not know, poor simple soule, God wote thou dost not
                                        knowe,
From whome thou fleest. For if thou knew, thou wouldste not
                                     flee me so.
In Delphos is my chiefe abode, my Temples also stande
At Glaros and at Patara within the Lycian lande.
And in the Ile of Tenedos the people honour mee.
The king of Gods himselfe is knowne my father for to bee.
By me is knowne that was, that is, and that that shall ensue,

By mee men learne to sundrie tunes to frame sweete ditties true.
In shooting have I stedfast hand, but surer hand had hee
That made this wound within my heart that heretofore was free.
Of Phisicke and of surgerie I found the Artes for neede,
The powre of everie herbe and plant doth of my gift proceede.
Nowe wo is me that nere an herbe can heale the hurt of love
And that the Artes that others helpe their Lord doth helpelesse prove.
　　As Phoebus would have spoken more, away Penaeis stale
　　With fearful steppes, and left him in the midst of all his tale.
And as she ran the meeting windes hir garments backewarde blue,
So that hir naked skinne apearde behinde hir as she flue,
Hir goodly yellowe golden haire that hanged loose and slacke,
With every puff of ayre did wave and tosse behinde hir backe.
Hir running made hir seeme more fayre, the youthfull God therefore
Coulde not abyde to waste his wordes in dalyance any more.
But as his love advysed him he gan to mende his pace,
And with the better foote before, the fleeing Nymph to chace.

(TR. ARTHUR GOLDING)

This passage from the *Metamorphoses* begins with Apollo's admiring the beauty of the nymph Daphne and ends with his chasing after her. Somewhat later in the story, just as he is about to seize her, she prays to her father, the river Penaeus, to change her into a tree, which he does. After trying, unsuccessfully, to hug and kiss the tree, Apollo finally accepts defeat gracefully:

Well (quoth Apollo) though my Feere and spouse thou can not bee,
Assuredly from this time forth yet shalt thou be my tree.

Daphne has changed to a laurel tree, and Apollo says that wreaths of laurel will be worn by him and by all the most celebrated heroes.

Ovid's book is a collection of stories of all the most marvelous transformations (metamorphoses) of Greek and Latin mythology: Zeus into a bull, a swan, and a shower of gold; Io into a cow; etc. Ezra Pound called Golding's translation of the *Metamorphoses* the "most beautiful book in the English language."

The verse form is, like that of Chapman's translation of the *Iliad,* fourteener couplets. (Penaeis is another name for Daphne.)

LI BAI

CHINESE (701–762 A.D.)

THE CITY OF CHOAN

The phoenix are at play on their terrace.
The phoenix are gone, the river flows on alone.
Flowers and grass
Cover over the dark path
    where lay the dynastic house of the Go.
The bright cloths and bright caps of Shin
Are now the base of old hills.

The Three Mountains fall through the far heaven,
The isle of White Heron
    splits the two streams apart.
Now the high clouds cover the sun
And I can not see Choan afar
And I am sad.

(TR. EZRA POUND)

ON CLIMBING IN NAN-KING
TO THE TERRACE OF PHŒNIXES

Phœnixes that played here once, so that the place was named for
    them,
Have abandoned it now to this desolate river;
The paths of Wu Palace are crooked with weeds;
The garments of Chin are ancient dust.
. . . Like this green horizon halving the Three Peaks,
Like this Island of White Egrets dividing the river,
A cloud has arisen between the Light of Heaven and me,
To hide his city from my melancholy heart.

(TR. W. H. BYNNER)

CLIMBING PHOENIX TERRACE AT CHIN-LING

The phoenix birds once frolicked on phoenix terrace.
The birds are gone, the terrace empty, and the river flows on.
Flourishing flowers of Wu Palace are buried beneath dark trails.
Caps and gowns of Tsin times all lie in ancient mounds.
The three-peaked mountain half visible under the blue sky,
The two-forked stream separated by White-egret Isle.
It's always the clouds that block the sun,
I do not see Ch'ang-an and I grieve.

(TR. JOSEPH J. LEE)

These are three translations of the same poem about visiting the now abandoned site of where was once an imperial palace. A noteworthy part of this palace was a terrace where there were many phoenixes (peacocklike birds). Pound's version is a good example of his making translations dramatic and new. In line one he shows us the phoenix; in line two they are gone. The loss of the phoenix, and the disappearance of the whole palace, is, in his translation, an experience we have—not something that is merely described.

KIYOTSUGU

JAPANESE (PROBABLY FIFTEENTH CENTURY)

from *Sotoba Komachi*

ONO

I am the ruins of Ono,
The daughter of Ono no Yoshizane.

WAKI AND TSURE
(*together*)

How sad a ruin is this:
Komachi was in her day a bright flower;
She had the blue brows of Katsura;
She used no powder at all;
She walked in beautiful raiment in palaces.
Many attended her verse in our speech
And in the speech of the foreign court.

White of winter is over her head,
Over the husk of her shoulders;
Her eyes are no more like the colour on distant mountains.
She is like a dull moon that fades in the dawn's grip.
The wallet about her throat has in it a few dried beans,
A bundle is wrapped on her back, and on her shoulder is a
      basket of woven roots;
She cannot hide it at all.
She is begging along the road;
She wanders, a poor, daft shadow.

(TR. ERNEST FENOLLOSA WITH EZRA POUND)

This is a brief excerpt from a Japanese Noh play. The main character of a
Noh play is often a wandering spirit. The characters, along with the chorus,
speak lines and also describe what is happening. Music accompanies the
action and some lines are sung or chanted. The directness and intensity of
Noh plays, with their concentration on one overwhelming dramatic
moment, along with their brevity and their otherworldly atmosphere and

their strange theatrical conventions, appealed to modern poets who wanted to write plays free of both Shakespeare and all other kinds of conventional Western theater. Among others, Yeats, Paul Goodman, and Frank O'Hara wrote Noh-like plays. Pound and Donald Keene have done excellent translations.

RYOTA

JAPANESE (1718–1787)

Communion

From them no words come:
the guest, the host, the white
chrysanthemum.

(TR. HAROLD HENDERSON)

No one spoke
The host, the guest,
The white chrysanthemums

(TR. KENNETH REXROTH)

Mono-twazu | *kayaku* | *to* | *teishu* | *to* | *shira-giku* | *to*
Not-saying-anything | guest | [and] | host | [and] |
white-chrysanthemum | [and]

(THIS WORD-FOR-WORD TRANSCRIPTION
IS ALSO BY HAROLD HENDERSON)

I think Rexroth found better resources in the poetry language than did the other translator, who may have given up too much in order to get a rhyme—*come/chrysanthemum.* The trouble with "no words come" is that it's awkward and no one ever says it; it takes away from the believability and the drama of the poem. This is a scene one has to get into quickly: "No one spoke" is just right. Actually, Rexroth's version has quite a lot of music, and it doesn't interfere with the drama or the sense—the music of the ō sounds in *no/spoke/host;* and the music of the *t* sounds in *host/guest/white.*

DANTE ALIGHIERI

ITALIAN (1265–1321)

Sonnet to Guido Cavalcanti

Sonetto

Guido, vorrei che tu e Lapo ed io
  Fossimo presi per incantamento,
  E messi ad un vascel, ch'ad ogni vento
  Per mare andasse a voler vostro e mio;

Sicchè fortuna, od altro tempo rio
  Non ci potesse dare impedimento,
  Anzi, vivendo sempre in un talento,
  Di stare insieme crescesse il disio.

E monna Vanna e monna Lagia poi,
  Con quella ch'è sul numero del trenta,
  Con noi ponesse il buono incantatore:

E quivi ragionar sempre d'amore;
  E ciascuna di lor fosse contenta,
  Siccome io credo che sariamo noi.

SONNET

Guido, I would that Lapo, thou, and I,
  Led by some strong enchantment, might ascend
  A magic ship, whose charmed sails should fly
  With winds at will, wheree'er our thoughts might wend,
And that no change, nor any evil chance,
  Should mar our joyous voyage; but it might be
  That even satiety should still enhance
  Between our hearts their strict community,
And that the bounteous wizard then would place
  Vanna and Bice and my gentle love,
  Companions of our wandering, and would grace

With passionate talk, wherever we might rove,
   Our time, and each were as content and free
   As I believe that thou and I should be.

(TR. PERCY BYSSHE SHELLEY)

SONNET

Guido, I wish that you and Lapo and I
   Were carried off by magic
And put in a boat, which, every time there was wind,
   Would sail on the ocean exactly where we wanted.

In this way storms and other dangerous weather
   Wouldn't be able to harm us—
And I wish that, since we all were of one mind,
   We'd go on wanting more and more to be together.

And I wish that Vanna and Lagia too
   And she whose name on the list is number thirty
Were put into our boat by the magician

And that we all did nothing but talk about love
   And I wish that they were just as glad to be there
   As I believe the three of us would be.

(TR. KENNETH KOCH)

Young Dante imagines a magical boat trip in which he and two men poet friends and their three girlfriends could ride about pleasantly forever and do nothing but talk about love. I translated this poem twenty-five years ago; last year I was somewhat startled at finding a translation of it by Shelley. Shelley's translation gets the exhilaration and the "magic" of the situation—Shelley's poetry is marvelous at getting such effects. In order to do so, he takes a few liberties—in line 2, one doesn't really "ascend" a boat; in line 4, a literal translation of Dante's line would be "would move on the sea according to your will and mine"—"wheree'er our thoughts might wend" seems a bit unclear; lines 7 and 8 are a free and inventive translation of what Dante says; in the last line Shelley says "thou and I" but I think Dante means all three of the young men, not just two of them. None of these "liberties" falsifies Dante's poem and the result, musically, is quite beautiful. In

154 • *An Anthology of Poems*

my translation I tried to be accurate and simple, even plain, and at the same time to get some of the excitement of Dante's invitation to a magical boat ride. The original has qualities that aren't in either translation, but with two English versions—Shelley's exhilarating one and my plain one— the reader may get an idea of this poem that, in Italian, is plain and exhilarating at the same time.

Dante's tenth line is a problem to translate (literally, "with her who is on the number thirty"). The poet seems to wish to conceal his love's name—the number thirty may be where her name appears on a church registry, or on a list that Dante himself made of the sixty most beautiful women of Florence.

DANTE ALIGHIERI

ITALIAN (1265–1321)

Sestina

I have reached, alas, the long shadow
and short day of whitening hills
when color is lost in the grass.
My longing, all the same, keeps green
it is so hooked in the hard stone
that speaks and hears like a woman.

In that same way this new woman
stands as cold as snow in shadow,
less touched than if she had been stone
by the sweet time that warms the hills
and brings them back from white to green,
dressing them in flowers and grass.

Who, when she wreathes her hair with grass,
thinks of any other woman?
The golden waves so mix with green
that Love himself seeks its shadow
that has me fixed between small hills
more strongly than cemented stone.

More potent than a precious stone,
her beauty wounds, and healing grass
cannot help; across plains and hills
I fled this radiant woman.
From her light I found no shadow
of mountain, wall, or living green.

I have seen her pass, dressed in green,
and thought the sight would make a stone
love, as I, even her shadow.
And I have walked with her on grass,
speaking like a lovesick woman,
enclosed within the highest hills.

But streams will flow back to their hills
before this branch, sappy and green,
catches fire (as does a woman)
from me, who would bed down on stone
and gladly for his food crop grass
just to see her gown cast shadow.

The heavy shadow cast by hills
this woman's light can change to green,
as one might hide a stone in grass.

(TR. JAMES SCHUYLER)

The sestina is a poetic form that was invented by the troubadour poet
Arnaut Daniel. There are six words that end every line, and these words
occur in a regular pattern. The six end-words here are *shadow, hills, grass,
green, stone,* and *woman.* The poem is a sort of variation on a theme of these
six words. The last end-word of stanza one is the first end-word of stanza
two, which makes for an echoing connection between stanzas. The pattern
in which the end-words change is this: if the words in stanza one are considered as 1 2 3 4 5 6, then the order in stanza two will be 6 1 5 2 4 3; in
stanza 3, 3 6 4 1 2 5, and so on. This is true of the six six-line stanzas. In the
final, three-line stanza, end-words 1 and 2 are in line 1; 3 and 4 in line 2; 5
and 6 in line 3. The form is easier to write in than it seems. One way a poet
might procede is to pick out six favorite, meaningful, malleable words that
resonate well together and suggest dramatic and poetic possibilities. The end
words can be set in place even before the poem is written. There are good
sestinas in English by Spenser, Kipling, Pound, Auden, Elizabeth Bishop, and
John Ashbery, among others. The unusual non-rhyming repeating music of
the form has appealed to a number of modern poets.

Dante's *Sestina* is on the familiar theme of passionate and unrequited
love, but, in this beautiful translation by James Schuyler, is as fresh, moving, and unfamiliar as one would expect any poem by Dante to be.

PETRARCH

ITALIAN (1304–1374)

Sonnet

Quanta invidia io ti porto, avara terra,
ch' abbracci quella cui veder m'è tolto
e mi contendi l'aria del bel volto
dove pace trovai d'ogni mia guerra!

Quanta ne porto al ciel, che chiude e serra
e sì cupidamente à in sé raccolto
lo spirto da le belle membra sciolto
e per altrui sì rado si diserra!

Quanta invidia a quell'anime che 'n sorte
ànno or sua santa e dolce compagnia,
la qual io cercai sempre con tal brama!

Quant' a la dispietata e dura morte,
ch' avendo spento in lei la vita mia,
stassi ne' suoi begli occhi, e me non chiama!

HE IS JEALOUS OF THE HEAVENS AND THE EARTH

What a grudge I am bearing the earth that has its arms about her
and is holding that face away from me, where I was finding peace
from great sadness.

What a grudge I am bearing the Heavens that are after taking her,
and shutting her in with greediness, the Heavens that do push their
bolt against so many.

What a grudge I am bearing the blessed saints that have got her
sweet company, that I am always seeking; and what a grudge I am
bearing against Death, that is standing in her two eyes, and will
not call me with a word.

(TR. J. M. SYNGE)

How much envy I bear you, greedy earth,
Embracing her whose sight is taken from me
Denying me the beauty of that face
Where I found peace from every war!

How much I bear heaven, which closes and locks up,
Having so stingily gathered it to itself
Her soul now separate from her beautiful limbs,
Heaven which for anyone else so seldom opens!

How much envy I feel for all those souls
Who have her sweet and sainted company
That I sought after always with such longing!

How much for hard and ruthless death,
Who having ended my life by ending hers,
Stands in her beautiful eyes and does not call me!

(TR. KENNETH KOCH)

Petrarch wrote three hundred and sixty-six love poems to Laura, and their relationship was limited to the poems. Most of the poems are sonnets and are full of old-fashioned varieties of poetic devices such as, in this sonnet, the personification of Earth, Heaven, and Death. The poems, in Italian, are beautiful in their language and their form, neither of which is easy to get in an English version; and the ideas, being old and by now conventionally poetic ones, by themselves aren't enough to make the beauty of the poems interesting to contemporary readers. In order to bring the beauty and drama of Petrarch's poetry into English, John Synge did a very free translation, something it's worth doing if the result is saving poetry that would otherwise be lost. Petrarch's original poem is a sonnet; Synge's version is not in any recognizable poetic form but is three long sentences, and not even in standard English but in the kind of Irish-English spoken in the Arran Islands.

ANONYMOUS

BRITISH (PROBABLY FIFTEENTH OR SIXTEENTH CENTURY)

The Unquiet Grave

1

"The wind doth blow today, my love,
　And a few small drops of rain;
I never had but one true-love,
　In cold grave she was lain.

2

"I'll do as much for my true-love
　As any young man may;
I'll sit and mourn all at her grave
　For a twelvemonth and a day."

3

The twelvemonth and a day being up,
　The dead began to speak:
"Oh who sits weeping on my grave,
　And will not let me sleep?"

4

" 'Tis I, my love, sits on your grave,
　And will not let you sleep;
For I crave one kiss of your clay-cold lips,
　And that is all I seek."

5

"You crave one kiss of my clay-cold lips,
　But my breath smells earthy strong;
If you have one kiss of my clay-cold lips,
　Your time will not be long.

6

" 'Tis down in yonder garden green,
  Love, where we used to walk,
The finest flower that e'er was seen
  Is withered to a stalk.

7

"The stalk is withered dry, my love,
  So will our hearts decay;
So make yourself content, my love,
  Till God calls you away."

Ballads like these were sung on London streets, and elsewhere. Often the words weren't written down; the ballads would pass from one singer to another—there are over forty versions of this one. The ballads are pure storytelling, no decoration, all action and suspense. The stories almost always have to do with death and are told in a surprising and frightening way. The stanzas are in "ballad meter," with only lines 2 and 4 rhyming, but here there are sometimes repeated words at the ends of lines 1 and 3 and there is an extra rhyme in stanza 6.

QUEEN ELIZABETH I

BRITISH (1533–1603)

When I Was Fair and Young

When I was fair and young, and favor graced me,
   Of many was I sought, their mistress for to be;
But I did scorn them all, and answered them therefore,
    Go, go, go, seek some otherwhere,
      Impórtune me no more!

How many weeping eyes I made to pine with woe,
   How many sighing hearts, I have no skill to show;
Yet I the prouder grew, and answered them therefore,
    Go, go, go, seek some otherwhere,
      Impórtune me no more!

Then spake fair Venus' son, that proud victorious boy,
   And said: Fine dame, since that you be so coy,
I will so pluck your plumes that you shall say no more,
    Go, go, go, seek some otherwhere,
      Impórtune me no more!

When he had spake these words, such change grew in my breast
   That neither night nor day since that, I could take any rest.
Then lo! I did repent that I had said before,
    Go, go, go, seek some otherwhere,
      Impórtune me no more!

Political power and poetic power haven't often gone together. Though powerful, however, Elizabeth shows herself just as much subject to the poetic conventions of her time as any lesser-born writer—in her conversation with Cupid, for example, which, had it really taken place, would have been a summit meeting of an unusual kind. The poem has an admirable sprightliness.

EDMUND SPENSER

BRITISH (1552?–1599)

from *The Faerie Queene*, Book I

1

A Gentle Knight was pricking on the plaine,
    Y cladd in mightie armes and silver shielde,
    Wherein old dints of deepe wounds did remaine,
    The cruell markes of many a bloudy fielde;
    Yet armes till that time did he never wield:
    His angry steede did chide his foming bitt,
    As much disdayning to the curbe to yield:
    Full jolly knight he seemd, and faire did sitt,
As one for knightly giusts and fierce encounters fitt.

2

But on his brest a bloudie Crosse he bore,
    The deare remembrance of his dying Lord,
    For whose sweete sake that glorious badge he wore,
    And dead as living ever him ador'd:
    Upon his shield the like was also scor'd,
    For soveraine hope, which in his helpe he had:
    Right faithfull true he was in deede and word,
    But of his cheere did seeme too solemne sad,
Yet nothing did he dread, but ever was ydrad.

3

Upon a great adventure he was bond,
    That greatest Gloriana to him gave,
    That greatest Glorious Queene of Faerie lond,
    To winne him worship, and her grace to have,
    Which of all earthly things he most did crave;
    And ever as he rode, his hart did earne
    To prove his puissance in battell brave
    Upon his foe, and his new force to learne;
Upon his foe, a Dragon horrible and stearne.

A lovely Ladie rode him faire beside,
    Upon a lowly Asse more white than snow,
    Yet she much whiter, but the same did hide
    Under a vele, that wimpled was full low,
    And over all a blacke stole she did throw,
    As one that inly mourned: so was she sad,
    And heavie sat upon her palfrey slow;
    Seemèd in heart some hidden care she had,
And by her in a line a milke white lambe she lad.

5

So pure an innocent, as that same lambe,
    She was in life and every vertuous lore,
    And by descent from Royall lynage came
    Of ancient Kings and Queenes, that had of yore
    Their scepters stretcht from East to Westerne shore,
    And all the world in their subjection held;
    Till that infernall feend with foule uprore
    Forwasted all their land, and then expeld:
Whom to avenge, she had this Knight from far compeld.

6

Behind her farre away a Dwarfe did lag,
    That Lasie seemd in being ever last,
    Or wearied with bearing of her bag
    Of needments at his backe. Thus as they past,
    The day with cloudes was suddeine overcast,
    And angry *Jove* an hideous storme of raine
    Did pour into his Lemans lap so fast,
    That every wight to shrowd it did constrain,
And this faire couple eke to shroud themselves were fain.

7

Enforst to seeke some covert nigh at hand,
    A shadie grove not far away they spide,
    That promist ayde the tempest to withstand:
    Whose loftie trees yclad with sommers pride,

Did spred so broad, that heavens light did hide,
Not perceable with power of any starre:
And all within were pathes and alleies wide,
With footing worne, and leading inward farre:
Faire harbour that them seemes; so in they entered arre.

8

And foorth they passe, with pleasure forward led,
Joying to heare the birdes sweete harmony,
Which therein shrouded from the tempest dred,
Seemd in their song to scorne the cruell sky.
Much can they prayse the trees so straight and hy,
The sayling Pine, the Cedar proud and tall,
The vine-prop Elme, the Poplar never dry,
The builder Oake, sole king of forrests all,
The Aspine good for staves, the Cypresse funerall.

9

The Laurell, meed of mightie Conquerours
And Poets sage, the Firre that weepeth still,
The Willow worne of forlorne Paramours,
The Eugh obedient to the benders will,
The Birch for shaftes, the Sallow for the mill,
The Mirrhe sweete bleeding in the bitter wound,
The warlike Beech, the Ash for nothing ill,
The fruitfull Olive, and the Platane round,
The carver Holme, the Maple seeldom inward sound.

10

Led with delight, they thus beguile the way,
Untill the blustring storme is overblowne;
When weening to returne, whence they did stray,
They cannot finde that path, which first was showne,
But wander too and fro in wayes unknowne,
Furthest from end then, when they neerest weene,
That makes them doubt, their wits be not their owne:
So many pathes, so many turnings seene,
That which of them to take, in diverse doubt they been.

The Faerie Queen is over thirty-five thousand lines long. It is a collection of wonderfully told fantastic medieval stories which are also allegories: that is, stories in which not everything but certain important things, and all the characters, stand for something else: chastity, hypocrisy, falsehood, temptation, etc. The main characters are knights, ladies, and the monstrous beings who threaten them. Somewhat surprisingly, the poem is fascinating—surprisingly, because the very idea of allegory seems a little boring: it seems too simple, too one-on-one, that one thing should stand for another. Also we tend not to believe in absolute distinctions between good and evil. Spenser, however, turns the situation around in such a way that the allegory becomes part of the fascination: the reader is always wondering what represents what and is pleased to catch the fleeting meaning and to get it right. Also pleasing is the suspense: it's not clear how anything is going to turn out. With its multitude of characters and situations, the story is complicated and surprising. There is also a lot of sensuousness in the poetry, and many pleasantly fantastic digressions—like the description of the various trees in stanzas eight and nine above. As for the charms of the allegory, notice the shadow of evil portent in the knight's and lady's going into the forest to escape the storm, in stanza seven. Everything *seems* lovely: "a shadie grove," and "loftie trees yclad with sommers pride." One doesn't, at first, pay much attention to the word "pride"; but one may start to feel a little chill in the next line, reading of these trees that "Did spred so broad, that heaven's light did hide," and were "Not perceable with power of any starre." Later in the stanza we are reassured: the paths and "allies" are wide, and the forest seems "faire harbour." And then, beginning the next stanza, "And foorth they passe, with pleasure forward led,/Joying to heare the birdes sweete harmony"; and then there is the interesting and delightful list of different kinds of trees and their respective virtues. Surely all of this is good, and the reader feels safe and happy, as the characters do; but it may still linger in one's mind that this forest blocks out heaven's light, which can't be good. And indeed a little later, the forest turns out to be an evil and dangerous place, in which they end up encountering a deadly monster, who represents (allegorically) Error, "Most lothsom, filthie, foule, and full of vile disdaine" (Stanza 14).

The reader will have noticed the oddness of Spenser's spelling but needn't be put off by it. The poet wanted to write his medieval adventure stories in medieval language. Ben Jonson said that Spenser, in "affecting the Ancients . . . writ no language." Jonson left out mention of the pleasure there was in this odd, sensuous, decorative language that has something of the charm of medieval tapestries. John Ashbery said reading *The Faerie Queene* was like reading an endless beautiful comic strip.

CHRISTOPHER MARLOWE

BRITISH (1564–1593)

from *Tamburlaine*

Zenocrate lovelier than the love of Jove,
Brighter than is the silver Rhodope,
Fairer than whitest snow on Scythian hills,
Thy person is more worth to Tamburlaine
Than the possession of the Persian crown,
Which gracious stars have promised at my birth.
A hundred Tartars shall attend on thee,
Mounted on steeds swifter than Pegasus;
Thy garments shall be made of Median silk,
Enchas'd with precious jewels of mine own,
More rich and valorous than Zenocrate's;
With milk-white harts upon an ivory sled
Thou shalt be drawn amidst the frozen pools,
And scale the icy mountains' lofty tops,
Which with thy beauty will be soon resolv'd.

Here, Tamburlaine, the great conqueror, gives a glorious speech in order to win the heart of the beautiful Zenocrate. He praises her, says how much he wants her, mentions his own coming greatness, and promises her wonderful gifts. This and other passages of Christopher Marlowe's work are among the rare moments when part of the history of the poetic language is taking place, as it were, on stage—here it is the creation of a kind of blank verse that flows on from line to line in an even and musical way, and in which groups of lines are even more harmonious, like longer parts of a musical composition. One can see this by reading any of the first five lines separately and then reading them all together. This kind of music didn't exist before Marlowe's plays: Marlowe invented it and passed it on to Shakespeare, who made good use of it.

WILLIAM SHAKESPEARE

from *Romeo and Juliet*

Enter Romeo and Juliet aloft [at the window].

Juliet. Wilt thou be gone? It is not yet near day.
   It was the nightingale, and not the lark,
   That pierced the fearful hollow of thine ear.
   Nightly she sings on yond pomegranate tree.
   Believe me, love, it was the nightingale.
Romeo. It was the lark, the herald of the morn;
   No nightingale. Look, love, what envious streaks
   Do lace the severing clouds in yonder East.
   Night's candles are burnt out, and jocund day
   Stands tiptoe on the misty mountain tops.
   I must be gone and live, or stay and die.
Juliet. Yond light is not daylight; I know it, I.
   It is some meteor that the sun exhales
   To be to thee this night a torchbearer
   And light thee on thy way to Mantua.
   Therefore stay yet; thou need'st not to be gone.
Romeo. Let me be ta'en, let me be put to death.
   I am content, so thou wilt have it so.
   I'll say yon grey is not the morning's eye,
   'Tis but the pale reflex of Cynthia's brow;
   Nor that is not the lark whose notes do beat
   The vaulty heaven so high above our heads.
   I have more care to stay than will to go.
   Come, death, and welcome! Juliet wills it so.
   How is't, my soul? Let's talk; it is not day.
Juliet. It is, it is! Hie hence, be gone, away!
   It is the lark that sings so out of tune,
   Straining harsh discords and unpleasing sharps.
   Some say the lark makes sweet division;
   This doth not so, for she divideth us.
   Some say the lark and loathèd toad change eyes;
   O, now I would they had changed voices too,
   Since arm from arm that voice doth us affray,

Hunting thee hence with hunt's-up to the day.
O, now be gone! More light and light it grows.
Romeo. More light and light—more dark and dark our
woes.

Enter Nurse [hastily].

Nurse. Madam!
Juliet. Nurse?
Nurse. Your lady mother is coming to your chamber.
The day is broke; be wary, look about.   [*Exit.*]
Juliet. Then, window, let day in, and let life out.
Romeo. Farewell, farewell! One kiss, and I'll descend.
                                        [*He goeth down.*]
Juliet. Art thou gone so, love-lord, ay husband-friend?
I must hear from thee every day in the hour,
For in a minute there are many days.
Or, by this count I shall be much in years
Ere I again behold my Romeo!
Romeo. Farewell!
I will omit no opportunity
That may convey my greetings, love, to thee.
Juliet. O, think'st thou we shall ever meet again?
Romeo. I doubt it not; and all these woes shall serve
For sweet discourses in our times to come.
Juliet. O God, I have an ill-divining soul!
Methinks I see thee, now thou art below,
As one dead in the bottom of a tomb.
Either my eyesight fails, or thou lookest pale.
Romeo. And trust me, love, in my eye so do you.
Dry sorrow drinks our blood. Adieu, adieu! [*Exit.*]
Juliet. O Fortune, Fortune! All men call thee fickle.
If thou art fickle, what dost thou with him
That is renowned for faith? Be fickle, Fortune,
For then I hope thou wilt not keep him long
But send him back.   [*She goeth down from the window.*]

(ACT III, SCENE V)

Romeo and Juliet have just spent their first night together; Romeo has to
leave before daylight or be taken and killed. He sees the first light of dawn;
Juliet wants so much for him to stay that she says it's still night; finally she
realizes the danger he is in and urges him to go. The scene is a good exam-

ple of what the "language of theater" can add to the "language of poetry." As readers of poetry we feel the beauty of the dawn, with its streaks that "lace the severing clouds," but as readers (or spectators) of a play, who identify with the characters, we also feel the danger of it. The scene is mostly in blank verse, but there are also six rhyming couplets which help give it more the sweet, sad, lyrical sound of a love duet.

WILLIAM SHAKESPEARE

(BRITISH 1564–1616)

from *Hamlet*

To be, or not to be, that is the question—
Whether 'tis nobler in the mind to suffer
The slings and arrows of outrageous fortune,
Or to take arms against a sea of troubles,
And by opposing end them.

(ACT III, SCENE I)

Hamlet's speech is full of the language of poetry—there is the repetition of "to be"; the repeating music of all the *DUM* dah two-syllable words at the ends of lines and also inside them: *question, nobler, suffer, arrows, fortune, troubles,* and then the two word *DUM* dah to end the series: *end them.* And *end them* rhymes a little bit with *question,* a rhyme that rounds off and finishes the thought. There are also Fortune, personified as an archer, and troubles, imagined as a sea against which one could battle. Hamlet's question, that is to say, the skeleton of it, can be stated in ordinary English. "Is it better to go on suffering the pains imposed by bad fortune or wouldn't it be a nobler thing to do to take an active role against despair by killing oneself?" In the actual poetry language (Shakespearean version) one can linger over each of its details as one would over those of a sonata, experiencing the nobility, the unhappiness, the fancifulness, even the slight pretentiousness and self-deception of an individual mind (Hamlet's) at a moment of trouble and indecision.

WILLIAM SHAKESPEARE

BRITISH (1564–1616)

Oh Mistress Mine

Oh mistress mine! where are you roaming?
Oh! stay and hear; your true love's coming,
　　That can sing both high and low.
Trip no further, pretty sweeting;
Journeys end in lovers meeting,
　　Every wise man's son doth know.

What is love? 'Tis not hereafter;
Present mirth hath present laughter;
　　What's to come is still unsure:
In delay there lies no plenty;
Then come kiss me, sweet and twenty,
　　Youth's a stuff will not endure.

The love songs of Shakespeare and other seventeenth-century poets often bring in the themes of time, change, and death, which gives them a kind of seriousness that songs haven't had since—at least until our own time, when there have been some attempts to write love songs that go beyond prettiness and desire.

Songs like this one are meant to be sung. Songs don't usually introduce new ideas but, rather, arrange already familiar ones. Shakespeare's songs manage to be beautiful and surprising while doing so.

WILLIAM SHAKESPEARE

BRITISH (1564–1616)

Sonnet LXXIII

That time of year thou mayst in me behold
When yellow leaves, or none, or few, do hang
Upon those boughs which shake against the cold,
Bare ruined choirs, where late the sweet birds sang.
In me thou see'st the twilight of such day
As after sunset fadeth in the west,
Which by and by black night doth take away,
Death's second self, that seals up all in rest.
In me thou see'st the glowing of such fire,
That on the ashes of his youth doth lie,
As the deathbed whereon it must expire,
Consumed with that which it was nourished by.
    This thou perceiv'st, which makes thy love more strong,
    To love that well which thou must leave ere long.

Shakespeare compares his aging self to three things: a winter day, twilight, and a dying fire. Each comparison occupies four lines of this fourteen-line poem. This division of the sense of what is said into three four-line "boxes" followed by a two-line conclusion is typical of how ideas are presented in Shakespeare's sonnets. *Choirs* in line 4 doesn't mean the singers but the part of the church where they sang; in this case, the singers are the birds and the "choirs" are the branches of the trees. "Black night" is personified as "Death's second self." The third comparison is difficult at first: the body, which sustains life (fire) is also consumed by life (fire) and turns to used-up body (ashes), which finally kills the life (fire).

BEN JONSON

BRITISH (1572–1637)

To Celia

Drink to me only with thine eyes,
And I will pledge with mine;
Or leave a kiss but in the cup,
And I'll not look for wine.
The thirst that from the soul doth rise,
Doth ask a drink divine;
But might I of Jove's nectar sup,
I would not change for thine.

I sent thee late a rosy wreath,
Not so much honoring thee,
As giving it a hope, that there
It could not withered be.
But thou thereon did'st only breathe,
And sent'st it back to me;
Since when it grows and smells, I swear,
Not of itself, but thee.

This song, like other Jonson poems, is witty and formally elegant. The complicated rhyme scheme (the mixture of rhymes two lines apart—*mine* and *wine*—with those four lines apart—*eyes* and *rise*) is one thing that makes the song seem very "well made," even, almost, "perfect." The tone is "sophisticated" and so is the content. The lady refuses the poet's gift of flowers but he goes on praising her anyway.

JOHN DONNE

BRITISH (1572–1631)

The Good-Morrow

I wonder, by my troth, what thou and I
Did, till we loved? were we not weaned till then?
But sucked on country pleasures, childishly?
Or snorted we in the Seven Sleepers' den?
'Twas so; but this, all pleasures fancies be.
If ever any beauty I did see,
Which I desired, and got, 'twas but a dream of thee.

And now good-morrow to our waking souls,
Which watch not one another out of fear;
For love, all love of other sights controls,
And makes one little room an everywhere.
Let sea-discoverers to new worlds have gone,
Let maps to other, worlds on worlds have shown,
Let us possess one world, each hath one, and is one.

My face in thine eye, thine in mine appears,
And true plain hearts do in the faces rest;
Where can we find two better hemispheres,
Without sharp North, without declining West?
Whatever dies was not mixed equally;
If our two loves be one, or, thou and I
Love so alike that none do slacken, none can die.

Donne brings geography, world conquest, optics, chemistry, medicine, and religious history into this poem about waking up with a woman he loves. The intellectual content causes no decrease of passion; on the contrary, it makes the passion more inclusive and more convincing. It's a change in the language of poetry, an opening up of the ways love can be talked about. Let explorers travel and discover as many worlds as they like, Donne says, for us one world is enough. Each of us is one world and each of us possesses one world (the other person). The idea in the first line of the last stanza can be understood by looking into someone's eyes: there in the pupil you see a reflection of your own face. Hearts appear in the faces not in this same optical way but only figuratively: our love for each other shows in our faces, thus there are hearts in our faces. There's a shift, then, to geography: each face is compared to a hemisphere; but these are better than the real hemispheres which have a north, where it's cold, and a west, where the sun sets. In us, Donne suggests, there's no sharp cold and no decline of light and warmth. The last three lines refer to an idea of the Greek physician Galen (second century A.D.) that death was the result of an imbalance of elements in the body; Donne says if they love each other with equal force there'll be no imbalance and they'll live (and love) forever. It is hard to believe that the two lovers will never die, but not hard, in the spell of the poem, to believe in the poet's feeling that they won't.

ROBERT HERRICK

BRITISH (1591–1674)

The Vision

Sitting alone (as one forsook)
Close by a Silver-shedding Brook;
With hands held up to Love, I wept;
And after sorrowes spent, I slept:
Then in a Vision I did see
A glorious forme appeare to me:
A Virgins face she had; her dresse
Was like a sprightly *Spartanesse.*
A silver bow with green silk strung,
Down from her comely shoulders hung:
And as she stood, the wanton Aire
Dandled the ringlets of her haire.
Her legs were such *Diana* shows,
When tuckt up she a hunting goes;
With Buskins shortned to descrie
The happy dawning of her thigh:
Which when I saw, I made accesse
To kisse that tempting nakednesse:
But she forbad me, with a wand
Of Mirtle she had in her hand:
And chiding me, said, Hence, Remove,
Herrick, thou art too coorse to love.

To Dianeme

Sweet, be not proud of those two eyes,
Which Star-like sparkle in their skies:
Nor be you proud, that you can see
All hearts your captives; yours, yet free:
Be you not proud of that rich haire,

Which wantons with the Love-sick aire:
When as that *Rubie*, which you weare,
Sunk from the tip of your soft eare,
Will last to be a precious Stone,
When all your world of Beautie's gone.

Herrick makes fun of himself in his poetic account of a "dream vision." The beautiful dream-woman tells him he is too coarse to love. His poem is anything but coarse, having a most elegant music to go with its sensuousness and its humor. "The happy dawning of her thigh" is one of the remarkable images often to be found in Herrick's poems.

"To Dianeme" seems between two stages of the poetry language of the seventeenth century. The comparison of the lady's eyes to stars is old-fashioned, as is the idea of hearts being her captives. However, the image of her hair moving seductively in the air (which is in love with it) is new; and the "Rubie," "Sunk from the tip of your soft eare" is fresh, physical, and immediate, a step forward in sensuous description.

GEORGE HERBERT

BRITISH (1593–1633)

Prayer

Prayer, the church's banquet, angels' age,
   God's breath in man returning to his birth,
   The soul in paraphrase, heart in pilgrimage,
The Christian plummet sounding heaven and earth;

Engine against th' Almighty, sinner's tower,
   Reverséd thunder, Christ-side-piercing spear,
   The six-days' world transposing in an hour,
A kind of tune, which all things hear and fear;

Softness, and peace, and joy, and love, and bliss,
   Exalted manna, gladness of the best,
   Heaven in ordinary, man well dressed,
The Milky Way, the bird of Paradise,

   Church bells beyond the stars heard, the soul's blood,
   The land of spices; something understood.

"Prayer" is like the definition(s) of the word *prayer* in some sort of sublime Dictionary of the Poetic Language. Herbert may have found all his "definitions" of prayer in his own mind and heart. (Another way to create such a poem might be to go through other poems and find all the ways "prayer"— or "love" or "night," say—is metaphorically described.) The different definitions aren't connected to each other, and all together they don't make a sentence; they are simply a list. Some parts of the list are likely to be unclear at first, either because of the speed and conciseness of the writing or because of the reader's not knowing certain aspects of Christian doctrine. It was a long time before I understood all of this poem, though there was always enough that I understood to make me want to go on reading.

"Engine against th' Almighty" and "sinner's tower" refer to the kind of warfare that used to be conducted in order to conquer a walled city: the "engine" would be a sort of cannon, and the "tower" a construction that enabled soldiers to get over the top of the wall.

JOHN MILTON

BRITISH (1608–1674)

from *Paradise Lost*

> Not that fair field
> Of *Enna,* where *Proserpin* gath'ring flow'rs
> Herself a fairer Flow'r by gloomy *Dis*
> Was gather'd, which cost *Ceres* all that pain
> To seek her through the world; not that sweet Grove
> Of *Daphne* by *Orontes,* and th' inspir'd
> *Castalian* Spring might with this Paradise
> Of *Eden* strive; nor that *Nyseian* Isle
> Girt with the River *Triton,* where old *Cham,*
> Whom Gentiles *Ammon* call and *Lybian Jove,*
> Hid *Amalthea* and her Florid Son,
> Young *Bacchus,* from his Stepdame *Rhea's* eye;
> Nor where *Abassin* Kings thir issue Guard,
> Mount *Amara,* though this by some suppos'd
> True Paradise under the *Ethiop* Line
> By *Nilus* head, enclos'd with shining Rock,
> A whole day's journey high, but wide remote
> From this *Assyrian* Garden, where the Fiend
> Saw undelighted all delight, all kind
> Of living Creatures new to sight and strange . . .

(BOOK IV, 268–287)

Characteristic of Milton is the plentiful use of proper names; one is positively bombarded by them. Characteristic, too, is the long sentence: this passage is part of a sentence that ends twenty-four lines later. In the sentence, too, words are suspended: one doesn't quite know what goes with what: subjects, objects, and verbs come in unexpected places—Milton writes English somewhat as if it were Latin.

This passage describes all the most famous gardens that ever existed and states that none was so beautiful as the Garden of Eden, which Satan (the Fiend) is now seeing for the first time. It's obvious that at first a lot more will be seen and heard than will be understood. The best policy is to give in to it (what else can one do?), enjoy the names and the music and catch on to whatever sense one can. One may, for example, know the story of Proserpina (in Greek, Persephone), who, out picking flowers one day, was kidnapped by Dis, the god of the underworld, and taken there to be his bride (Ceres was her mother). Whatever one knows, the impression Milton gives of knowing everything and bringing in the whole universe at once is dramatic and grand.

ANNE BRADSTREET

AMERICAN (1612?–1672)

To My Dear and Loving Husband

If ever two were one, then surely we.
If ever man were loved by wife, then thee;
If ever wife was happy in a man,
Compare with me, ye women, if you can.
I prize thy love more than whole mines of gold
Or all the riches that the East doth hold.
My love is such that rivers cannot quench,
Nor ought but love from thee, give recompense.
Thy love is such I can no way repay,
The heavens reward thee manifold, I pray.
Then while we live, in love let's so persevere
That when we live no more, we may live ever.

These neat, concise couplets contain surprises that make them varied and dramatic—such as the change, in line three, from talking to the husband to talking to "ye women"; the happy exaggeration of "whole mines of gold"; the change of tone in the last two lines.

ANDREW MARVELL

BRITISH (1621–1678)

Ametas and Thestylis Making Hay-Ropes

I

Ametas
Think'st Thou that this Love can stand,
Whilst Thou still dost say me nay?
Love unpaid does soon disband:
Love binds Love as Hay binds Hay.

II

Thestylis
Think'st Thou that this Rope would twine
If we both should turn one way?
Where both parties so combine,
Neither Love will twist nor Hay.

III

Ametas
Thus you vain Excuses find,
Which your selves and us delay:
And Love tyes a Womans Mind
Looser than with Ropes of Hay.

IV

Thestylis
What you cannot constant hope
Must be taken as you may.

V

Ametas
Then let's both lay by our Rope,
And go kiss within the Hay.

The charm of this poem is in the songlike music of the simple elegant stanzas, in the philosophical arguments of the shepherd and shepherdess, and in the atmosphere of complete youthfulness, loveliness, and permissiveness of the world in which they seem to exist. This is an example of "pastoral" poetry, a genre peopled mostly by amorous and philosophical tenders of sheep; these imaginary lovers have exquisite feelings and time for amorous dallyings and, being poor, are free of the burdens of responsibility, and, being children of nature, are free of falseness. What might be called the pastoral fantasy inspired poets as early as Theocritus (third century B.C.); it appears only rarely after the seventeenth century.

The poem can be seen as a little (very little) play that begins and ends quickly.

WILLIAM BLAKE

BRITISH (1757–1827)

London

I wander thro' each charter'd street,
Near where the charter'd Thames does flow,
And mark in every face I meet
Marks of weakness, marks of woe.

In every cry of every man,
In every Infant's cry of fear,
In every voice, in every ban,
The mind-forg'd manacles I hear.

How the Chimney-sweeper's cry
Every blackening Church appalls;
And the hapless Soldier's sigh
Runs in blood down Palace walls.

But most thro' midnight streets I hear
How the youthful Harlot's curse
Blasts the new-born Infant's tear,
And blights with plagues the Marriage hearse.

This is a taking-a-walk poem that turns out to be a terrifying vision of what's wrong with a whole society. The meter and rhyme are regular in an almost mechanical way, which adds to the effect the poem gives of simplicity, directness, and unobstructed truth. What is wrong with the society is that everything has been regulated (chartered) and restricted in disastrous ways. The streets and the river are regulated and controlled, but these are just emblematic of the worse regulation of people's behavior; the people are in chains and the chains are the "rules" other people have made to control them (the "mind-forg'd manacles"). The last two stanzas give specific instances; in them, Blake tells us what he sees on the surface of life and what he sees underneath, simultaneously; it's as though he had a kind of X-ray vision that enabled him to see the true moral nature of things. The young boys who clean chimneys cry out and their crying drapes the church in deadly white ("appalls" it). The soldiers sigh and their sighs are blood on the palace walls. The church sanctions chimney sweeping and (in Blake's vision) is disgraced and disfigured by it. The government sponsors wars, and (in Blake's vision) the misery of the soldiers is visible in the bloody walls. In the last stanza Blake's vision is of the evil done by laws that inhibit sexual freedom: these cause prostitution to exist, and prostitutes spread venereal disease—babies are born "blasted" by it and it turns weddings into funerals. Blake's direct, visionary way of writing was a startling addition to the language of poetry.

WILLIAM WORDSWORTH

BRITISH (1770–1850)

To My Sister

It is the first mild day of March:
Each minute sweeter than before,
The redbreast sings from the tall larch
That stands beside our door.

There is a blessing in the air,
Which seems a sense of joy to yield
To the bare trees, and mountains bare,
And grass in the green field.

My sister! ('tis a wish of mine)
Now that our morning meal is done,
Make haste, your morning task resign;
Come forth and feel the sun.

Edward will come with you;—and, pray,
Put on with speed your woodland dress;
And bring no book: for this one day
We'll give to idleness.

No joyless forms shall regulate
Our living calendar:
We from to-day, my Friend, will date
The opening of the year.

Love, now a universal birth,
From heart to heart is stealing,
From earth to man, from man to earth:
—It is the hour of feeling.

One moment now may give us more
Than years of toiling reason:
Our minds shall drink at every pore
The spirit of the season.

Some silent laws our hearts will make,
Which they shall long obey:
We for the year to come may take
Our temper from to-day.

And from the blessed power that rolls
About, below, above,
We'll frame the measure of our souls:
They shall be tuned to love.

Then come, my Sister! come, I pray,
With speed put on your woodland dress;
And bring no book: for this one day
We'll give to idleness.

This "let's take a walk" poem written at the end of the eighteenth century is new in its simplicity and directness, as well as in its being quite personal, casual, and familiar—in being addressed "To My Sister," for example, and in the mention of "our door." There's a sweet springlike feeling of happiness. Wordsworth, like Blake, disliked "joyless forms" (in Blake's "London," the "charter'd" things and "mind-forg'd manacles") but his walk, unlike Blake's, is amidst the joyful ones.

WILLIAM WORDSWORTH

BRITISH (1770–1850)

from *The Prelude*

Meanwhile, abroad
The heavy rain was falling, or the frost
Raged bitterly, with keen and silent tooth,
And, interrupting oft the impassion'd game,
From Esthwaite's neighbouring Lake the splitting ice,
While it sank down towards the water, sent,
Among the meadows and the hills, its long
And dismal yellings, like the noise of wolves
When they are howling round the Bothnic Main.

This passage is a memory of childhood: while he and his friends were indoors playing cards, Wordsworth says, nature outside was lively, even violent, and sometimes frightening. Esthwaite is a lake, and the exploding sounds Wordsworth describes come from the splitting up of the ice on its surface.

Wordsworth used blank verse (unrhymed iambic pentameter) in a deliberately plain, flat way; it has a sound of sincerity, of someone talking, talking in a rather meditative and sometimes emotional way, but staying as close to the plain truth as possible—the emotion he feels is a part of this truth but doesn't overwhelm the plain and level tone.

There are two personifications—of ice and of the "pent-up air." The comparison to howling troops of wolves is quite wild for Wordsworth.

The "Bothnic Main" must refer to the Gulf of Bothnia, which is an arm of the Baltic Sea, between Finland and Sweden. It's hard to know if Wordsworth chose it for its geographical and zoological accuracy or for its wonderful sound, or both.

LORD BYRON

BRITISH (1788–1824)

from *Don Juan,* Canto II

CLXXI

When Juan woke he found some good things ready,
    A bath, a breakfast, and the finest eyes
That ever made a youthful heart less steady,
    Besides her maid's, as pretty for their size;
But I have spoken of all this already—
    And repetition's tiresome and unwise—
Well—Juan, after bathing in the sea,
Came always back to coffee and Haidée.

CLXXII

Both were so young, and one so innocent,
    That bathing pass'd for nothing; Juan seem'd
To her, as 'twere, the kind of being sent,
    Of whom these two years she had nightly dream'd,
A something to be loved, a creature meant
    To be her happiness, and whom she deem'd
To render happy; all who joy would win
Must share it—Happiness was born a twin.

CLXXIII

It was such pleasure to behold him, such
    Enlargement of existence to partake
Nature with him, to thrill beneath his touch,
    To watch him slumbering, and to see him wake:
To live with him forever were too much;
    But then the thought of parting made her quake:
He was her own, her ocean-treasure, cast
Like a rich wreck—her first love, and her last.

CLXXIV

And thus a moon roll'd on, and fair Haidée
    Paid daily visits to her boy, and took
Such plentiful precautions, that still he
    Remain'd unknown within his craggy nook;
At last her father's prows put out to sea,
    For certain merchantmen upon the look,
Not as of yore to carry off an Io,
But three Ragusan vessels bound for Scio.

CLXXV

Then came her freedom, for she had no mother,
    So that, her father being at sea, she was
Free as a married woman, or such other
    Female, as where she likes may freely pass,
Without even the encumbrance of a brother,
    The freest she that ever gazed on glass:
I speak of Christian lands in this comparison,
Where wives, at least, are seldom kept in garrison.

CLXXVI

Now she prolong'd her visits and her talk
    (For they must talk), and he had learnt to say
So much as to propose to take a walk—
    For little had he wander'd since the day
On which, like a young flower snapp'd from the stalk,
    Drooping and dewy on the beach he lay—
And thus they walk'd out in the afternoon,
And saw the sun set opposite the moon.

CLXXVII

It was a wild and breaker-beaten coast,
    With cliffs above, and a broad sandy shore,
Guarded by shoals and rocks as by an host,
    With here and there a creek, whose aspect wore
A better welcome to the tempest-tost;
    And rarely ceased the haughty billow's roar,
Save on the dead long summer days, which make
The outstretch'd ocean glitter like a lake.

CLXXVIII

And the small ripple split upon the beach
　　Scarcely o'erpass'd the cream of your champagne,
When o'er the brim the sparkling bumpers reach,
　　That spring-dew of the spirit! the heart's rain!
Few things surpass old wine; and they may preach
　　Who please—the more because they preach in vain—
Let us have wine and woman, mirth and laughter,
Sermons and soda-water the day after.

CLXXIX

Man, being reasonable, must get drunk;
　　The best of life is but intoxication:
Glory, the grape, love, gold, in these are sunk
　　The hopes of all men, and of every nation;
Without their sap, how branchless were the trunk
　　Of life's strange tree, so fruitful on occasion:
But to return—Get very drunk; and when
You wake with headache, you shall see what then!

CLXXX

Ring for your valet—bid him quickly bring
　　Some hock and soda-water, then you'll know
A pleasure worthy Xerxes the great king;
　　For not the blest sherbet, sublimed with snow,
Nor the first sparkle of the desert-spring,
　　Nor Burgundy in all its sunset glow,
After long travel, ennui, love, or slaughter,
Vie with that draught of hock and soda-water!

CLXXXI

The coast—I think it was the coast that I
　　Was just describing—Yes, it *was* the coast—
Lay at this period quiet as the sky,
　　The sands untumbled, the blue waves untost,
And all was stillness, save the sea-bird's cry,
　　And dolphin's leap, and little billow crost
By some low rock or shelve, that made it fret
Against the boundary it scarcely wet.

CLXXXII

And forth they wander'd, her sire being gone,
    As I have said, upon an expedition;
And mother, brother, guardian, she had none,
    Save Zoe, who, although with due precision
She waited on her lady with the sun,
    Thought daily service was her only mission,
Bringing warm water, wreathing her long tresses,
And asking now and then for cast-off dresses.

CLXXXIII

It was the cooling hour, just when the rounded
    Red sun sinks down behind the azure hill,
Which then seems as if the whole earth it bounded,
    Circling all nature, hush'd, and dim, and still,
With the far mountain-crescent half surrounded
    On one side, and the deep sea calm and chill
Upon the other, and the rosy sky,
With one star sparkling through it like an eye.

CLXXXIV

And thus they wander'd forth, and hand in hand,
    Over the shining pebbles and the shells,
Glided along the smooth and harden'd sand,
    And in the worn and wild receptacles
Work'd by the storms, yet work'd as it were plann'd,
    In hollow halls, with sparry roofs and cells,
They turn'd to rest; and, each clasp'd by an arm,
Yielded to the deep twilight's purple charm.

CLXXXV

They look'd up to the sky, whose floating glow
    Spread like a rosy ocean, vast and bright;
They gazed upon the glittering sea below,
    Whence the broad moon rose circling into sight;
They heard the waves splash, and the wind so low,
    And saw each other's dark eyes darting light
Into each other—and, beholding this,
Their lips drew near, and clung into a kiss;

CLXXXVI

A long, long kiss, a kiss of youth, and love,
  And beauty, all concentrating like rays
Into one focus, kindled from above;
  Such kisses as belong to early days,
Where heart, and soul, and sense, in concert move,
  And the blood's lava, and the pulse a blaze,
Each kiss a heart-quake—for a kiss's strength,
I think, it must be reckon'd by its length.

CLXXXVII

By length I mean duration; theirs endured
  Heaven knows how long—no doubt they never reckon'd;
And if they had, they could not have secured
  The sum of their sensations to a second:
They had not spoken; but they felt allured,
  As if their souls and lips each other beckon'd,
Which, being join'd, like swarming bees they clung—
Their hearts the flowers from whence the honey sprung.

CLXXXVIII

They were alone, but not alone as they
  Who shut in chambers think it loneliness;
The silent ocean, and the starlight bay,
  The twilight glow, which momently grew less,
The voiceless sands, and dropping caves, that lay
  Around them, made them to each other press,
As if there were no life beneath the sky
Save theirs, and that their life could never die.

CLXXXIX

They fear'd no eyes nor ears on that lone beach,
  They felt no terrors from the night, they were
All in all to each other; though their speech
  Was broken words, they *thought* a language there—
And all the burning tongues the passions teach
  Found in one sigh the best interpreter
Of nature's oracle—first love—that all
Which Eve has left her daughters since her fall.

CXC

Haidée spoke not of scruples, ask'd no vows,
    Nor offr'd any; she had never heard
Of plight and promises to be a spouse,
    Or perils by a loving maid incurr'd;
She was all which pure ignorance allows,
    And flew to her young mate like a young bird;
And, never having dreamt of falsehood, she
Had not one word to say of constancy.

CXCI

She loved, and was beloved—she adored,
    And she was worshipp'd; after nature's fashion,
Their intense souls, into each other pour'd,
    If souls could die, had perish'd in that passion—
But by degrees their senses were restored,
    Again to be o'ercome, again to dash on;
And, beating 'gainst *his* bosom, Haidée's heart
Felt as if never more to beat apart.

CXCII

Alas! they were so young, so beautiful,
    So lonely, loving, helpless, and the hour
Was that in which the heart is always full,
    And, having o'er itself no further power,
Prompts deeds eternity cannot annul,
    But pays off moments in an endless shower
Of hell-fire—all prepared for people giving
Pleasure or pain to one another living.

CXCIII

Alas! For Juan and Haidée! they were
    So loving and so lovely—till then never,
Excepting our first parents, such a pair
    Had run the risk of being damn'd for ever;
And Haidée, being devout as well as fair,
    Had, doubtless, heard about the Stygian river,
And hell and purgatory—but forgot
Just in the very crisis she should not.

They look upon each other, and their eyes
  Gleam in the moonlight; and her white arm clasps
Round Juan's head, and his around her lies
  Half buried in the tresses which it grasps;
She sits upon his knee, and drinks his sighs,
  He hers, until they end in broken gasps;
And thus they form a group that's quite antique,
Half naked, loving, natural, and Greek.

CXCV

And when those deep and burning moments pass'd,
  And Juan sunk to sleep within her arms,
She slept not, but all tenderly, though fast,
  Sustain'd his head upon her bosom's charms;
And now and then her eye to heaven is cast,
  And then on the pale cheek her breast now warms,
Pillow'd on her o'erflowing heart, which pants
With all it granted, and with all it grants.

I've included a long passage from Byron's great poem *Don Juan* because I think it takes a fairly long passage to show what it's like. Its way of telling a story, slowly and in detail, with affection and with suspense, yet at the same time with what seem unending witty comments and digressions, doesn't become quite clear in just a few stanzas. These stanzas are from the second Canto of the poem. The young hero Don Juan is washed up almost dead on a small Greek island after a shipwreck. He is nursed back to health by beautiful Haidée, who lives on the island. The stanza form, ottava rima, gives Byron ideal circumstances for telling a story and continually digressing from it. In the first place, being a stanza, an eight-line contained unit, it can start off from a different place each time—or be continuous with the preceding stanza. But even better, this is a stanza divided into two different kinds of parts—one of six lines that has alternating rhymes and is good for storytelling; and the other, a two-line part that is a rhyming couplet and is especially good for changing the subject, making witty comments, or summing up. Byron doesn't always use the two parts this way (which, I think, would become tedious) but does so often enough—here, for example, in stanzas CLXXI, CLXXIV, CLXXV, CLXXVIII, and in at least six others. Sometimes the changes in the couplet are changes of tone—usually from rather high-poetic to something less exalted and wittier, and sometimes with funny, unexpected rhymes:

> I speak of Christian lands in this comparison,
> Where wives, at least, are seldom kept in garrison.
> (CLXXV)

Byron is a storyteller; his story is reassuring to listen to. The reader feels as brilliant and sophisticated as the poet. The wit, as is apparent in these stanzas and perhaps especially in the second-to-last one, never interferes with either the sensuousness or the tenderness but enhances both. Byron brought his storytelling stanza into English from Renaissance Italian poets like Pulci, Boiardo, and Ariosto.

PERCY BYSSHE SHELLEY

BRITISH (1792–1822)

Ode to the West Wind

1

O wild West Wind, thou breath of Autumn's being,
Thou, from whose unseen presence the leaves dead
Are driven, like ghosts from an enchanter fleeing,

Yellow, and black, and pale, and hectic red,
Pestilence-stricken multitudes: O thou,
Who chariotest to their dark wintry bed

The wingèd seeds, where they lie cold and low,
Each like a corpse within its grave, until
Thine azure sister of the Spring shall blow

Her clarion o'er the dreaming earth, and fill
(Driving sweet buds like flocks to feed in air)
With living hues and odors plain and hill:

Wild Spirit, which art moving everywhere;
Destroyer and preserver; hear, oh, hear!

2

Thou on whose stream, mid the steep sky's commotion,
Loose clouds like earth's decaying leaves are shed,
Shook from the tangled boughs of Heaven and Ocean,

Angels of rain and lightning: there are spread
On the blue surface of thine aëry surge,
Like the bright hair uplifted from the head

Of some fierce Maenad, even from the dim verge
Of the horizon to the zenith's height,
The locks of the approaching storm. Thou dirge

Of the dying year, to which this closing night
Will be the dome of a vast sepulcher,
Vaulted with all thy congregated might

Of vapors, from whose solid atmosphere
Black rain, and fire, and hail will burst: oh, hear!

3

Thou who didst waken from his summer dreams
The blue Mediterranean, where he lay,
Lulled by the coil of his crystàlline streams,

Beside a pumice isle in Baiae's bay,
And saw in sleep old palaces and towers
Quivering within the wave's intenser day,

All overgrown with azure moss and flowers
So sweet, the sense faints picturing them! Thou
For whose path the Atlantic's level powers

Cleave themselves into chasms, while far below
The sea-blooms and the oozy woods which wear
The sapless foliage of the ocean, know

Thy voice, and suddenly grow gray with fear,
And tremble and despoil themselves: oh, hear!

4

If I were a dead leaf thou mightest bear;
If I were a swift cloud to fly with thee;
A wave to pant beneath thy power, and share

The impulse of thy strength, only less free
Than thou, O uncontrollable! If even
I were as in my boyhood, and could be

The comrade of thy wandering over Heaven,
As then, when to outstrip thy skyey speed
Scarce seemed a vision; I would ne'er have striven

As thus with thee in prayer in my sore need.
Oh, lift me as a wave, a leaf, a cloud!
I fall upon the thorns of life! I bleed!

A heavy weight of hours has chained and bowed
One too like thee: tameless, and swift, and proud.

5

Make me thy lyre, even as the forest is:
What if my leaves are falling like its own!
The tumult of thy mighty harmonies

Will take from both a deep, autumnal tone,
Sweet though in sadness. Be thou, Spirit fierce,
My spirit! Be thou me, impetuous one!

Drive my dead thoughts over the universe
Like withered leaves to quicken a new birth!
And, by the incantation of this verse,

Scatter, as from an unextinguished hearth
Ashes and sparks, my words among mankind!
Be through my lips to unawakened earth

The trumpet of a prophecy! O Wind,
If Winter comes, can Spring be far behind?

Nature is very much personified: the West Wind, Autumn, Spring, the earth, rain, lightning, the Mediterranean all appear as sentient beings. Shelley apostrophizes (that is he talks to) the West Wind about all of them. He hails and praises the wind, tells it what it does, then asks it to do something for him: first, in stanza IV, he wishes the wind could lift him up and carry him and give him its power; then in the last stanza, he finds a possibly fulfillable form of this wish: that the wind spread his life-giving poems everywhere on earth. Talking to the wind permits Shelley to be completely carried away in what he says and in doing so both he and his poem get to be much like the wind, full of excitement and power.

The form is a variation on terza rima, the stanza Dante used in the *Divine Comedy*. Shelley wrote most of the poem during pauses on a walk in the Cascine Gardens outside Florence. He wrote it out, leaving blank spaces to be filled in later. He also later changed some already-written lines. His change of the last line must be one of the greatest revisions a poet ever made: at first it was "When Winter comes, Spring lags not far behind." How the word "lags" got past Shelley in the first place is unclear—he must have been writing in a great rush.

A reader is likely to be excited by the details of this poem even before understanding everything; and meanwhile there is the experience of standing out in a windstorm of gorgeous words.

JOHN KEATS

BRITISH (1795–1821)

from *Endymion*

On gold sand empearled
With lily shells, and pebbles milky white
Poor Cynthia greeted him, and sooth'd her light
Against his pallid face; he felt the charm
To breathlessness, and suddenly a warm
Of his heart's blood; 'twas very sweet: he stay'd
His wandering steps, and half-entranced laid
His head upon a tuft of straggling weeds,
To taste the gentle moon, and freshening beads
Lashed from the crystal roof by fishes' tails,
And so he kept, until the rosy veils
Mantling the east, by Aurora's peering hand
Were lifted from the water's breast, and fann'd
Into sweet air; and sober'd morning came
Meekly through billows ...

(III, 102–117)

Keats's poem *Endymion* is about the love of a young man, Endymion, for the moon. One reads it, as one reads other poems by Keats, for sensations, sensuousness, sweetness, lusciousness. Keats is a good storyteller, also, but his story is unusual in being mainly a story of sensations—one could almost say the "plot" consisted of every color, fragrance, warmth, taste, or other strong sensation his characters feel. There is in Keats an attention to sensuousness that's new to the language of poetry: "pebbles milky white" and "to taste the gentle moon, and freshening beads/Lashed from the crystal roof" are examples of the mixture of senses called synesthesia and are also very delicious to say. Of course there was attention to the sensuousness of words before Keats wrote—in Marlowe, in Spenser, in Milton, and certainly in Shakespeare—but no poet had taken it so far nor made it the main thing. In the scene from *Romeo and Juliet* (p. 168), for example, the coming of day is beautifully described, but the emphasis is on the effect the dawn may have on the lovers' lives. Here, in Keats's poem, both night and day are important for the paradiselike feelings they give to Endymion—and to the reader.

JOHN KEATS

BRITISH (1795–1821)

Bright Star

Bright star! would I were steadfast as thou art—
　　Not in lone splendor hung aloft the night
And watching, with eternal lids apart,
　　Like nature's patient, sleepless Eremite,
The moving waters at their priestlike task
　　Of pure ablution round earth's human shores,
Or gazing on the new soft-fallen mask
　　Of snow upon the mountains and the moors—
No—yet still steadfast, still unchangeable,
　　Pillowed upon my fair love's ripening breast,
To feel forever its soft fall and swell,
　　Awake forever in a sweet unrest,
Still, still to hear her tender-taken breath,
And so live ever—or else swoon to death.

This poem is talked about in the chapter on Reading. It seemed a good idea to also have it here by itself.

WALT WHITMAN

AMERICAN (1819–1892)

from "Song of Myself"

I am the poet of the body,
And I am the poet of the soul.

The pleasures of heaven are with me, and the pains of hell are with me,
The first I graft and increase upon myself.... the latter I translate into a
    new tongue.

I am the poet of the woman the same as the man,
And I say it is as great to be a woman as to be a man,
And I say there is nothing greater than the mother of men.

I chant a new chant of dilation or pride.
We have had ducking and deprecating about enough,
I show that size is only development.

Have you outstript the rest? Are you the President?
It is a trifle.... they will more than arrive there every one, and still pass on.

I am he that walks with the tender and growing night;
I call to the earth and sea half-held by the night.

Press close barebosomed night! Press close magnetic nourishing night!
Night of south winds! Night of the large few stars!
Still nodding night! Mad naked summer night!

Smile O voluptuous coolbreathed earth!
Earth of the slumbering and liquid trees!
Earth of departed sunset! Earth of the mountains misty-topt!
Earth of the vitreous pour of the full moon just tinged with blue!
Earth of shine and dark mottling the tide of the river!
Earth of the limpid gray of clouds brighter and clearer for my sake!
Far-swooping elbowed earth! Rich apple-blossomed earth!
Smile, for your lover comes!

Whitman showed poets a way to be conversational and plain-seeming and yet grand at the same time.

His use of apostrophe here is of quite a new kind. He not only talks to the night and to the earth but proposes himself as their lover. The boasting ("The pleasures of heaven are with me"), the teasing ("Are you the President?"), the wild almost egomaniacal sensuousness ("Press close bare-bosomed night!"), the questions, the exclamations, the asides, the plain talk side by side with elevated poetic talk, all these together give a good idea of Whitman's poetic language.

Wonderful as Whitman's poetry is, it's possible at first not to like it, and a reader shouldn't feel bad about it. When I first read Whitman, he seemed to me long-winded, patriotic, phonily religious, old-fashioned, and boring. That's probably because of what I happened to read of him in my high-school literature books: "I Hear America Singing," "O Captain! My Captain!" and other inflated and trite-seeming works. When I read all of "Song of Myself" finally, though, it seemed to change everything I felt about poetry. A problem in reading poets of the past is that their original discoveries are used by other poets till they begin to seem dull and are also supplanted by yet newer discoveries. However, in a great past poet like Whitman, the excitement is always there to be found, whenever you have the good luck to find it.

CHARLES BAUDELAIRE

FRENCH (1821–1867)

La Beauté

Je suis belle, ô mortels! comme un rêve de pierre,
Et mon sein, où chacun s'est meutri tour à tour,
Est fait pour inspirer au poète un amour
Eternel et muet ainsi que la matière.

Je trône dans l'azur comme un sphinx incompris;
J'unis un cœur de neige à la blancheur des cygnes;
Je hais le mouvement qui déplace les lignes,
Et jamais je ne pleure et jamais je ne ris.

Les poètes, devant mes grandes attitudes,
Que j'ai l'air d'emprunter aux plus fiers monuments,
Consumeront leurs jours en d'austères études;

Car j'ai, pour fasciner ces dociles amants,
De purs miroirs qui font toutes choses plus belles:
Mes yeux, mes larges yeux aux clartés éternelles!

I am beautiful, o mortals, like a dream of stone
And my breast on which everyone has been bruised in his turn
Is made so as to inspire in the poet a love
That is mute and eternal, as matter is.

I reign in the blue sky like an ununderstood sphinx;
I have both a heart of snow and the whiteness of a swan;
I hate any movement that displaces the lines,
And I never weep and I never laugh.

Poets, in the presence of my grand postures
Which I seem to borrow from the proudest monuments
Will consume their days in austere study;

For I have, to fascinate these docile lovers,
Pure mirrors that make everything more beautiful:
My eyes, my large eyes of eternally flashing light.

(TR. KENNETH KOCH)

Baudelaire is inspired by the mysterious. His poems don't resolve mysteries but make them even more mysterious. Discovering him at age seventeen, I was amazed at finding a poet who was, as I secretly was, fascinated by sex, by dreams, even by horror and evil, and who could write great poems about them. This poem is discussed in the Reading chapter, on p. 132. My translation is awkward, but the reader may be able to use it to "read through" to the original.

CHRISTINA ROSSETTI

BRITISH (1830–1894)

Song

When I am dead, my dearest,
   Sing no sad songs for me;
Plant thou no roses at my head,
   Nor shady cypress tree:
Be the green grass above me
   With showers and dewdrops wet;
And if thou wilt, remember,
   And if thou wilt, forget.

I shall not see the shadows,
   I shall not feel the rain;
I shall not hear the nightingale
   Sing on, as if in pain:
And dreaming through the twilight
   That doth not rise nor set,
Haply I may remember,
   And haply may forget.

The contrast between what's being said and the tone of saying it is considerable. The poet is imagining her death in a lightly lyrical and gentle way. The phrase "when I am dead" is a good example of the resources language offers for speed and compression: the word "when" exists, and it can be put in front of any statement, no matter how impossible or distant, and it makes it possible and nearby—so one may say "When beauty breaks and falls asunder" (Louise Bogan), "When God at first made man" (Herbert), and so on. The poem is full of physical sensations that the poet is saying she won't be aware of. The lovely, easy tone makes everything seem much easier than one would think it could be. The poet won't die, she will simply be dead and even when dead she'll be capable of remembering and forgetting.

On first reading, the word *be* in line five may be confusing: Rossetti may be telling her lover to be, himself, the grass above her grave. On re-reading, it seems most likely, however, that what is meant by *be* is "Let the green grass be...." Still, the "mistaken" sense of "be" is there and adds to the feeling of ease about grief, and the repeated "if thou wilt" makes the tremendous difference between remembering and forgetting seem negligible—the parallel phrasing makes the choice seem easy.

EMILY DICKINSON

AMERICAN (1830–1886)

I would not paint—a picture—

I would not paint—a picture—
I'd rather be the One
Its bright impossibility
To dwell—delicious—on—
And wonder how the fingers feel
Whose rare—celestial—stir—
Evokes so sweet a Torment—
Such sumptuous—Despair—

I would not talk, like Cornets—
I'd rather be the One
Raised softly to the Ceilings—
And out, and easy on—
Through Villages of Ether—
Myself endued Balloon
By but a lip of Metal—
The pier to my Pontoon—

Nor would I be a Poet—
It's finer—own the Ear—
Enamored—impotent—content—
The License to revere,
A privilege so awful
What would the Dower be,
Had I the Art to stun myself
With Bolts of Melody!

Bright, delicious, rare, celestial, sweet, torment, sumptuous, despair—and this is just the first stanza. The poem is filled with wild sensations; and these are the first things a reader is likely to get on reading it: being raised to the ceiling, passing through Villages of Ether, being stunned by Bolts of Melody. This exhilarated stuff is set forth in plain and simple stanzas. Dickinson's poems are like high explosives hidden in small, neat boxes. The music is altered, and the drama increased, by her odd use of capital letters and dashes. Both add rests to the already existing ones of line endings, causing the reader to pause, to stop and start, to read interruptedly, as if unexpectedly slowed down, or speeded up, by feelings.

GERARD MANLEY HOPKINS

BRITISH (1844–1889)

The Windhover

To Christ our Lord

I caught this morning morning's minion, king-
    dom of daylight's dauphin, dapple-dawn-drawn Falcon, in
      his riding
Of the rolling level underneath him steady air, and striding
High there, how he rung upon the rein of a wimpling wing
In his ecstasy! then off, off forth on swing,
    As a skate's heel sweeps smooth on a bow-bend: the hurl
      and gliding
Rebuffed the big wind. My heart in hiding
Stirred for a bird,—the achieve of, the mastery of the thing!

Brute beauty and valour and act, oh, air, pride, plume, here
    Buckle! AND the fire that breaks from thee then, a billion
Times told lovelier, more dangerous, O my chevalier!

No wonder of it: shéer plód makes plough down sillion
Shine, and blue-bleak embers, ah my dear,
    Fall, gall themselves, and gash gold-vermilion.

This is a good example of a poem that a reader can begin to enjoy immediately but that may take a long time to become completely clear. The music is
of a sort that takes the breath away, and one is excited before quite knowing
what is going on. The poem has a very high content of obvious kinds of poetic
music: alliteration—"morning's minion," "steady"/"striding," "Brute beauty,"
etc.—which is so frequent that it accompanies the other (metrical and
rhyming) music of the poem like a constant drumbeat; there are also internal rhyme ("dawn-drawn," "stirred for a bird," "fall, gall"); and plain repetition
("morning morning's," "off, off," "the achieve of, the mastery of"). The
music creates rush and richness, a spring windstorm of sound in which it is
possible to find the excitement of the oneness Hopkins finds in the falcon (the
"windhover") and Christ, both most beautiful when they "fall."

ARTHUR RIMBAUD

FRENCH (1854–1891)

Aube

J'ai embrassé l'aube d'été.

Rien ne bougeait encore au front des palais. L'eau était morte. Les camps d'ombres ne quittaient pas la route du bois. J'ai marché, réveillant les haleines vives et tièdes, et les pierreries regardèrent, et les ailes se levèrent sans bruit.

La première enterprise fut, dans le sentier déjà empli de frais et blêmes éclats, une fleur qui me dit son nom.

Je ris au wasserfall blond qui s'échevela à travers les sapins: à la cime argentée je reconnus la déesse.

Alors je levai un à un les voiles. Dans l'allée, en agitant les bras. Par la plaine, où je l'ai dénoncée au coq. À la grand'ville, elle fuyait parmi les clochers et les dômes, et, courant comme un mendiant sur les quais de marbre, je la chassais.

En haut de la route, près d'un bois de lauriers, je l'ai entourée avec ses voiles amassés, et j'ai senti un peu son immense corps. L'aube et l'enfant tombèrent au bas du bois.

Au réveil il était midi.

Dawn

I embraced the summer dawn.

Nothing was stirring yet in front of the palaces. The water lay lifeless. Encamped shadows did not leave the woodland road. I stepped forth, arousing breaths alive and warm, and precious stones kept watch, and wings rose up without a sound.

My first enterprise was, in the path already filled with cool, pale glints, a flower that told me her name.

I laughed at the blond waterfall which tossed disheveled hair across the pines: on the silvery summit I espied the goddess.

Then, one by one, I lifted her veils. In the lanes waving my arms. On the plain, where I gave the cock notice of her coming. In the city, she fled among the steeples and domes, and, running like a beggar across the marble quays, I pursued her.

On the upper part of the road, near a grove of laurels, I surrounded her with her massed veils, and sensed somewhat her immeasurable body. Dawn and the child plunged to the bottom of the wood.

When I awoke, it was noon.

(TR. ENID RHODES PESCHEL)

The exhilaration of being awake and outside during the coming of dawn is caught in a story: the young poet searches for dawn, sees her (she is personified as a woman), then chases her through country and city, and finally catches her and takes her in his arms. The ecstasy of morning is communicated by the ecstasy of love. Rimbaud's poems often treat experiences of nature in a sexual way.

"Aube" ("Dawn") is a "prose poem," which means it is written out as prose and not divided into lines. Prose poems have been written mainly by French poets of the nineteenth and twentieth centuries—among them, Baudelaire, Rimbaud, Jacob, Reverdy, Michaux, Ponge—though there are also some in English. Prose poems replace the music caused by line divisions with music caused by other stops and interruptions, and of course they use the other inclinations of the poetry language (personification, comparison, lies, etc.) as well. One charm of reading prose poems is being taken by surprise by what seems to be ordinary prose but turns out not to be.

WILLIAM BUTLER YEATS

IRISH (1865–1939)

Her Triumph

I did the dragon's will until you came
Because I had fancied love a casual
Improvisation, or a settled game
That followed if I let the kerchief fall:
Those deeds were best that gave the minute wings
And heavenly music if they gave it wit;
And then you stood among the dragon-rings.
I mocked, being crazy, but you mastered it
And broke the chain and set my ankles free,
Saint George or else a pagan Perseus;
And now we stare astonished at the sea,
And a miraculous strange bird shrieks at us.

Here, ordinary experience is transformed into something intense and mythological. Myth has been defined as truth attempting to escape from reality. The point of doing this is to escape trivial, limiting, everyday details (age, income, social class, occupation, hometown, etc.) and get to the essence and powerful universality of what takes place. Yeats's "real-life," pre-mythological subject seems to be a young woman who thought love was simply a matter of idle flirtation until she met a man she loved passionately. Yeats brings to this rather ordinary situation a dragon, chained ankles, Saint George, Perseus, and "a miraculous strange bird." The obvious reference is to the story of Andromeda, who was chained to a rock and guarded by a dragon; Perseus killed the dragon and freed her. Saint George was also a dragon killer.

Both Yeats's poem and the preceding Rimbaud poem are fantastic accounts of experiences—Yeats's of falling in love, Rimbaud's of being enthralled by the beauty of morning. Yeats uses classical mythology and a music of slightly syncopated iambic pentameter-rhymed quatrains. Rimbaud makes up a mythology of his own and writes a proselike poetry with no meter and no rhyme.

WILLIAM BUTLER YEATS

IRISH (1865–1939)

Crazy Jane Talks with the Bishop

I met the Bishop on the road
And much said he and I.
"Those breasts are flat and fallen now,
Those veins must soon be dry;
Live in a heavenly mansion,
Not in some foul sty."

"Fair and foul are near of kin,
And fair needs foul," I cried.
"My friends are gone, but that's a truth
Nor grave nor bed denied,
Learned in bodily lowliness
And in the heart's pride.

"A woman can be proud and stiff
When on love intent;
But Love has pitched his mansion in
The place of excrement;
For nothing can be sole or whole
That has not been rent."

Crazy Jane is an old woman who has had an active and enjoyable love life.
The Bishop tells her, well, that's finished now, you are old, you should give
up your earthly concerns and give yourself to God, live in His House not
"in some foul sty." Jane (who may be presumed to have Yeats's point of
view) replies that fair and foul need each other; and, the implication is,
she's not going to change her ways. The poem is a highly charged philosophical treatise condensed into eighteen lines of almost childlike, old-
fashioned ballad-meter verse; the philosophical point is the inextricable
unity of fair and foul. The last four lines of stanza two may be hard to catch
on to at first. The "truth" that's not denied by death (grave) or lovemaking
(bed) is that "fair needs foul." It is not, as one might be misled into think-

ing, that "My friends are gone." Yeats's poems are sometimes so violently condensed that several readings of the same passage may be possible.

This is a much earthier poem about love than the preceding Yeats poem, "Her Triumph," written two years earlier (in 1929).

GERTRUDE STEIN

AMERICAN (1874–1946)

from *Say It with Flowers, a Play*

George Henry, Henry Henry and Elisabeth
Henry.
Subsidiary characters.
Elisabeth and William Long.
Time Louis XI
Place Gisors.
Action in a cake shop and the sea shore.
Other interests.

The welcoming of a man and his dog and the
wish that they would come back sooner.
George Henry and Elisabeth Henry and Henry
Henry ruminating.
Elisabeth and William Long.
Waiting.
Who has asked them to be amiable to me.
She said she was waiting.
George Henry and Elisabeth Henry and
Henry Henry.
Who might be asleep if they were not waiting for me.
She.
Elisabeth Henry and Henry Henry and
George Henry.
She might be waiting with me.
Henry Henry absolutely ready to be here with me.
Scenery.
The home where they were waiting for William Long to ask them
to come along and ask them not to be waiting for them.
Will they be asleep while they are waiting.
They will be pleased with everything.
What is everything.
A hyacinth is everything.
Will they be sleeping while they are waiting for everything.

William Long and Elisabeth Long were so silent you might have heard an egg shell breaking. They were busy all day long with everything.

Elisabeth and William Long were very busy waiting for him to come and bring his dog along.

Why did they not go with him.

Because they were busy waiting.

Stein's work can be at first, bewildering. If you want to enjoy it, you simply have to give in to it and read it word by word, phrase by phrase, letting it say things in the odd way it seems to want to say them. In the end, this is likely to be interesting.

This text is characteristic of much of Stein's poetry (and prose), saying things again and again with only slight variations, which, however, may lead to brilliant surprises like "What is everything./A hyacinth is everything./Will they be sleeping while they are waiting for everything." Without the repetition and the apparent "meaninglessness," the dazzle of this almost-clear meaning wouldn't be there.

A director who did this play as a play would have to decide who was speaking which lines. Maybe there is action on stage and a narrator speaking, or maybe no action and a narrator speaking. Maybe George Henry, Henry Henry, and Elisabeth Henry alternate speaking; maybe they all speak at once. Gertrude Stein wrote plays that break down the barriers between plays and everything else. One can't tell if they are stories or poems or plays; what they are depends on how one reads them, or, as plays, on how one puts them on.

RAINER MARIA RILKE

GERMAN (1875–1926)

Archaic Torso of Apollo

Wir kannten nicht sein unerhörtes Haupt,
darin die Augenäpfel reiften. Aber
sein Torso glüht noch wie ein Kandelaber,
in dem sein Schauen, nur zurückgeschraubt,

sich hält und glänzt. Sonst könnte nicht der Bug
der Brust dich blenden, und im leisen Drehen
der Lenden könnte nicht ein Lächeln gehen
zu jener Mitte, die die Zeugung trug.

Sonst stünde dieser Stein entstellt und kurz
unter der Schultern durchsichtigem Sturz
und flimmerte nicht so wie Raubtierfelle;

und bräche nicht aus allen seinen Rändern
aus wie ein Stern: denn da ist keine Stelle,
die dich nicht sieht. Du mußt dein Leben ändern.

We cannot know his legendary head
with eyes like ripening fruit. And yet his torso
is still suffused with brilliance from inside,
like a lamp, in which his gaze, now turned to low,

gleams in all its power. Otherwise
the curved breast could not dazzle you so, nor could
a smile run through the placid hips and thighs
to that dark center where procreation flared.

Otherwise this stone would seem defaced
beneath the translucent cascade of the shoulders
and would not glisten like a wild beast's fur:

would not, from all the borders of itself,
burst like a star: for here there is no place
that does not see you. You must change your life.

(TR. STEPHEN MITCHELL)

Rilke found inspiration in paintings and statues. He wrote two books of poems about them. He seemed to have the gift of being so intimate with them that what they were "saying" excited, exalted, or afflicted him as if they were persons he loved. Here his object is an early (sixth or seventh century B.C.) torso of Apollo with its head broken off. There is such power in the sculpture of the body, Rilke says, that seeing it will oblige a person to change his life. Keats's "Ode on a Grecian Urn" is a much earlier example of poetry about art, in which the work of art contains an important truth.

RAINER MARIA RILKE

GERMAN (1875–1926)

from *Duino Elegies*

THE FIRST ELEGY

Who, if I cried out, would hear me among the angels'
hierarchies? and even if one of them pressed me
suddenly against his heart: I would be consumed
in that overwhelming existence. For beauty is nothing
but the beginning of terror, which we still are just able to endure,
and we are so awed because it serenely disdains
to annihilate us. Every angel is terrifying.
    And so I hold myself back and swallow the call-note
of my dark sobbing. Ah, whom can we ever turn to
in our need? Not angels, not humans,
and already the knowing animals are aware
that we are not really at home in
our interpreted world. Perhaps there remains for us
some tree on a hillside, which every day we can take
into our vision; there remains for us yesterday's street
and the loyalty of a habit so much at ease
when it stayed with us that it moved in and never left.
    Oh and night: there is night, when a wind full of infinite space
gnaws at our faces. Whom would it not remain for—that longed-after
mildly disillusioning presence, which the solitary heart
so painfully meets. Is it any less difficult for lovers?
But they keep on using each other to hide their own fate.
    Don't you know *yet*? Fling the emptiness out of your arms
into the spaces we breathe; perhaps the birds
will feel the expanded air with more passionate flying.

Yes—the springtimes needed you. Often a star
was waiting for you to notice it. A wave rolled toward you
out of the distant past, or as you walked
under an open window, a violin
yielded itself to your hearing. All this was mission.
But could you accomplish it? Weren't you always
distracted by expectation, as if every event

announced a beloved? (Where can you find a place
to keep her, with all the huge strange thoughts inside you
going and coming and often staying all night.)
But when you feel longing, sing of women in love;
for their famous passion is still not immortal. Sing
of women abandoned and desolate (you envy them, almost)
who could love so much more purely than those who were gratified.
Begin again and again the never-attainable praising;
remember: the hero lives on; even his downfall was
merely a pretext for achieving his final birth.
But Nature, spent and exhausted, takes lovers back
into herself, as if there were not enough strength
to create them a second time. Have you imagined
Gaspara Stampa intensely enough so that any girl
deserted by her beloved might be inspired
by that fierce example of soaring, objectless love
and might say to herself, "Perhaps I can be like her"?
Shouldn't this most ancient of sufferings finally grow
more fruitful for us? Isn't it time that we lovingly
freed ourselves from the beloved and, quivering, endured:
as the arrow endures the bowstring's tension, so that
gathered in the snap of release it can be more than
itself. For there is no place where we can remain.

Voices. Voices. Listen, my heart, as only
saints have listened: until the gigantic call lifted them
off the ground; yet they kept on, impossibly,
kneeling and didn't notice at all:
so complete was their listening. Not that you could endure
God's voice—far from it. But listen to the voice of the wind
and the ceaseless message that forms itself out of silence.
It is murmuring toward you now from those who died young.
Didn't their fate, whenever you stepped into a church
in Naples or Rome, quietly come to address you?
Or high up, some eulogy entrusted you with a mission,
as, last year, on the plaque in Santa Maria Formosa.
What they want of me is that I gently remove the appearance
of injustice about their death—which at times
slightly hinders their souls from proceeding onward.

Of course, it is strange to inhabit the earth no longer,
to give up customs one barely had time to learn,

not to see roses and other promising Things
in terms of a human future; no longer to be
what one was in infinitely anxious hands; to leave
even one's own first name behind, forgetting it
as easily as a child abandons a broken toy.
Strange to no longer desire one's desires. Strange
to see meanings that clung together once, floating away
in every direction. And being dead is hard work
and full of retrieval before one can gradually feel
a trace of eternity.—Though the living are wrong to believe
in the too-sharp distinctions which they themselves have created.
Angels (they say) don't know whether it is the living
they are moving among, or the dead. The eternal torrent
whirls all ages along in it, through both realms
forever, and their voices are drowned out in its thunderous roar.

In the end, those who were carried off early no longer need us:
they are weaned from earth's sorrows and joys, as gently as children
outgrow the soft breasts of their mothers. But we, who do need
such great mysteries, we for whom grief is so often
the source of our spirit's growth—: could we exist without *them*?
Is the legend meaningless that tells how, in the lament for Linus,
the daring first notes of song pierced through the barren numbness;
and then in the startled space which a youth as lovely as a god
had suddenly left forever, the Void felt for the first time
that harmony which now enraptures and comforts and helps us.

(TR. STEPHEN MITCHELL)

This is the first of the ten *Duino Elegies;* Duino is the name of the castle
where Rilke wrote the first two Elegies and some parts of others. The
"angels" in the poem aren't the conventional Christian angels but powerful
beings imagined by Rilke who are somewhere between gods and humans.
Rilke begins the Elegy by asking if any angel would even hear him if he
cried out (apparently in bewilderment and pain) and then by imagining
what would happen if an angel actually embraced him—angels are so
powerful, he says, that such an embrace would destroy him. Whom, then,
can we turn to for sympathy and help? Rilke wonders if lovers are any better off because they have each other but then says no, they are not—all that
they have in their arms is emptiness. Longing for love, it may be, is the best
thing we can have; the example of young women who died of unfulfilled
love can give us strength. The second-to-last stanza of the poem is about

how it feels to be dead. Rilke imagines death as a kind of continuation of life: life and death are much closer to each other than we imagine. At the end of the Elegy, Rilke suggests that grief for the dead was the origin of poetry. The god Apollo, grieving for his young friend Linus, sang the first song, which was the first poem.

These are only a few of the themes in this first Elegy and they are themes that continue throughout the Elegies. An elegy is normally a poem of mourning for the dead; but these elegies mourn for the living and for our almost hopelessly unhappy state, we who long for a kind of permanence and connectedness that we don't know how to achieve. With love rejected as a solution, one possible answer to our emptiness and loneliness, as becomes clearer in the later Elegies, is to transform the world into words, into poetry.

Once one catches on to the main themes—loneliness, longing, and seeking—the Elegies are easier to understand. They are a joy to read, however, before that. They have a wonderfully touching, confiding, and easygoing tone, a strange tone, really, for talking about such urgent and mysterious subjects. And they are full of surprising perceptions, like the description of beauty (lines 4 and 5) as "Nothing/but the beginning of terror, which we still are just able to endure."

WALLACE STEVENS

AMERICAN (1879–1955)

Metaphors of a Magnifico

Twenty men crossing a bridge,
Into a village,
Are twenty men crossing twenty bridges,
Into twenty villages,
Or one man
Crossing a single bridge into a village.

This is old song
That will not declare itself ...

Twenty men crossing a bridge,
Into a village,
Are
Twenty men crossing a bridge
Into a village.

That will not declare itself
Yet is certain as meaning ...

The boots of the men clump
On the boards of the bridge.
The first white wall of the village
Rises through fruit-trees.
Of what was it I was thinking?
So the meaning escapes.

The first white wall of the village ...
The fruit-trees ...

The first time I read this poem I felt disbelief (and then relief): this couldn't be poetry! But then it turned out to be after all—that was the relief. Just by being a poem it shows how something so prosy and simple can be one. It has plainness and also music and surprise.

Lorenzo di Medici, a ruler of Renaissance Florence, also a poet, was called "Il Magnifico" (the Magnificent). What Stevens's "Magnifico" refers to as "song" is what would usually be called "philosophy" or "thinking." This "magnifico," a sort of ideal poet and man, is trying to figure out a philosophical problem by intellectual means, but he ends up "solving" it by being distracted from it by sensations—the clumping boots, the white wall, the fruit trees. The reader may conclude from this that sensations may be, after all, more important than human theories about them. (The theories may be too rigid, may be dead and unchanging, like the jar placed in Tennessee; see p. 117).

from "Le Monocle de Mon Oncle"

xi

If sex were all, then every trembling hand
Could make us squeak, like dolls, the wished-for
    words.
But note the unconscionable treachery of fate,
That makes us weep, laugh, grunt and groan, and
    shout
Doleful heroics, pinching gestures forth
From madness or delight, without regard
To that first, foremost law. Anguishing hour!
Last night, we sat beside a pool of pink,
Clippered with lilies scudding the bright chromes,
Keen to the point of starlight, while a frog
Boomed from his very belly odious chords.

This is one stanza of a twelve-part poem about being over forty years old and finding oneself in love. Each stanza plays a variation on this theme. In this one, Stevens begins by noting that sex alone could never make him feel the way he does. The last four lines depict a particular ecstatic, anguishing moment of the love he feels. The poetic language of these four lines is about as extreme in the direction of sensuality and "gorgeousness" as such language can be and still make ordinary sense: like certain of Hopkins's passages it is crowded with noises—the big vowel sounds of *boomed, odious,* and *chromes;* alliterations like "pool of pink" and "boomed from his very belly"—and with odd words used in odd, loud ways—*clippered, scudding,* and *chromes*—a crowding that makes it too busy, complex, and rich to be understood, at first, as anything but music and sensations.

WALLACE STEVENS

AMERICAN (1879–1955)

Thirteen Ways of Looking at a Blackbird

i

Among twenty snowy mountains,
The only moving thing
Was the eye of the blackbird.

ii

I was of three minds,
Like a tree
In which there are three blackbirds.

iii

The blackbird whirled in the autumn winds.
It was a small part of the pantomime.

iv

A man and a woman
Are one.
A man and a woman and a blackbird
Are one.

v

I do not know which to prefer,
The beauty of inflections
Or the beauty of innuendoes,
The blackbird whistling
Or just after.

vi

Icicles filled the long window
With barbaric glass.
The shadow of the blackbird
Crossed it, to and fro.
The mood
Traced in the shadow
An indecipherable cause.

vii

O thin men of Haddam,
Why do you imagine golden birds?
Do you not see how the blackbird
Walks around the feet
Of the women about you?

viii

I know noble accents
And lucid, inescapable rhythms;
But I know, too,
That the blackbird is involved
In what I know.

ix

When the blackbird flew out of sight,
It marked the edge
Of one of many circles.

x

At the sight of blackbirds
Flying in a green light,
Even the bawds of euphony
Would cry out sharply.

He rode over Connecticut
In a glass coach.
Once, a fear pierced him,
In that he mistook
The shadow of his equipage
For blackbirds.

xii

The river is moving.
The blackbird must be flying.

xiii

It was evening all afternoon.
It was snowing
And it was going to snow.
The blackbird sat
In the cedar-limbs.

This is an odd way of writing a poem: having thirteen numbered sections, each a different description of the same thing—in this case a blackbird. In fact, the thirteen parts aren't exactly descriptions but different ways in which a blackbird can be talked about surprisingly enough to make the reader experience a blackbird's presence each time. The "rhetorical form" is variations on a theme. The language is, mostly, plain and simple; the effect is strangeness.

This poem goes along with Stevens's idea of the poem as something that should be constantly changing; nothing in nature or in experience is fixed—the only way for poetry to keep up is to itself reflect change. The differing views of the blackbird in this poem might be seen as those of different fields of study; stanza one is cinematic, stanza two psychological, stanza three theatrical, stanza four philosophical, and so on.

WALLACE STEVENS

AMERICAN (1879–1955)

from *Notes Toward a Supreme Fiction*

On her trip around the world, Nanzia Nunzio
Confronted Ozymandias. She went
Alone and like a vestal long-prepared.

I am the spouse. She took her necklace off
And laid it in the sand. As I am, I am
The spouse. She opened her stone-studded belt.

I am the spouse, divested of bright gold,
The spouse beyond emerald or amethyst,
Beyond the burning body that I bear.

I am the woman stripped more nakedly
Than nakedness, standing before an inflexible
Order, saying I am the contemplated spouse.

Speak to me that, which spoken, will array me
In its own only precious ornament.
Set on me the spirit's diamond coronal.

Clothe me entire in the final filament,
So that I tremble with such love so known
And myself am pious for your perfecting.

Then Ozymandias said the spouse, the bride
Is never naked. A fictive covering
Weaves always glistening from the heart and mind.

Notes Toward a Supreme Fiction, of which this is one small section, is like a
philosophy book with gorgeous illustrations. The philosophical subject of
this passage is the nature of beauty. Instead of philosophizing, Stevens tells
the story of a striptease in the middle of the desert. Ozymandias is a mysterious sphinxlike being who possesses all wisdom. Nanzia Nunzio's name is
Italian, she seems perhaps the most beautiful of Italian movie stars. She

journeys to see Ozymandias so he can declare her the world's most beautiful and desirable woman and take her for his bride. But Ozymandias tells her she is making a mistake: the spouse, he says, is never naked. A "fictive covering," some new way of imagining the beauty we desire, is always necessary—like a new scarf, a new music, a new stanza; unchanging nakedness isn't it. The suggested aesthetic idea is that every poem should be different from every other and even that it should somehow change as it goes along—as "Thirteen Ways of Looking at a Blackbird" does, for example, or "Metaphors of a Magnifico."

Unlike Wordsworth, who likes the sound of plainness and plain sincerity in his blank verse lines, Stevens tends to make his lines as decorative and elegant as possible—here arranging the unrhymed lines in three-line stanzas, each with a strongly pronounced music of beginning, middle, and end.

Cœur Couronne et Miroir

Cœur Couronne et Miroir

```
    N                    N                            Q
  E                    O  C              L     R      U    M      R
R  V E RS É E   M         OE
  E                       U             ES    OIS     I   EU     ENT
    M                     R
      M                   P             TOUR         A          TOUR
      A                 A
        L             R                RENAISSENT AU COEUR DES POÈTES
       F        E
        E     E
         N  I
         U  L
          À
```

```
                    DANS
            FLETS          CE
        RE                  MI
       LES                 ROIR
       SONT                 JE
       ME                  SUIS
       COM    Guillaume     EN
       NON    Apollinaire  CLOS
       ET                   VI
       GES                 VANT
       AN                   ET
       LES                 VRAI
        NE                 COM
         GI                ME
            MA          ON
                   I
```

Heart Crown and Mirror

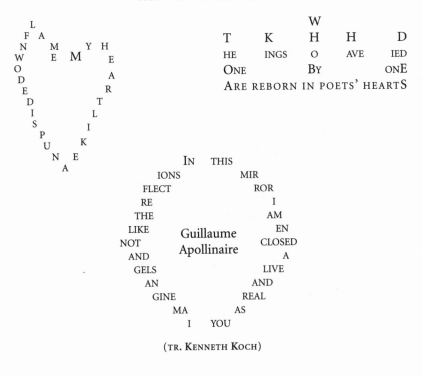

(TR. KENNETH KOCH)

Apollinaire invented this kind of poem which he called a calligramme. *Calligramme* combines the words *calligraphy* and *telegram* and is an appropriate name for a message sent by a picture. Calligrammes aren't written in lines but in shapes related to what they're about. The secret of successful ones is their being about something more than just what is pictured. "This is what my heart looks like," for example, wouldn't be as interesting a poem as Apollinaire's "My heart like an upside-down flame," which suggests, but doesn't say, that the poet is in love.

This poetry invention is an expansion of what a poem can do: it adds the space of art to poetry as poetic drama adds the space of theater.

MINA LOY

AMERICAN (1882–1966)

from "Three Moments in Paris"

1. One O'Clock at Night

Though you had never possessed me
I had belonged to you since the beginning of time
And sleepily I sat on your chair beside you
Leaning against your shoulder
And your careless arm across my back   gesticulated
As your indisputable male voice   roared
Through my brain and my body
Arguing dynamic decomposition
Of which I understand nothing
Sleepily
And the only less male voice of your brother
    pugilist of the intellect
Boomed   as it seemed to me   so sleepy
Across an interval of a thousand miles
An interim of a thousand years
But you who make more noise than any man
    in the world when you clear your throat
Deafening   woke me
And I caught the thread of the argument
Immediately assuming my personal mental
    attitude
And ceased to be a woman

Beautiful half-hour of being a mere woman
The animal woman
Understanding nothing of man
But mastery   and the security of imparted
    physical heat
Indifferent to cerebral gymnastics
Or regarding them as the self-indulgent
    play of children
Or the thunder of alien gods
But you woke me up

        Anyhow   who am I that I should criticize
            your theories of plastic velocity

    "Let us go home   she is tired   and
        wants to go to bed."

The poet seems to be speaking from different states of consciousness as she leans against a man friend's shoulder in a Paris café while he loudly discusses art with his brother. The poem speaks in very different tones—"since the beginning of time" and "sleepily I sat on your chair," for example. It is quiet, witty, and subversive; the men have no idea of what she's thinking or feeling—that she doesn't want to be part of their bombastic conversation but is happy to be there not paying much attention to it. Her friend simply thinks "she is tired."

WILLIAM CARLOS WILLIAMS

AMERICAN (1883–1963)

Queen-Ann's-Lace

Her body is not so white as
anemone petals nor so smooth—nor
so remote a thing. It is a field
of the wild carrot taking
the field by force; the grass
does not raise above it.
Here is no question of whiteness,
white as can be, with a purple mole
at the center of each flower.
Each flower is a hand's span
of her whiteness. Wherever
his hand has lain there is
a tiny purple blemish. Each part
is a blossom under his touch
to which the fibres of her being
stem one by one, each to its end,
until the whole field is a
white desire, empty, a single stem,
a cluster, flower by flower,
a pious wish to whiteness gone over—
or nothing.

A remarkable comparison in which nothing is openly compared. The field
full of white blossoms and the body of a woman are talked about simultaneously, in a way that catches the dizzying sensation of first perceiving a
likeness before knowing exactly what is what. Williams extends this fleeting moment of perception over a thoughtful poem of twenty-one lines.

WILLIAM CARLOS WILLIAMS

AMERICAN (1883–1963)

from "Della Primavera Trasportata al Morale"

PART 1: "APRIL"

the beginning—or
what you will:
>   the dress

in which the veritable winter
walks in Spring—

Loose it!
Let it fall (where it will)
—again

A live thing
the buds are upon it
the green shoot come between
the red flowerets
>   curled back

under whose green veil
strain trunk and limbs of
the supporting trees—

Yellow! the arched stick
pinning the fragile foil
—in abundance
>   or
the bush before the rose
pointed with green

bent into form
upon the iron frame

wild onion
swifter than the grass

the grass thick
at the post's base

iris blades unsheathed—

BUY THIS PROPERTY

—the complexion of the impossible
(you'll say)

never realized—
At a desk in a hotel in front of a

machine a year
later—for a day or two—

(Quite so—)
Whereas the reality trembles

frankly
in that though it was like this

in part
it was deformed

even when at its utmost to
touch—as it did

and fill and give and take
—a kind

of rough drawing of flowers
and April

STOP : GO

—she
opened the door! nearly
six feet tall, and I . . .
wanted to found a new country—

For the rest, virgin negress
at the glass
in blue-glass Venetian beads—

> a green truck
> dragging a concrete mixer
> passes
> in the street—

> the clatter and true sound
> of verse—

—the wind is howling
the river, shining mud—

Moral
> it looses me

Moral
> it supports me

Moral
> it has never ceased
> to flow

Moral
> the faded evergreen

Moral
> I can laugh

Moral
> the redhead sat
> in bed with her legs
> crossed and talked
> rough stuff

Moral
> the door is open

Moral
         the tree moving diversely
         in all parts—

—the moral is love, bred of
the mind and eyes and hands—

         But in the cross-current
         between what the hands reach
         and the mind desires

         and the eyes see
         and see starvation, it is

         useless to have it thought
         that we are full—

         But April is a thing
         comes just the same—

         and in it we see now
         what then we did not know—

                  STOP : STOP

I believe
         in the sound patriotic and
         progressive Mulish policies
         and if elected—

I believe
         in a continuance of the pro-
         tective tariff because—

I believe
         that the country can't do
         too much—

I believe
         in honest law enforcement—
         and I also believe—

I believe
in giving the farmer and
land owner adequate protection

I believe

I believe

I believe
in equality for the negro—

THIS IS MY PLATFORM

I believe in your love
the first dandelion
flower at the edge of—

taraaaaaaa!—taraaaaaaa!

—the fishman's bugle announces
the warm wind—

reminiscent of the sea
the plumtree flaunts
its blossom-encrusted
branches—

I believe
Moving to three doors
above—May 1st.

I believe
ICE—and warehouse site

No parking between tree and corner

You would "kill me with kindness"
I love you too, but I love you
too—

Thus, in that light and in that
light only can I say—

Winter : Spring

abandoned to you. The world lost—
in you

Is not that devastating enough
for one century?

I believe
    Spumoni $1.00
    French Vanilla   .70
    Chocolate   .70
    Strawberry   .70
    Maple Walnut   .70
    Coffee   .70
    Tutti Frutti   .70
    Pistachio   .70
    Cherry Special   .70
    Orange Ice   .70
    Biscuit Tortoni
                 25c per portion

trees—seeming dead:
        the long years—

    tactus eruditus

    Maple, I see you have
    a squirrel in your crotch—

    And you have a woodpecker
    in your hole, Sycamore

—a fat blonde, in purple (no trucking
on this street)

        POISON!

I believe

WOMAN'S WARD

PRIVATE

The soul, my God, shall rise up
—a tree
    But who are You?
in this mortal wind
that I at least can understand
having sinned willingly

The forms
of the emotions are crystalline,
geometric-faceted. So we recognize
only in the white heat of
understanding, when a flame
runs through the gap made
by learning, the shapes of things—
the ovoid sun, the pointed trees

lashing branches

The wind is fierce, lashing

the long-limbed trees whose
branches
wildly toss—

The title is Italian and can be translated, roughly, "Springtime considered from the point of view of philosophy and ethics." The question the poem keeps playing with in one way and another is "What does April mean?" or "What does the way I feel in April mean?" "April" appears in the poem first as trees, leaves, grass, and flowers; then as a brief love affair; a stoplight; a woman opening a door; a concrete mixer; a set of "morals" and a set of political "beliefs"; a few remarks to a woman; a new set of "beliefs" (spumoni, etc.); various things seen; a speculation on the meaning of it all. Williams's "Della Primavera Trasportata al Morale" is one of the most inventive (and exhilarating) of twentieth-century poems, one of the great new poems—like Apollinaire's "Zone" and certain poems of O'Hara—that expand the possibilities of what the "subject" of a lyric poem can be. There is a subject here, of course, a main theme that gives a unity to all the various parts—springtime's energy and joy—but this subject is not so much "dealt with" as exemplified: there is example after example of it, sometimes accompanied by questioning and sometimes not. The examples come one after another like the events of a day. And the form of the poem, and in a sense its true subject, seems in fact to be a day, a short span of time and everything that happens in it, a day of excitements and thoughts.

WILLIAM CARLOS WILLIAMS

AMERICAN (1883–1963)

The Locust Tree in Flower

Among
of
green

stiff
old
bright

broken
branch
come

white
sweet
May

again

The Locust Tree in Flower

[*First Version*]

Among
the leaves
bright

green
of wrist-thick
tree

and old
stiff broken
branch

ferncool
swaying
loosely strung—

come May
again
white blossom

clusters
hide
to spill

their sweets
almost
unnoticed

down
and quickly
fall

Williams said that he made his revision of this poem because in the first version one "couldn't see the locust tree." This might be translated as "couldn't see the locust tree and nothing but the locust tree." There are, in the first version, some details that might get in the way—"loosely strung" isn't entirely visual (one has to think for a moment about *loosely*), and "hide/to spill/their sweets/almost/unnoticed/down" is practically theoretical compared with the rest of the poem. The second, one-word-in-a-line version gets a nice musical variation from the occurrence of two-syllable words in lines 1, 7, and 13. The poem has to be read word for word, with pauses: read straight-out as a prose sentence, it doesn't make sense; read as "poetry language" (which can be cavalier about conventional connections), it does.

WILLIAM CARLOS WILLIAMS

AMERICAN (1883–1963)

The Three Graces

We have the picture of you in mind,
when you were young, posturing
(for a photographer) in scarves
(if you could have done it) but now,
for none of you is immortal, ninety-
three, the three, ninety and three,
Mary, Ellen and Emily, what
beauty is it clings still about you?
Undying? Magical? For there is still
no answer, why we live or why
you will not live longer than I
or that there should be an answer why
any should live and whatever other
should die. Yet you live. You live
and all that can be said is that
you live, time cannot alter it—
and as I write this Mary has died.

Williams uses his clear, plain-spoken American language to talk about the
mysterious subjects of beauty, change, and death, as he used it in earlier
poems to talk about flowers, trees, and streets.

D. H. LAWRENCE

BRITISH (1885–1930)

The White Horse

The youth walks up to the white horse, to put its halter on
And the horse looks at him in silence.
They are so silent, they are in another world.

A very short poem—like Pound's "Alba" and Williams's "The Locust Tree in Flower"—but which uses the real event it describes to suggest an "elsewhere" (in this case, "another world") rather than concentrating on the physical reality of what is there. The poem gets a certain musical unification from the repeated word *horse* in lines 1 and 2, and the *silence/silent* repetition in lines 2 and 3. Some of its words, even before "another world," are somewhat mysteriously suggestive: "youth," "white horse," and "in silence." If these are replaced, say, by "young man," "brown horse," and "quietly," the mysterious atmosphere is pretty much gone. The repetition of "they are" in the third line helps to make the second statement—"they are in another world"—as easy to accept as the first one.

EZRA POUND

AMERICAN (1885–1972)

The Garden

En robe de parade
—SAMAIN

Like a skein of loose silk blown against a wall
She walks by the railing of a path in Kensington Gardens,
And she is dying piecemeal
　　　of a sort of emotional anemia.

And round about there is a rabble
Of the filthy, sturdy, unkillable infants of the very poor.
They shall inherit the earth.

In her is the end of breeding.
Her boredom is exquisite and excessive.
She would like someone to speak to her,
And is almost afraid that I
　　　will commit that indiscretion.

The variability of tones and kinds of language in this poem is an important
contribution to the language of poetry. Traditionally, poems had the same
kind of language and the same level of "poeticalness" throughout. Here
Pound goes from the relatively "high" language of "a skein of loose silk
blown against a wall" to the very low-on-the-poetry-thermometer language of "piecemeal" and "emotional anemia." This high-low tone variation makes possible a new kind of poetic music.

EZRA POUND

AMERICAN (1885–1972)

Alba

As cool as the pale wet leaves
                    of lily-of-the-valley
She lay beside me in the dawn.

The apparent subject is the coolness of the woman's body but the real subject seems to be something else: a moment of happiness. *Alba* means *dawn* in Spanish (and in the medieval language Provençal). To stop with the one sensation is characteristic of one kind of twentieth-century art. Earlier poets (think of Tennyson, for example) would almost certainly have gone on with the "story"—

And then she sighed, the Lady Guinevere,
And turned to me and said, "I must be gone," etc.

EZRA POUND

AMERICAN (1885–1972)

from *Canto LXXX*

Nancy where art thou?
Whither go all the vair and the cisclatons
and the wave pattern runs in the stone
on the high parapet (Excideuil)
Mt Segur and the city of Dioce
Que tous les mois avons nouvelle lune
What the deuce has Herbiet (Christian)
      done with his painting?
Fritz still roaring at treize rue Gay de Lussac
with his stone head still on the balcony?
Orage, Fordie, Crevel too quickly taken

    de mis soledades vengan

lay there till Rossetti found it remaindered
    at about two pence
(Cythera, in the moon's barge whither?
      how hast thou the crescent for car?)

or did they fall because of their loose taste in music
    "Here! none of that mathematical music!"
Said the Kommandant when Münch offered Bach to the regiment

or Spewcini the all too human
    beloved in the eyetalian peninsula
for quite explicable reasons
    so that even I can now tolerate
    man seht but with the loss of criteria
and the wandering almost-tenor explained to me:
    well, the operas in the usual repertoire
have been sifted out, there's a reason

Les hommes ont je ne sais quelle peur étrange,
    said Monsieur Whoosis, de la beauté

La beauté, "Beauty is difficult, Yeats" said Aubrey Beardsley
    when Yeats asked why he drew horrors
    or at least not Burne-Jones
    and Beardsley knew he was dying and had to
    make his hit quickly

hence no more B-J in his product.

        So very difficult, Yeats, beauty so difficult.

    "I am the torch" wrote Arthur "she saith"
in the moon barge βροδοδάκτυλο('Ηφ(

with the veil of faint cloud before her
    Κύθηρα δεινα as a leaf borne in the current
pale eyes as if without fire

all that Sandro knew, and Jacopo
        and that Velásquez never suspected
lost in the brown meat of Rembrandt
        and the raw meat of Rubens and Jordaens

"This alone, leather and bones between you and το πα∞ν<"
                  [toh pan, the all]
      (Chu Hsi's comment)

This part of a Canto is on the subject of beauty—beauty of clothes (vair
and cisclatons), of architecture, of painting, of sculpture; then, later, of
music; Aphrodite, goddess of beauty, herself comes into it, in Greek as
Kythera deina (dread Aphrodite). Many of the people named are friends of
Pound's, all engaged with beauty through art, acquaintances who talk
about art, or famous artists of one kind or another. One Poundian addition to the language of poetry is the free and fragmentary use of other languages; another, of course, is the extreme fragmentation of meaning and
the rapidity of the transitions from one thing to another. These qualities
give pleasure and also cause difficulty—in Pound's *Cantos* it's especially
clear how these two can be one. If the Spanish line (it's by Lope de Vega)
"de mis soledades vengan" (Let them come out of my solitude) had to be
identified or translated one would miss the quick pleasure of its unexpected appearance; and the same goes for everything else in the passage.
No matter how difficult the Canto may be at any point, it consistently

offers the pleasures of a radical new prosy kind of verse and of surprising juxtapositions. There is much to be gained from going on reading. A useful attitude to start with might be, I'll be surprised if I understand anything; I'm just going to read this. This will probably get good results; it's hard not to enjoy Spewcini, Monsieur Whoosis, and, even in the first line, the striking combination of old and new in "Nancy where art thou?" As is the case with other long poems, the Cantos teach you how to best read them, though it may take a while. In the meantime, obscurity itself can be an attraction: the "intellectual" tone, suggesting clarity, may give an exciting sensation of being always on the verge of understanding.

MARIANNE MOORE

AMERICAN (1887–1972)

To a Steam Roller

The illustration
is nothing to you without the application.
   You lack half wit. You crush all the particles down
      into close conformity, and then walk back and forth
      on them.

Sparkling chips of rock
are crushed down to the level of the parent block.
   Were not "impersonal judgment in aesthetic
      matters, a metaphysical impossibility," you

might fairly achieve
it. As for butterflies, I can hardly conceive
   of one's attending upon you, but to question
      the congruence of the complement is vain, if it exists.

More new music in the language of poetry. The first two lines of each stanza rhyme (*illustration/application,* etc.), and yet everything else seems as proselike as it could be. There is, however, a largely unnoticeable, yet present, musical element: there are the same number of syllables in each first line (five), second line (twelve), third (twelve), and fourth (fifteen), of all three stanzas. Having the same number of syllables—this is called "syllabic verse"—creates a different effect from meter, which means having the same number of stressed and unstressed syllables: a much subtler sense of sameness. For the poet, it sets limits that may inspire her to say things differently. A mixed poetic/prosy music has been attractive to other modern poets, but none has organized it so systematically as Moore.

    The subject matter, the whole idea of talking so seriously to a steamroller, is funny. A reader may suppose, too, on the basis of Moore's other poems, that the "steamroller" probably represents a person Moore doesn't like, perhaps a literary critic. In which case, who knows what the "butterfly" may represent?—perhaps the "steam roller" 's mistress or wife. The identity of these two is not a "hidden meaning" but simply something else to think about—the steamroller and the butterfly are enough.

BLAISE CENDRARS

FRENCH (1887–1961)

Réveil

Je suis nu
J'ai déjà pris mon bain
Je me frictionne à l'eau de Cologne
Un voilier lourdement secoué passe dans mon hublot
Il fait froid ce matin
Il y a de la brume
Je range mes papiers
J'établis un horaire
Mes journées seront bien remplies
Je n'ai pas une minute à perdre
J'écris

Waking Up

I'm naked
I've already taken my bath
I rub on some cologne
A sailboat is buffeted across my porthole
It's cold this morning
There's some fog
I straighten my papers
I set up a schedule
My days will be busy
I don't have a minute to lose
I write

(TR. RON PADGETT)

Aube

A l'aube je suis descendu au fond des machines
J'ai écouté pour une dernière fois la respiration profonde des pistons
Appuyé à la fragile main-courante de nickel j'ai senti pour une dernière
       fois cette sourde vibration des arbres de couche pénétrer en moi
       avec le relent des huiles surchauffées et la tiédeur de la vapeur
Nous avons encore bu un verre le chef mécanicien cet homme tranquille
       et triste qui a un si beau sourire d'enfant et qui ne cause jamais et
       moi
Comme je sortais de chez lui le soleil sortait tout naturellement de la mer
       et chauffait déjà dur
Le ciel mauve n'avait pas un nuage
Et comme nous pointions sur Santos notre sillage décrivait un grand arc-
       de-cercle miroitant sur la mer immobile

Dawn

At dawn I went down among the machines
For the last time I listened to the deep breathing of the pistons
Leaning on the fragile nickel-plated handrail I felt for the last time the
    dull vibration of the drive shafts sink into me with the musty smell of
    the overheated oil and the tepidness of the steam
We had one more drink me and the chief mechanic that sad quiet man
    who has such a beautiful childlike smile and who never indulges in
    small talk
As I was leaving the engine room the sun naturally was leaving the sea
    and already getting hot
There was not one cloud in the purple sky
And as we swung toward Santos our wake described a big arc glistening
    on the unmoving sea

These are two poems about early mornings on the steamship the poet is taking to South America. In the first, he is naked, happy, and writing poetry. In the second, he is busily leaving the ship. The poems proceed line by line, each line telling a part of what's happening. The poems seem so simple and transparent that it's almost hard to see how they can be poems at all. The trick is probably in getting everything just right—hot off the feelings, as it were—simple but excited, which Padgett gets perfectly in the translations, as well. One false "literary" note and all would be lost.

T. S. ELIOT

AMERICAN (1888–1965)

from *Sweeney Agonistes*

FRAGMENT OF A PROLOGUE

DUSTY. DORIS.

DUSTY: How about Pereira?
DORIS: What about Pereira?
    I don't care.
DUSTY: You don't care!
    Who pays the rent?
DORIS: Yes he pays the rent
DUSTY: Well some men don't and some men do
    Some men don't and you know who
DORIS: You can have Pereira
DUSTY: What about Pereira?
DORIS: He's no gentleman, Pereira:
    You can't trust him!
DUSTY: Well that's true.
    He's no gentleman if you can't trust him
    And *if* you can't trust him—
    Then you never know what he's going to do.
DORIS: No it wouldn't do to be too nice to Pereira.
DUSTY: Now Sam's a gentleman through and through.
DORIS: I like Sam
DUSTY: *I* like Sam
    Yes and Sam's a nice boy too.
    He's a funny fellow
DORIS: He *is* a funny fellow
    He's like a fellow once I knew.
    He could make you laugh.
DUSTY: Sam can make you laugh:
    Sam's all right
DORIS: But Pereira won't do.
    We can't have Pereira
DUSTY: Well what you going to do?
TELEPHONE: Ting a ling ling
                   Ting a ling ling

DUSTY: That's Pereira
DORIS: Yes that's Pereira
DUSTY: Well what you going to do?
TELEPHONE: Ting a ling ling
                        Ting a ling ling
DUSTY: That's Pereira
DORIS: Well can't you stop that horrible noise?
        Pick up the receiver
DUSTY: What'll I say!
DORIS: Say what you like: say I'm ill,
        Say I broke my leg on the stairs
        Say we've had a fire
DUSTY: Hello Hello are you there?
        Yes this is Miss Dorrance's *flat*—
        Oh Mr. Pereira is that you? how do you do!
        Oh I'm *so* sorry. I *am* so sorry
        But Doris came home with a terrible chill. . . .

This dialogue is from an early play by T. S. Eliot in which he uses a variation of English music-hall patter—a rapid, jokey exchange of simple and banal remarks—as a form of dramatic poetry. Dusty and Doris are two young women living in London. This kind of verse seems a great, promising one for modern plays, but Eliot never used it again, and, in fact, didn't finish writing this work.

ANNA AKHMATOVA

RUSSIAN (1889–1966)

from "Requiem"

INTRODUCTION

It was a time when only the dead
smiled, happy in their peace.
And Leningrad dangled like a useless pendant
at the side of its prisons.
At a time when, tortured out of their minds,
the convicted walked in regiments,
and the steam whistles sang
their short parting song.
Stars of death stood over us,
and innocent Russia squirmed
under the bloody boots,
under the wheels of Black Marias.

1

They took you away at dawn,
I walked after you as though you were being borne out,
the children were crying in the dark room,
the candle swam by the ikon-stand.
The cold of the ikon on your lips.
Death sweat on your brow . . . Do not forget!
I will howl by the Kremlin towers
like the wives of the Streltsy.

2

The quiet Don flows quietly,
the yellow moon goes into the house,

goes in with its cap askew,
the yellow moon sees the shadow.

This woman is sick,
this woman is alone,

husband in the grave, son in prison,
pray for me.

3

No, this is not me—someone else suffers.
I couldn't stand this: let black drapes
cover what happened,
and let them take away the street lights . . .
Night.

. . .

5

For seventeen months I have been screaming,
calling you home.
I flung myself at the executioner's feet.
You are my son and my terror.
Everything is confused forever,
and I can no longer tell
beast from man,
and how long I must wait for the execution.
Only the dusty flowers,
the clank of censers, and tracks
leading from somewhere to nowhere.
An enormous star
looks me straight in the eye
and threatens swift destruction.

6

Weightless weeks fly by,
I will never grasp what happened.
How the white nights looked
at you, my son, in prison,
how they look again
with the burning eye of the hawk,

Requiem • 263

they speak of your tall cross,
they speak of death.

7

Verdict

The stone wall fell
on my still living breast.
Never mind, I was prepared,
somehow I'll come to terms with it.

Today I have much work to do:
I must finally kill my memory,
I must, so my soul can turn to stone,
I must learn to live again.

Or else . . . the hot summer rustle,
like holiday time outside my window.
I have felt this coming for a long time,
this bright day and the empty house. . . .

(TR. RICHARD McKANE)

These are six parts of a long poem composed by Akhmatova at the time of
the terrible Stalinist purges of 1935–1940. Akhmatova says in a prefatory note
to the poem that she "spent seventeen months standing in line in front of the
Leningrad prisons," when her son, Lev, and others close to her were prison-
ers there. According to one account, Akhmatova wrote different parts of the
poem on scraps of paper, which she destroyed as soon as she had the lines
memorized; a few friends memorized them also; and the poem was carried
in her and their memories till it seemed finally safe to publish it, more than
twenty years later, in 1963. The second section, above (1) refers to the arrest
of a close friend, N. N. Punin. The "Streltsy" were a special military unit
defeated—and eight hundred of them executed—by Peter I in 1698. Her former husband, referred to in (2) was executed as a "counterrevolutionary" in
1921. There are a number of references to her son's imprisonment, and the
poem is dedicated to him. This poem has about it an urgency that seems to
come from great suffering and the specific events that caused it. Bertolt Brecht
said, on the subject of "political poetry," that "you can't write poems about
trees when the woods are full of policemen."

BORIS PASTERNAK

RUSSIAN (1890–1960)

Hops

Beneath the willow, wound round with ivy,
We take cover from the worst
Of the storm, with a greatcoat round
Our shoulders and my hands around your waist.

I've got it wrong. That isn't ivy
Entwined in the bushes round
The wood, but hops. You intoxicate me!
Let's spread the greatcoat on the ground.

(TR. JON STALLWORTHY AND PETER FRANCE)

The apparent digression in the second stanza is a surprise that gives the poem power. By getting "off the subject" (concerned with whether the vine he's looking at is ivy or hops) Pasternak in fact really is on the subject—which is a moment of great excitement with his mind racing all over the place while he tries to concentrate on getting the best place to lie down with the woman he is crazy about. This on-the-subject way of being off the subject is mainly an achievement of modern poets; you can find it in Williams and in O'Hara, among others.

Pasternak, Russian friends tell me, is "impossible to translate." "Difficult" must be closer to the truth. Something certainly comes through here. When I read Pasternak's poems, I read three or four translations of each poem when that's possible.

VLADIMIR MAYAKOVSKY

RUSSIAN (1893–1930)

from *I Love*

ТАК И СО МНОЙ

Флоты—и то стекаются в гавани.
Поезд—и то к вокзалу гонит.
Ну, а меня к тебе и подавней
—я же люблю!—
тянет и клонит.
Скупой спускается пушкинский рыцарь.
подвалом своим любоватьсяп рытвся.
Так я
к тебе возвращаюсь, любимая.
Мое это сердце,
любуюсь моим я.
Домой возвращаетесь радостно.
Грязь вы
с себя соскребаете, бреясь и моясь.
Так я
к тебе возвращаюсь,—
разве,
к тебе идя,
не иду домой я?!
Зелных принимает земное лоно.
К конечной мы возвращаемся цели.
Так я
к тебе
тянусь неуклонно,
еле расстались,
развиделсь еле.

It's That Way with Me

Fleets! They too flow to port.
A train likewise speeds to a station.
And I, even more, am pulled and tugged
towards you—
for I love.
Pushkin's covetous knight
visits his cellar to rummage and gloat.
In the same way,
my beloved,
I return to you.
This is my heart,
and I marvel at it.
People gladly go home
and scrape off their dirt,
washing and shaving.
In the same way
I return to you—
for in going towards you,
am I not returning home?
Man of earth in earth is laid.
We return to our destination.
Thus steadily
I am drawn back
towards you
as soon as we part
or stop seeing each other.

(TR. MAX HAYWARD AND GEORGE REAVEY)

Mayakovsky brought a new kind of violent intensity into love poetry. Here
he compares the way he is irresistibly drawn to the woman he loves to the
way ships are drawn to ports, trains to stations, misers to their gold, dirty

working men to their homes to get clean, and, finally, to the way the human body is drawn back to the earth, in death. These are "inner-body sensations" he's talking about, not outward sensations, things merely seen or heard.

BESSIE SMITH

AMERICAN (1894?–1937)

Black Mountain Blues

Back in Black Mountain
                     a child will smack your face
Back in Black Mountain
                     a child will smack your face
Babies crying for liquor
                     and all the birds sing bass

Black Mountain people
                     are bad as they can be
Black Mountain people
                     are bad as they can be
They uses gun powder
                     just to sweeten their tea

On the Black Mountain
                     can't keep a man in jail
On the Black Mountain
                     can't keep a man in jail
If the jury finds them guilty
                     the judge'll go their bail

Had a man in Black Mountain
                     sweetest man in town
Had a man in Black Mountain
                     the sweetest man in town
He met a city gal
                     and he throwed me down

I'm bound for Black Mountain
                     me and my razor and my gun
Lord, I'm bound for Black Mountain
                     me and my razor and gun
I'm gonna shoot him if he stands still
                     and cut him if he run

Down in Black Mountain
                they all shoots quick and straight
Down in Black Mountain
                they all shoots quick and straight
The bullet'll get you
                if you starts a-dodging too late

Got the devil in my soul
                and I'm fulla bad booze
Got the devil in my soul
                and I'm fulla bad booze
I'm out here for trouble
                and I've got the Black Mountain Blues

(TR. ERIC SACKHEIM)

Blues were written to be sung. The singing rhythm they have carries over onto the page, and it's hard to read the two repeating lines and the third that rhymes with it without hearing it. Langston Hughes, among others, was influenced in his poetry by blues.

E. E. CUMMINGS

AMERICAN (1894–1962)

Spring is like a perhaps hand

Spring is like a perhaps hand
(which comes carefully
out of Nowhere)arranging
a window, into which people look(while
people stare
arranging and changing placing
carefully there a strange
thing and a known thing here)and

changing everything carefully

spring is like a perhaps
Hand in a window
(carefully to
and fro moving New and
Old things, while
people stare carefully
moving a perhaps
fraction of flower here placing
an inch of air there)and

without breaking anything.

Cummings's poem seems a transcription of something just about inexpressible: an incredible lightness of feeling that comes with the beginning of spring, a lightness that brings change. The poem takes part in the change by itself turning things upside down—syntax, punctuation, and the usual way of making sense—but only slightly and lightly—still, definitively, as spring does.

JOHN WHEELWRIGHT

AMERICAN (1897–1940)

Father

An East Wind asperges Boston with Lynn's sulphurous brine.
Under the bridge of turrets my father built,—from turning sign
of CHEVROLET, out-topping our gilt State House dome
to burning sign of CARTER'S INK,—drip multitudes
of checker-board shadows. Inverted turreted reflections
sleeting over axle-grease billows, through all directions
cross-cut parliamentary gulls, who toss like gourds.

 Speak. Speak to me again, as fresh saddle leather
 (Speak; talk again) to a hunter smells of heather.
 Come home. Wire a wire of warning without words.
 Come home and talk to me again, my first friend. Father,
 come home, dead man, who made your mind my home.

The accuracy, drama, and clarity of the depiction of the Boston cityscape in the first stanza carry over to and make more convincing the more difficult, more purely emotional second stanza. The feelings sound real partly because the city description is so plain and unidealized: with its Chevrolet sign, its Carter's Ink ad, its checkerboard shadows and "axle-grease billows." Wheelwright combines clear, straightforward, educated American talk with such classic poetry-language devices as repetition and alliteration. As for technical form, this poem is Wheelwright's variation of a sonnet, with twelve lines instead of fourteen and with a different, more pounding sort of rhyme scheme (more rhyming couplets). (Lynn is a town on the Atlantic Ocean, near Boston.)

MELVIN B. TOLSON

from "The Harlem Gallery"

Once, twice,
Hideho sneaked a swig.
"On the house," he said, proffering the bottle
as he lorded it under the table.
Glimpsing the harpy eagle at the bar,
I grimaced,
"I'm not the house snake of the Zulu Club."

A willow of a woman,
bronze as knife money,
executed, near our table, the Lenox Avenue Quake.
Hideho winked at me and poked
that which
her tight Park Avenue skirt vociferously advertised.
Peacocking herself, she turned like a ballerina,
her eyes blazing drops of rum on a crêpe suzette.
"Why, you—"
A sanitary decree, I thought. "Don't *you* me!" he fumed.
The lips of a vixen exhibited a picadill flare.
"*What* you smell isn't cooking," she said.
Hideho sniffed.
"Chanel No. 5," he scoffed,
"from Sugar Hill."
I laughed and clapped him on the shoulder.
"A bad metaphor, *poet.*"
His jaws closed
like an alligator squeezer.
"She's a willow," I emphasized,
"a willow by a cesspool."
Hideho mused aloud,
"Do I hear The Curator rattle Eliotic bones?"

Out of the Indigo Combo
flowed rich and complex polyrhythms.
Like surfacing bass,

The Harlem Gallery • 273

exotic swells and softenings
of the veld vibrato
emerged
. . .
Was that Snakehips Briskie
gliding out of the aurora australis of the Zulu Club
into the kaleidoscopic circle?
. . .
Etnean gasps!
Vesuvian acclamations!

This poem has an amazing number of words one has to stop and pay atten-
tion to, both for their meaning and their music—in the first stanza:
*Hideho, swig, proffering, bottle, lorded, harpy eagle, grimaced, house snake,
Zulu Club.* There's a similar effect of a proliferation of percussive words in
Dylan Thomas, in Hopkins, in Césaire, and in Senghor, but Tolson's poem
has its own particular wrenching music and its bizarre variations:

His jaws closed
like an alligator squeezer.
"She's a willow," I emphasized . . .

FEDERICO GARCÍA LORCA

SPAIN (1899–1936)

The Moon Rises

Cuando sale la luna
se pierden las campanas
y aparecen las sendas
impenetrables.

Cuando sale la luna,
el mar cubre la tierra
y el corazón se siente
isla en el infinito.

Nadie come naranjas
bajo la luna llena.
Es preciso comer
fruta verde y helada.

Cuando sale la luna
de cien rostros iguales,
la moneda de plata
solloza en el bolsillo.

When the moon comes up
the bells are lost
and there appear
impenetrable paths.

When the moon comes up
the sea blankets the earth
and the heart feels
like an island in infinity.

No one eats oranges
under the full moon.
One must eat
cold green fruit.

When the moon comes up
with a hundred equal faces,
silver money
sobs in the pocket.

(TR. WILLIAM B. LOGAN)

This is a poem of repetitions: each stanza tells of one or two things that happen when the moon comes up. Some are more fantastic than others—the prohibition against eating oranges, and especially the sobbing coins. (Finally, one figures out that the coins are probably miserable because when they see the moon, which they look like, they long to be with it, where they belong, in the sky.) Even before understanding the events, the reader may be fascinated by them. They take place in a world where sensations and feelings determine reality: a sharp sensation of heat on your shoulder may mean that the sun is cutting you with its knife. These fantastic things are said in simple, direct language. Anything in a translation not in such language damages the effect—translating "moneda de plata," for example, as one translator did, as "silver coinage"—"silver money" is better.

LAURA RIDING

AMERICAN (1901–1991)

You or You

How well, you, you resemble!
Yes, you resemble well enough yourself
For me to swear the likeness
Is no other and remarkable
And matchless and so that
I love you therefore.

And all else which is very like,
Perfect counterfeit, pure almost,
Love, high animation, loyal unsameness—
To the end true, unto
Unmasking, self.

I am for you both sharp and dull.
I doubt thoroughly
And thoroughly believe.
I love you doubly,
How well, you, you deceive,
How well, you, you resemble.
I love you therefore.

Through a musical maze of rather general, unspecific words—abstractions arranged as a song—the reader gets a sense of a changeable, deceiving, excitable person who is loved by the poet. The poem gives a sense of the thrill of being vague and evasive while at the same time praising and affirming a feeling. It is as though the poet were staying far away from particular details so as to be able to write this way. In some of Auden's poems, abstractions are the subject, but here they don't seem to be.

LANGSTON HUGHES

AMERICAN (1902–1967)

from *Montage of a Dream Deferred*

NEIGHBOR

Down home
he sets on a stoop
and watches the sun go by.
In Harlem
when his work is done
he sets in a bar with a beer.
He looks taller than he is
and younger than he ain't.
He looks darker than he is, too.
And he's smarter than he looks,

> *He ain't smart.*
> *That cat's a fool.*

Naw, he ain't neither.
He's a good man,
except that he talks too much.
In fact, he's a great cat.
But when he drinks,
he drinks fast.

> *Sometimes*
> *he don't drink.*

True,
he just
lets his glass
set there.

REQUEST

Gimme $25.00
and the change.
I'm going
where the morning
and the evening
won't bother me.

FACT

There's been an eagle on a nickel,
An eagle on a quarter, too.
But there ain't no eagle
On a dime.

These are three of a long series of short poems on life in Harlem. In the series the characters and the scenes change, but the voice one hears is always the same—direct, coversational and convincing, with the kind of insider humor and know-how of someone who has been with the subjects he's talking about for a long time. The poems say a lot—some of it quite surprising—with very few words.

LÉOPOLD SÉDAR SENGHOR

SENEGALESE (1906–)

Elegy of Midnight

Summer, splendid Summer feeding the Poet on the milk of your light.
I who grew up like the wheat of Spring which made me drunk
From the green water, the green streaming in the gold of Time.
Ah! no longer can I tolerate your light, the lamplight,
Your atomic light which disintegrates my whole being.
No more can I tolerate the midnight light.
The splendor of such honors resembles the Sahara,
An immense void with neither erg nor rocky plateau,
With no grass, no twinkling eye, no beating heart.
Day in and day out like this, and my eyes wide open
Like Father Cloarec's, crucified on a boulder by Joal pagans
Who worshipped snakes. In my eyes the Portuguese lighthouse
Turns round and round, day in day out,
A precise and restless mechanism, until the end of time.

I jumped out of bed, a leopard about to be snared,
A sudden gust from Simoun filling my throat with sand.
Ah! if I could just crumple down in the dung and blood in the void.
I turn around among my books watching me with their deep eyes.
Six thousand lamps burning twenty-four hours a day.
I stand up lucid, strangely lucid. And I am handsome,
Like the one-hundred meter runner, like the black stallion
Rutting in Mauritania. I carry in my blood a river of seeds
That can fertilize all the plains of Byzance.
And the hills, the austere hills.
I am the Lover and the locomotive with a well-oiled piston.

Her sweet strawberry lips, her thick stone body,
Her secret softness ripe for the catch, her body
A deep field open to the black sower.
The spirit germinates under the groin, in the matrix of desire.
Sex is one antenna among many where flashing messages are exchanged.
Love music can no longer cool me down, nor the holy rhythm of poetry.

Against this despair, Lord, I need all my might
—A soft dagger in the heart as deep as remorse.
I am not sure of dying. Then this must be Hell: the lack of sleep
This desert of the Poet, this pain of living, this dying
From not being able to die, this agony of gloom, this passion
For death and light like moths on the hurricane lamp at night
In the horrible rotting of virgin forests.

Lord of light and darkness,
You, Lord of the Cosmos, let me rest in Joal-of-the-Shades,
Let me be born again in the Kingdom of Childhood full of dreams,
Let me be the shepherd of my shepherdess on the Dyilor flats
Where dead men gather, let me burst out applauding
When Tening-Ndyare and Tyagoum-Ndyare enter the circle
And let me dance like the Athlete to the drum of this year's Dead.
This is only a prayer. You know my peasant's patience.
Peace will come, the Angel of dawn will come, the singing of birds
Never heard before will come. The light of dawn will come.
I will sleep a death-like sleep that nourishes the poet.
—O You who give the sleeping sickness to newborns,
And to Marone the Woman Poet, to Kotye Barma the Just!
I will sleep at dawn, my pink doll in my arms,
My green and gold-eyed doll with a voice so marvelous,
It is the very tongue of poetry.

(TR. MELVIN DIXON)

Senghor, with Aimé Césaire, was founder of the Negritude movement. It came, Senghor wrote, from a "desire to divest ourselves of our borrowed attire—that of assimilation—to assert our being, that is to say our negritude." In Surrealism, wild and close to the unconscious, the poets saw a way to do this, adapting surrealist methods to African themes and rhythms. Senghor said African Surrealism was unlike European Surrealism in being mystical and metaphysical. The surreal images in this poem are meant not to be dreams but realities, parts of an invisible divine universe of life forces.

W. H. AUDEN

ENGLISH (1907–1973)

This Lunar Beauty

This lunar beauty
Has no history,
Is complete and early;
If beauty later
Bear any feature,
It had a lover
And is another.

This like a dream
Keeps other time,
And daytime is
The loss of this;
For time is inches
And the heart's changes,
Where ghost has haunted,
Lost and wanted.

But this was never
A ghost's endeavour
Nor, finished this,
Was ghost at ease;
And till it pass
Love shall not near
The sweetness here,
Nor sorrow take
His endless look.

Auden's poems are full of sometimes difficult and sophisticated ideas and it's possible at first to find them too difficult and too abstract, too purely intellectual—compared with Williams's, for example, which are constantly giving one things—beds, plums, trees, etc. These are different kinds of poetry. When I got to like Auden, even when I didn't understand all he was saying, I was fascinated by the charm with which he said it. Reading him was clearly an experience at the same time intellectual and artistic: he seemed to know and understand everything, and, as far as the art of poetry is concerned, to be constantly using different poetic forms and inventing new ones.

The form of this poem is a surprise—and a creation of Auden's: short lines with obvious but almost always imperfect (or partial) rhymes (*beauty/history, later/feature,* and so on). The two-strong-stressed lines make for a tone of inevitability and regularity. The "off-ness" of the rhymes, along with the oddly clipped style—"has no history,/Is complete and early"—make for roughness, which translates, emotionally, into sincerity. The poem is original also for being a lyric poem completely suffused with intellectuality; the lunar beauty is being thought about and connected to abstract ideas, not looked at and described. Auden was the inventor of this kind of intellectual lyric poem—certainly for our time.

W. H. AUDEN

ENGLISH (1907–1973)

from *Paid on Both Sides*

[*Enter* KURT *and others with prisoner.*]

KURT. We found this chap hiding in an outhouse.
JOHN. Bring him here. Who are you?
STEPHEN. I know him. I saw him once at Eickhamp. He's Seth Shaw's
    brother.
JOHN. He is, is he. What do you come here for? You know what we do to
    spies. I'll destroy the whole lot of you. Take him out.
SPY. You may look big, but we'll get you one day, Nower.

[*Exeunt all but* JOHN, STEPHEN *following.*]

STEPHEN. Don't go, darling.

[JOHN *sits. A shot outside followed by cheers.*]

[*Enter* ZEPPEL.]

ZEPPEL. Will you be wanting anything more to-night, sir?
JOHN.   No, that will be all thank you.
ZEPPEL. Good night, sir.
JOHN.   Always the following wind of history
      Of others' wisdom makes a buoyant air
      Till we come suddenly on pockets where
      Is nothing loud but us; where voices seem
      Abrupt, untrained, competing with no lie
      Our fathers shouted once. They taught us war,
      To scamper after darlings, to climb hills,
      To emigrate from weakness, find ourselves
      The easy conquerors of empty bays:
      But never told us this, left each to learn,
      Hear something of that soon-arriving day
      When to gaze longer and delighted on
      A face or idea be impossible.
      Could I have been some simpleton that lived

Before disaster sent his runners here:
Younger than worms, worms have too much to bear.
Yes, mineral were best: could I but see
These woods, these fields of green, this lively world
Sterile as moon.

CHORUS. The Spring unsettles sleeping partnerships,
Foundries improve their casting process, shops
Open a further wing on credit till
The winter. In summer boys grow tall
With running races on the froth-wet sand,
War is declared there, here a treaty signed;
Here a scrum breaks up like a bomb, there troops
Deploy like birds. But proudest into traps
Have fallen. These gears which ran in oil for week
By week, needing no look, now will not work;
Those manors mortgaged twice to pay for love
Go to another.
                                O how shall man live
Whose thought is born, child of one farcical night,
To find him old? The body warm but not
By choice, he dreams of folk in dancing bunches,
Of tart wine spilt on home-made benches,
Where learns, one drawn apart, a secret will
Restore the dead; but comes thence to a wall.
Outside on frozen soil lie armies killed
Who seem familiar but they are cold.
Now the most solid wish he tries to keep
His hands show through; he never will look up,
Say "I am good". On him misfortune falls
More than enough. Better where no one feels,
The out-of-sight, buried too deep for shafts.

[*Enter* FATHER CHRISTMAS. *He speaks to the audience.*]

FATHER CHRISTMAS. Ladies and Gentlemen: I should like to thank you all
very much for coming here to-night. Now we have a little surprise for
you. When you go home, I hope you will tell your friends to come
and bring the kiddies, but you will remember to keep this a secret,
won't you? Thank you. Now I will not keep you waiting any longer. . . .

This is a brief excerpt from Auden's verse play about an imaginary civil war in England. I've included, before and after the speeches by John and by the chorus, some "non-poetical" parts, to help give an idea of how the poetic parts sound in the play. Having a chorus—some sort of speaker or speakers who comment on the action of the play—is a dramatic device borrowed from Greek drama.

John's speech is in occasionally rhyming iambic pentameter. The chorus's speech is in consonant-rhyming couplets: *partnerships/shops, till/tall, sand/signed.*

John's speech in particular is a good example of the way Auden brings contemporary ideas of history and psychology into poetry.

ELIZABETH BISHOP

AMERICAN (1911–1979)

Arrival at Santos

Here is a coast; here is a harbor;
here, after a meager diet of horizon, is some scenery:
impractically shaped and—who knows?—self-pitying mountains,
sad and harsh beneath their frivolous greenery,

with a little church on top of one. And warehouses,
some of them painted a feeble pink, or blue,
and some tall, uncertain palms. Oh, tourist,
is this how this country is going to answer you

and your immodest demands for a different world,
and a better life, and complete comprehension
of both at last, and immediately,
after eighteen days of suspension?

Finish your breakfast. The tender is coming,
a strange and ancient craft, flying a strange and brilliant rag.
So that's the flag. I never saw it before.
I somehow never thought of there *being* a flag,

but of course there was, all along. And coins, I presume,
and paper money; they remain to be seen.
And gingerly now we climb down the ladder backward,
myself and a fellow passenger named Miss Breen,

descending into the midst of twenty-six freighters
waiting to be loaded with green coffee beans.
Please, boy, do be more careful with that boat hook!
Watch out! Oh! It has caught Miss Breen's

skirt! There! Miss Breen is about seventy,
a retired police lieutenant, six feet tall,
with beautiful bright blue eyes and a kind expression.
Her home, when she is at home, is in Glens Fall

s, New York. There. We are settled.
The customs officials will speak English, we hope,
and leave us our bourbon and cigarettes.
Ports are necessities, like postage stamps, or soap,

but they seldom seem to care what impression they make,
or, like this, only attempt, since it does not matter,
the unassertive color of soap, or postage stamps—
wasting away like the former, slipping the way the latter

do when we mail the letters we wrote on the boat,
either because the glue here is very inferior
or because of the heat. We leave Santos at once;
we are driving to the interior.

The seemingly careless rhymes and the general atmosphere of being in a
big hurry to get everything done on time and at once makes this poem
exhilaratingly close to the speech of a bright, sensitive, witty person thinking out loud and mysteriously accompanied by some equally quick music.
One feels one would like to listen a long time if she would go on talking.
The poem is, too, a case of making poetry out of what seem unpromising
poetic materials and in a way that brings some new music into the poetic
language: "Watch out! Oh! It has caught Miss Breen's/skirt!"

ANNE PORTER

AMERICAN (1911–)

Lovers

I can still see
The new weather
Diamond-clear
That flowed down from Canada
That day
When the rain was over

I can still see
The main street two blocks long
The weedy edges of the wilderness
Around that sawmill town

And the towering shadows
Of a virgin forest
Along the log-filled river

We walked around
In a small traveling carnival
I can still hear
Its tinny music
And smell its dusty elephants
I can still feel your hand
Holding my hand
That day

When human, quarrelsome
But stronger
Then death or anger
A love began.

The dramatic shock of the poem is in the last four lines. After the slow detailed description of one day, the reader finds out suddenly that the loved person has died and that the two had a long, happy, sometimes difficult time together. The music—which is mostly two strong beats in every line—contributes to the sense of urgency and inevitability: "I can STILL SEE/The NEW WEATHer/DIAmond-CLEAR/That FLOWED down from CANada. . . ." (Regular stresses in lines of unequal length have a similar effect in Gary Snyder's "Siwashing it out." The sudden shock of awareness at the end of "Lovers" has some similarity to the shock at the end of Yeats's "A Deep-Sworn Vow.")

AIMÉ CÉSAIRE

MARTINIQUE (1913–)

Tam-tam de nuit

train d'okapis facile aux pleurs la rivière aux doigts charnus
fouille dans le cheveu des pierres mille lunes miroirs tournants
mille morsures de diamants mille langues sans oraison
fièvre entrelacs d'archet caché à la remorque des mains de pierre
chatouillant l'ombre des songes plongés aux simulacres de la mer

Night Tom-Tom

file of okapis easily in tears the river with fleshy fingers
searches in the hair of stones a thousand moons mirrors revolving
a thousand diamond bites a thousand prayerless tongues
a fever loopings of a hidden violin bow towed by stone hands
tickling the shade of dreams plunged into the simulacra of the sea

(TR. CLAYTON ESHELMAN)

Phrase

Et pourquoi pas la haie de geysers les obélisques des heures le cri lisse des
nuages la mer en écart vert pâle fienté d'oiseaux vauriens et
l'espérance roulant ses billes sur les faîtes et entrefaîtes des maisons et
les déchirures en dorades des surgeons bananiers

dans les hautes branches du soleil sur le cœur heurté des matins sur le
tableau âcre du ciel un jour de craie de faucon de pluie et d'acacia sur
un portulan d'îles premières secouant leurs cheveux de sel interjetés
de doigts de mâts en toute main à toute fin sous le battement de cil du
hasard aux délices chantées d'ombre un assassin vêtu d'étamines
riches et calmes comme un chant de vin dur

Sentence

And why not the hedge of geysers the obelisk of hours the smooth scream
of clouds the sea's quartered pale green spattered by good-for-noth-
ing birds and hope playing marbles on the beams and betweens of
houses and the dolphin-like rips of banana tree suckers

in the top branches of the sun on the stubbed heart of mornings on the
acrid canvas of the sky a day of chalk of falcons of rain and acacia on
a portulan of primeval islands shaking their saline hair interposed by
fingers of masts handwritten for any purpose under the blink of
chance with its shadow sung delights an assassin clad in rich and
calm muslins like a chant of hard wine

(TR. CLAYTON ESHELMAN)

Aimé Césaire, a poet from Martinique, was, along with the Senegalese poet
Léopold Sédar Senghor, the creator of Negritude. His poems are full of the
violent excitement of the constant change of connections: everything is
part of everything else and may *be* something else—the river has fingers,
there is hair of stones, diamonds bite, a violin bow is towed by stone hands.
Nothing is still, and nothing is certain except for the continuing wild inter-
action of one thing with another. In the midst of all this, there are memorable discoveries, like "un chant de vin dur" (a song of hard wine), "a day of
chalk of falcons of rain and acacia." To make his changes and connections,
Césaire makes very free use of prepositions such as *of, with,* and *on.*

JAMES SCHUYLER

AMERICAN (1923–1991)

A White City

My thoughts turn south
a white city
we will wake in one another's arms.
I wake
and hear the steampipe knock
like a metal heart
and find it has snowed.

This very short poem communicates a lot while actually saying very little, and even what it says, in the first three lines, isn't immediately clear: it's only after reading line four that one knows the person speaking was asleep and, thus, that his thoughts of being in a "white city" in the South with his lover were part of a dream. So, reading the first three lines, the reader has the experience—which then turns out to be a dream. What is actually said in the last three lines is that the steampipe knocks and that, looking outside, the speaker sees snow on the ground. What the reader knows, without its being said, is that the person when he actually wakes up is not with his lover but alone—and lonely. The metal steampipe seems to mock his love by knocking like a metal (unfeeling) heart (somewhat frighteningly). The reader, along with the speaker, is comforted at the end by the snow, which has created a "white city" of another kind. None of this is explicitly stated; the reader has one experience after another, and the understanding of the poem is in the way these separate experiences come together. There is no other way to understand it. Schuyler's twentieth-century poem is somewhat remarkably like Li Bai's "Still Night Thoughts" (p. 131) written in China twelve hundred years earlier, though the details of the poems are quite different.

ALLEN GINSBERG

AMERICAN (1926–1997)

A Supermarket in California

What thoughts I have of you tonight, Walt Whitman, for I walked down the sidestreets under the trees with a headache self-conscious looking at the full moon.

In my hungry fatigue, and shopping for images, I went into the neon fruit supermarket, dreaming of your enumerations!

What peaches and what penumbras! Whole families shopping at night! Aisles full of husbands! Wives in the avocados, babies in the tomatoes!— and you, García Lorca, what were you doing down by the watermelons?

I saw you, Walt Whitman, childless, lonely old grubber, poking among the meats in the refrigerator and eyeing the grocery boys.

I heard you asking questions of each: Who killed the pork chops? What price bananas? Are you my Angel?

I wandered in and out of the brilliant stacks of cans following you, and followed in my imagination by the store detective.

We strode down the open corridors together in our solitary fancy tasting artichokes, possessing every frozen delicacy, and never passing the cashier.

Where are we going, Walt Whitman? The doors close in an hour. Which way does your beard point tonight?

(I touch your book and dream of our odyssey in the supermarket and feel absurd.)

Will we walk all night through solitary streets? The trees add shade to shade, lights out in the houses, we'll both be lonely.

Will we stroll dreaming of the lost America of love past blue automobiles in driveways, home to our silent cottage?

Ah, dear father, graybeard, lonely old courage-teacher, what America did you have when Charon quit poling his ferry and you got out on a smoking bank and stood watching the boat disappear on the black waters of Lethe?

Allen Ginsberg, deliberately writing in the Whitmanesque version of the language of poetry, plays variations on it. He is focusing the "Whitman machine" on America in 1955 and not, as Whitman did, in 1855. Whitman (in "Song of Myself"): "Seasons pursuing each other the indescribable crowd is gathered.... it is the Fourth of July.... What salutes of cannon and small arms!" Ginsberg (in "A Supermarket in California"): "What peaches and what penumbras! Whole families shopping at night! Aisles full of husbands! Wives in the avocados, babies in the tomatoes!" Ginsberg's tone is ironic and yet excited at the same time: it all really is amazing even if it is a supermarket. The poem is very funny in this first stanza. In the last stanza there are desolation and death; but the exhilarating tone goes through to the end.

FRANK O'HARA

AMERICAN (1926–1966)

Meditations in an Emergency

Am I to become profligate as if I were a blonde? Or religious as if I were French?

Each time my heart is broken it makes me feel more adventurous (and how the same names keep recurring on that interminable list!), but one of these days there'll be nothing left with which to venture forth.

Why should I share you? Why don't you get rid of someone else for a change?

I am the least difficult of men. All I want is boundless love.

Even trees understand me! Good heavens, I lie under them, too, don't I? I'm just like a pile of leaves.

However, I have never clogged myself with the praises of pastoral life, nor with nostalgia for an innocent past of perverted acts in pastures. No. One need never leave the confines of New York to get all the greenery one wishes—I can't even enjoy a blade of grass unless I know there's a subway handy, or a record store or some other sign that people do not totally *regret* life. It is more important to affirm the least sincere; the clouds get enough attention as it is and even they continue to pass. Do they know what they're missing? Uh huh.

My eyes are vague blue, like the sky, and change all the time; they are indiscriminate but fleeting, entirely specific and disloyal, so that no one trusts me. I am always looking away. Or again at something after it has given me up. It makes me restless and that makes me unhappy, but I cannot keep them still. If only I had grey, green, black, brown, yellow eyes; I would stay at home and do something. It's not that I'm curious. On the contrary, I am bored but it's my duty to be attentive, I am needed by things as the sky must be above the earth. And lately, so great has *their* anxiety become, I can spare myself little sleep.

Now there is only one man I love to kiss when he is unshaven. Hetero-
sexuality! you are inexorably approaching. (How discourage her?)

St. Serapion, I wrap myself in the robes of your whiteness which is like
midnight in Dostoevsky. How am I to become a legend, my dear? I've tried
love, but that hides you in the bosom of another and I am always springing
forth from it like the lotus—the ecstasy of always bursting forth! (but one
must not be distracted by it!) or like a hyacinth, "to keep the filth of life
away," yes, there, even in the heart, where the filth is pumped in and slan-
ders and pollutes and determines. I will my will, though I may become
famous for a mysterious vacancy in that department, that greenhouse.

Destroy yourself, if you don't know!

It is easy to be beautiful; it is difficult to appear so. I admire you,
beloved, for the trap you've set. It's like a final chapter no one reads because
the plot is over.

"Fanny Brown is run away—scampered off with a Cornet of Horse; I do
love that little Minx, & hope She may be happy, tho' She has vexed me by
this Exploit a little too. —Poor silly Cecchina! Or F:B: as we used to call her.
—I wish She had a good Whipping and 10,000 pounds." —Mrs. Thrale.

I've got to get out of here. I choose a piece of shawl and my dirtiest sun-
tans. I'll be back, I'll re-emerge, defeated, from the valley; you don't want
me to go where you go, so I go where you don't want me to. It's only afternoon, there's a lot ahead. There won't be any mail downstairs. Turning, I
spit in the lock and the knob turns.

The "emergency" in O'Hara's poem is difficulty in love. The meditations
are brief and rapidly changing reflections on an upsetting situation. Like
Rimbaud's "Dawn," this is a prose poem. It has a less lofty and heroic tone
than Rimbaud's poem, and brings to the form new possibilities and new
pleasures—with its variety of tones, its wit, and its sound of everyday talk.

FRANK O'HARA

AMERICAN (1926–1966)

A True Account of Talking to the Sun at Fire Island

The Sun woke me this morning loud
and clear, saying "Hey! I've been
trying to wake you up for fifteen
minutes. Don't be so rude, you are
only the second poet I've ever chosen
to speak to personally
                              so why
aren't you more attentive? If I could
burn you through the window I would
to wake you up. I can't hang around
here all day."
                    "Sorry, Sun, I stayed
up late last night talking to Hal."

"When I woke up Mayakovsky he was
a lot more prompt" the Sun said
petulantly. "Most people are up
already waiting to see if I'm going
to put in an appearance."
                              I tried
to apologize "I missed you yesterday."
"That's better" he said. "I didn't
know you'd come out." "You may be
wondering why I've come so close?"
"Yes" I said beginning to feel hot
wondering if maybe he wasn't burning me
anyway.
              "Frankly I wanted to tell you
I like your poetry. I see a lot
on my rounds and you're okay. You may
not be the greatest thing on earth, but
you're different. Now, I've heard some
say you're crazy, they being excessively
calm themselves to my mind, and other
crazy poets think that you're a boring

reactionary. Not me.
Just keep on
like I do and pay no attention. You'll
find that people always will complain
about the atmosphere, either too hot
or too cold too bright or too dark, days
too short or too long.
If you don't appear
at all one day they think you're lazy
or dead. Just keep right on, I like it.

And don't worry about your lineage
poetic or natural. The Sun shines on
the jungle, you know, on the tundra
the sea, the ghetto. Wherever you were
I knew it and saw you moving. I was waiting
for you to get to work.

And now that you
are making your own days, so to speak,
even if no one reads you but me
you won't be depressed. Not
everyone can look up, even at me. It
hurts their eyes."
"Oh Sun, I'm so grateful to you!"

"Thanks and remember I'm watching. It's
easier for me to speak to you out
here. I don't have to slide down
between buildings to get your ear.
I know you love Manhattan, but
you ought to look up more often.
And
always embrace things, people earth
sky stars, as I do, freely and with
the appropriate sense of space. That
is your inclination, known in the heavens
and you should follow it to hell, if
necessary, which I doubt.
Maybe we'll
speak again in Africa, of which I too

am specially fond. Go back to sleep now
Frank, and I may leave a tiny poem
in that brain of yours as my farewell."

"Sun, don't go!" I was awake
at last. "No, go I must, they're calling
me."
      "Who are they?"
                  Rising he said "Some
day you'll know. They're calling to you
too." Darkly he rose, and then I slept.

This poem, from which this book takes its title (lines 51–52—"And now that
you/are making your own days") is a more intimate, two-sided, and humor-
ous conversation with a celestial body than most—Keats's "Bright Star" sonnet, for example. In this case, it's the sun who initiates the dialogue, shining
in Frank's window to tell him how much he likes his poetry and to give him
some encouraging advice about it. The poem was directly inspired by a very
similar poem by the Russian poet Mayakovsky—thus the sun's reference to
Mayakovsky's being "a lot more prompt." The people who, according to the
Sun, think Frank's poetry is "crazy", are, doubtless, the traditional academic
poets of the time (1959), as opposed to the "crazy poets" who think he's a
"boring reactionary." The Sun reassures Frank that he, the Sun, likes what
he's doing, and also considers that the two of them are doing the same sort
of work: making days—quite a beautiful and interesting conception of
what poetry is, for both writers and readers (which is why I chose it as a title
for the book). O'Hara's poems often seem more like days, or parts of days,
than most other poems, with their subject being at least in part simply what
happens to the poet over a certain period of time; they also tend to be hot,
bright, and even dazzling, as if the sun were part of them.

JOHN ASHBERY

AMERICAN (1927–)

Le Livre est sur la table

I

All beauty, resonance, integrity,
Exist by deprivation or logic
Of strange position. This being so,

We can only imagine a world in which a woman
Walks and wears her hair and knows
All that she does not know. Yet we know

What her breasts are. And we give fullness
To the dream. The table supports the book,
The plume leaps in the hand. But what

Dismal scene is this? The old man pouting
At a black cloud, the woman gone
Into the house, from which the wailing starts?

II

The young man places a bird-house
Against the blue sea. He walks away
And it remains. Now other

Men appear, but they live in boxes.
The sea protects them like a wall.
The gods worship a line-drawing

Of a woman, in the shadow of the sea
Which goes on writing. Are there
Collisions, communications on the shore

Or did all secrets vanish when
The woman left? Is the bird mentioned
In the waves' minutes, or did the land advance?

Each part of this poem begins with statements and ends with questions. Some of the statements are slightly incomprehensible; some of the questions are unanswerable. The prose sense of the poem remains unclear. However, the individual moments are fairly clear. The language throughout is rather formal and logical—it *sounds* as though it made perfect sense—"This being so," "yet," "But what," "Now," and so on. And the very specific physical images—hair, breasts, bird, black cloud, book, plume—give us enough real familiar experience to make the poem understandable as an "event"— something that happens—even if we don't entirely know what is happening. This permanently unclear poem suggests meanings it never explains.

JOHN ASHBERY

AMERICAN (1927–)

from *Europe*

1.

To employ her
construction ball
Morning fed on the
light blue wood
of the mouth

            cannot understand
feels deeply)

2.

A wave of nausea—
numerals

3.

a few berries

4.

the unseen claw
Babe asked today
The background of poles roped over
into star jolted them

5.

filthy or into backward drenched flung heaviness
lemons asleep pattern crying

6.

The month of elephant—
embroidery over where
ill page sees.

7.

What might have
        children singing
the horses
                the seven
breaths under tree, fog
clasped—absolute, unthinking
menace to our way of life.
uh unearth more cloth
This could have been done—
This could not be done . . .

This is the beginning of a poem twenty times this long and in 111 stanzas. The poetic device of line divisions is carried to its logical (for art) and illogical (for reason) end: in this excerpt, every line has an uncertain connection to the lines before and after it. Sometimes the lines are syntactically connected but even then make no kind of ordinary sense: "Morning fed on the/light blue wood/of the mouth." The excitement, and the poetic meaning, come from reading them for whatever sense they make. Is there a light blue wooden statue of a person that is being slowly eaten away by time? Accustomed to statements making sense, the reader jumps from one disconnected statement to another as if they did make sense: for example, from "the month of elephant" to "embroidery over where": neither line makes much sense itself, but some kind of suggestive meaning is created by the two together.

Writing in this fragmented way, a poet can put a lot of emotion and play into every line and be in no way committed to continuing it. Part 3, "a few berries" is intriguing, like a "significant" camera shot; but whatever it is "about" may never be known; it remains pure significance, an interesting new pleasure of poetry.

GARY SNYDER

AMERICAN (1930–)

I Went into the Maverick Bar

I went into the Maverick Bar
In Farmington, New Mexico.
And drank double shots of bourbon
                    backed with beer.
My long hair was tucked up under a cap
I'd left the earring in the car.

Two cowboys did horseplay
                    by the pool tables,
A waitress asked us
                    where are you from?
a country-and-western band began to play
"We don't smoke Marijuana in Muskokie"
And with the next song,
                    a couple began to dance.

They held each other like in High School dances
                    in the fifties;
I recalled when I worked in the woods
                    and the bars of Madras, Oregon.
That short-haired joy and roughness—
                    America—your stupidity.
I could almost love you again.

We left—onto the freeway shoulders—
                    under the tough old stars—
In the shadow of bluffs
                    I came back to myself,
To the real work, to
                    "What is to be done."

Something that's convincing about the social and political criticism in this
poem is the way Snyder portrays so strongly what it is he likes about the

kind of American life he's rejecting and doesn't want to live. The poem also gives pleasure by trusting the reader to understand some unexplained details—what earring? And why did you leave it in the car? "Tough old stars" is a great quick personification.

JOSEPH CERAVOLO

AMERICAN (1934–1988)

Drunken Winter

Oak oak! like like
it then
    cold some wild paddle
so sky then;
flea you say
"geese geese" the boy
June of winter
of again
Oak sky

This poem seems so compressed that while its strong "poetic content" may come across, its prose meaning may not. Possibly, that meaning could be something like this: you look at an oak tree, are impressed by it, and exclaim "Oak oak!" Excited, you want to compare it to something ("like like") or else you're saying that you like it, but in any case before you get any further with your statement, it's interrupted by new sensations, of cold and of paddling in cold water; then you're aware of the sky overhead; you're little, a little boy, little as a flea (maybe), and in the sky you see geese and cry out again, this time "geese geese." Either the boy represents the springtime (June) of winter—or the passage of geese which suggests a change in the seasons suggests springtime. As for the title, the winter may be "drunken" because of the excitement it makes you feel, which you transfer back to it; or you may be actually drunk and that's why you are seeing winter in such an excited way.

Mainly, though, the effect the poem gives is of the *things* in it—oak, paddle, sky, etc.; these are experiences, whether one "figures them out" or not. Even the words *like like* seem thinglike. The "difficulty" of the poem means that the reader has a fresh experience of "getting it" each time it's read—that is, of getting the physical experience.

Index

Mozart, Wolfgang Amadeus, 110, 130
Muse, 19, 81
music of poetry, 21–24, 25, 26, 27–49, 51,
    112, 113–15, 119, 167, 184, 251
    irregular rhyme, 44–46, 256
    line division, 29–30, 214
    meter, 30–36, 212, 256
    non-metrical, 36–40
    non-rhyming, 44–46
    in other languages, 130
    poetic forms, 47–48
    punctuation and, 210–11
    repetition, 28–29, 171, 250
    rhyme, 40–43, 212, 233
    rhythm, 28–29, 171
    stanzas, 47–48
myth, 215

narrative poetry, 102, 123–25
    and translation, 132–33
Negritude movement, 280, 291
newness, 68–69
Noh plays, 150–51
non-metrical poetry, 30, 36–40
non-rhyming poetry, 44–46
non-traditional poetry, see non-metrical
    poetry
nouns, 25
novels vs. poetry, 123, 124

obscurity, 255
O'Hara, Frank, 11, 13, 37, 39, 48, 52, 61, 71,
    89, 90, 94, 104, 105–6, 113, 151, 246,
    265, 295–99
other languages
    poetry in, 14, 129–33
    used in English poetry, 254
ottava rima, 47, 86, 196
Ovid, 32, 132–33, 146–47

Padgett, Ron, 257–59
parallel syntactical construction, 36, 209
partial rhyme, 40, 42, 46, 282
Pasternak, Boris, 27, 54, 86, 265
pastoral poetry, 184
Peele, George, 41
percussive words, 274
personification, 14, 24, 51, 57–63, 73, 112,
    159
    abstractions and, 58–59

in Elizabethan and Jacobean poets, 59,
    173
in Modern poets, 62, 305
in Romantic poets, 60, 189, 200
in talking to God, 59–60
Peschel, Enid Rhodes, 213–14
Petrarch, 48, 82, 158–59
Plato, 81–82
pleasure of poetry, 110, 113, 115, 121
poet, definition of, 19
poetic forms, 14, 47–48, 101–3
poetic inclinations, see inclinations,
    poetic
poetic truth, 64–67
poetry:
    critical misconceptions about, 111
    descriptive, 102, 180–81
    details in, 95–97, 102–3
    difficulty of, 109, 111, 119–23
    dramatic, 14, 102, 125–28
    epic, 124
    features of, 14
    heroic, 141–43
    inclinations of, see inclinations, poetic
    inspiration for, see inspiration
    learning to write, 71–77
    long, 14, 123–25
    lyric, 123, 124, 126, 144, 246, 282
    and music, see music of poetry
    narrative, 102, 123–25, 132–33, 141–43
    non–metrical, 30, 36–40
    non–traditional, see non–metrical
        poetry
    vs. novels, 123, 124
    in other languages, 14, 129–33, 254
    as party, 20
    pastoral, 184
    pleasure of, 110, 113, 115, 121
    political, 264
    prose, 214, 215, 296
    vs. prose, 21, 30, 109, 123, 131, 214, 248,
        256
    reading of, 14, 109–33
    as a separate language, 14, 19–26,
        27–49, 51–77, 93, 96, 103, 109–10,
        112, 113, 114, 123, 124, 126, 152, 171
    translatability of, 133
    in translation, see translation
    unfamiliarity of, 111
    as "verbal synthesizer," 19–20

writing of, *see* writing

poetry base, acquiring of, 71–77

poets, known through their work, 109

political poetry, 264

Pope, Alexander, 29

Porter, Anne, 288–89

Pound, Ezra, 13, 57, 61, 69, 71, 86, 91, 132,
  145, 147, 148, 149, 150, 151, 157,
  250, 251–55

prepositions, 291

pronouns, 25

prose:
  nonliterary, 27
  vs. poetry, 21, 30, 109, 123, 124, 131,
    214, 248, 256

prose poems, 214, 215, 296

prose sense, unclear, 301, 306

Pulci, Luigi, 86, 197

punctuation, 36, 210–11

Pythagoras, 27

quatrains 47, 102–3, 116, 215

reading poetry, 14, 109–33

"realm of resemblances," 54, 55, 57

Reavey, George, 267

Renaissance, 32, 54–55, 59, 124
  see also sonnets; *specific authors*

repetition, 28, 36, 38, 41, 121, 126, 157,
  171, 219, 250, 272, 275

Reverdy, Pierre, 214

reversed foot, 34

revision, 104–7

Rexroth, Kenneth, 152

rhetorical forms, 24, 101–3

rhyme, 14, 23, 35, 36, 37, 39, 40–43, 44–46,
  72, 119, 287
  absence of, 44–46
  comic effect of, 35, 43, 197
  complete, 40
  definition of, 40
  internal, 42, 110
  irregular, 41, 44–46
  organizing by, 42–43
  partial, 40, 42, 46, 282

rhyme scheme, 101, 174
  alternating lines, 40
  intricate, 41
  Petrarchan sonnet, 48
  Shakespearean sonnet, 48

rhythm, 14, 28–29, 30
  of colloquial prose, 45
  imposed metrical, 33
  of natural speech, 33, 36, 38, 45
  non-metrical, 37, 39

Riding, Laura, 276

Rieu, E. V., 142

Rilke, Rainer Maria, 53, 92, 98, 102, 129,
  220–25

Rimbaud, Arthur, 67, 102, 129, 130,
  213–14, 215

Rodin, Auguste, 92

Roethke, Theodore, 32, 112

Romanticism, 34, 55, 60
  see also specific authors

Rome, 124

Rossetti, Christina, 208–9

Sackheim, Eric, 269–70

Sackville, Thomas, 33

St-John Perse, 89

Saintsbury, George, 13, 49

Sappho, 95, 133, 144

Schuyler, James, 52, 54, 157, 292

secrets, telling of, 67–68

Senghor, Léopold Sédar, 274, 279–80, 291

sensations, 227, 275

sentence structure, 159, 180

sestinas, 47, 156–57

Sextus Propertius, 145

Shakespeare, William, 14, 21, 23, 26, 31, 33,
  34, 35, 40, 41, 46, 48, 49n, 52, 53, 55,
  58, 59, 64, 66, 71, 77, 83, 85, 86, 94,
  102, 111, 116, 117, 119, 121, 124,
  125–26, 128, 151, 167, 168–73, 202

Shapiro, David, 112

Shelley, Percy Bysshe, 46, 47, 52, 55, 58, 60,
  66, 71, 73–74, 77, 87, 94, 105,
  153–55, 198–201

shock, 122–23

Sidney, Sir Philip, 32, 54–55, 57–58, 95

similes, 54

Smith, Bessie, 269–70

Snyder, Gary, 95–97, 98, 102, 289, 304–5

social vision, 185–86

songs, 172, 174, 270, 276

sonnets, 47, 48, 94–95, 102–3, 116
  Petrarchan, 48, 158–59
  Shakespearean, 48, 173

Sophocles, 126

Permissions